"Our easy-going and approachable narrator gives us a charming and entertaining book that is part travelogue, part memoir. Readers will find themselves cheering Esmeralda—and her family—on."

—SCOTT EDWARD ANDERSON, author of *Falling Up* and *Azorean Suite*

"Esmeralda enthusiastically embraces the opportunity to live with her family in a beautiful fishing village near Lisbon. Sharing genuine conversation with folks she meets, exploring her love of fish, and constantly translating and interpreting for her husband and children, Esmeralda's journey is rooted in an awareness of history and culture, and in the dilemma of belonging."

—MARIA MANUELA VAZ MARUJO,
Professor Emerita, University of Toronto

"With the keen eye of a traveller, Esmeralda Cabral serves up close depictions of daily life in Costa da Caparica, including market days, pastéis de nata, and Portuguese hospitality. Told with warmth and layered with Cabral's nuanced reflections on home, belonging, and family, *How to Clean a Fish* is an enticing memoir that will connect with readers."

—MEAGHAN HACKINEN,
author of *South Away: The Pacific Coast on Two Wheels*

"These pages are as delicious as the Portuguese food the author so enthusiastically writes about. Any English speaker interested in Portugal will gladly savor Esmeralda Cabral's genuine narratives as a tasty introduction to Portuguese culture's joys, appeals, intricacies, and mysteries. She is well-versed with food, fado, the language, and even soccer, but she has to negotiate how to feel somewhat at home in the complex web of subtle Portuguese ways."

—ONÉSIMO TEOTÓNIO ALMEIDA, Brown University

T0285594

How to Clean a Fish

How to Clean a Fish

And Other Adventures in Portugal

Esmeralda Cabral

UNIVERSITY *of* **ALBERTA** PRESS

Published by

University of Alberta Press
1-16 Rutherford Library South
11204 89 Avenue NW
Edmonton, Alberta, Canada T6G 2J4
amiskwaciwâskahikan | Treaty 6 | Métis Territory
uap.ualberta.ca | uapress@ualberta.ca

LIBRARY AND ARCHIVES CANADA
CATALOGUING IN PUBLICATION

Title: How to clean a fish : and other adventures in
    Portugal / Esmeralda Cabral.
Names: Cabral, Esmeralda, author.
Series: Wayfarer (Edmonton, Alta.)
Description: Series statement: Wayfarer
Identifiers: Canadiana (print) 20220485852 |
    Canadiana (ebook) 20220486255 |
    ISBN 9781772126556 (softcover) |
    ISBN 9781772126884 (EPUB) |
    ISBN 9781772126891 (PDF)
Subjects: LCSH: Cabral, Esmeralda—Travel—
    Portugal. | LCSH: Portugal—Description
    and travel. | LCSH: Portugal—Social life and
    customs—21st century. | CSH: Portuguese
    Canadians—Biography. | LCGFT: Travel
    writing.
Classification: LCC DP526.5 .C33 2023 |
    DDC 946.904/4—dc23

First edition, first printing, 2023.
First printed and bound in Canada by Houghton
Boston Printers, Saskatoon, Saskatchewan.
Proofreading by Mary Lou Roy.
Map by Matt Hall.

University of Alberta Press gratefully
acknowledges the support received for its
publishing program from the Government of
Canada, the Canada Council for the Arts, and
the Government of Alberta through the Alberta
Media Fund.

Aos meus queridos pais, Manuel e Ermelinda

e

à querida Carminha

Lembrando o dia em que emigrámos para o Canadá

. . . .

Contents

XI   *A Word about Saudade*

XV   *Map*

INVERNO (WINTER)

3   A Harrowing Ride

8   How Did We Get Here?

16   Passport Woes and Flight Plans

22   Around Town

29   The First Big Storm

35   Portuguese Hospitality

47   A Rainy Day in Lisbon

55   Planning to Run

61   Winter Market Days

69   Ashes to Ashes

77   Belonging

86   A Phone Call from Canada

PRIMAVERA (SPRING)

93 The Lisbon Mini Marathon
101 Tracking the Passport
111 Lost in Alfama
120 Fado Concert
127 25th of April
140 Reflections on Duality
151 Our Guests
163 Matt's Arrival
169 A Weekend in Aldeia
178 Haircut
187 World Cup Friendly
193 Border Services 1
200 Spring Market Days

VERÃO (SUMMER)

209 A Dog's Life
220 Border Services 2
225 Summer Market Days
234 An Inheritance of Loss
245 Fado Bar
252 Sardine Season
257 Adeus Costa da Caparica
263 A Vacation in the North
272 Goodbye Lisbon
282 Back in Vancouver

287 *Recipes*
297 *Further Reading*
299 *Acknowledgements*

· · · ·

A Word about Saudade

I GREW UP WITH SAUDADE, that feeling of melancholy or nostalgia
said to be characteristic of the Portuguese temperament. It infused
our everyday language at home. Even before we immigrated to Canada,
I remember my mother talking about it. Two of her brothers and
her sister had left the Azores years earlier, before I was born—two
siblings went to Brazil and one to Canada. My mother missed them
and longed to talk to them, but we didn't have a telephone at home.
She would write letters, and on special occasions like birthdays and
Christmas, she would walk down to the post office to use the phone.
For urgent news, if someone they knew had died or became ill, she
would send a telegram. Later, after we came to Canada and had our
own phone, there were calls at Christmas, but they were always brief
because it was so expensive.

By the time we left our island of São Miguel, I was seven years old,
and saudade was already ingrained in me. Once we arrived in Canada,
I missed everything about our life back home: my grandparents, our
house, my friends, and the rocky piscina in my hometown of Lagoa,
where I would go swimming with my sisters or my father. My sister
Maria was seventeen; she missed her life on the island, her friends,

and the comfort of the familiar. My father, as an only child, missed his parents, and we all missed my oldest sister Antónia who had stayed behind in Lisbon to finish her university program.

Saudade is about more than missing our relatives though, and there are many layers of emotion that can be expressed with this one word. When we bought frozen sardines at the Portuguese grocer down the block in Edmonton, my mother would barbecue them, and then we'd say how much we missed eating sardines back home on the island, with my grandparents.

"Ai que saudades," my mother would say, and we would all nod our heads in agreement.

Even though I don't remember loving sardines as a young child, I treasured sitting around the kitchen table for those big, long lunches with our extended family.

There were times when we would absent-mindedly sing fado tunes around the house while we did chores. Fado is sometimes called the Portuguese blues, but it's also known as the music of saudade. Even at the age of five or six, I could rattle off songs by the famous fado singer Amália Rodrigues. I remember standing at the dock in Ponta Delgada, the capital city of São Miguel, as a five-year-old, belting out the words to "Casa da Mariquinhas." It was my goodbye send-off to Antónia. She was looking down at me from high up on the ship that would be taking her to Lisbon to start university. I remember that everyone around me went silent as I sang loudly, without inhibition. Later, my sister would tell me that my singing had invoked an intense feeling of saudade in her even before she had left. She told me that she had cried.

There were other songs too. I remember my mother singing another of Amália's songs, one about longing to be twenty years old again. I sensed that my mother missed her youth, and I couldn't wait to grow up and turn twenty to find out what was so wonderful about it. My father would listen to "Ó Tempo Volta Para Trás" by António

Mourão, and then whistle the tune, seemingly non-stop, when he was pottering around the house.

As an adult and an immigrant, saudade is part of me. I long for my island home, for the Azores and for Portugal. Listening to fado or eating a typically Portuguese meal like crispy fried stickleback can send my heart into a whirl of saudade. There is something about the slow, intentional way I take apart the small fish, pull the meat off the bone, then dip each morsel in a pool of freshly squeezed lemon juice before placing it in my mouth, that transports me to lunch-time in Lagoa. And yet, when I return to that homeland and spend an extended period of time there, I start to long for my Canada—for the landscape I cherish that includes mountains and green space and silence, even rain and snow.

Saudade is about missing someone or something and longing for them, or it, to return, while accepting that it will probably never happen. Saudade may be wistful, but it is expressed in short bursts. There is sadness woven into the word, but not always. Saudade is not about pining.

There have been numerous efforts to translate saudade, to capture it with one word in English, but all attempts fall short. This is because, in Portuguese, it is not just a word but a feeling. It is nostalgia and longing, "missing you" and yearning, but it's also so much more. It's a deep feeling within your soul of love and loss combined, of trying to capture what may never be again.

• • •

Perhaps it is saudade that pulls me back to visit my other country as often as possible. When the opportunity arose for our family to live in Costa da Caparica for several months, it took only minutes to decide. We were going.

In writing this book, I relied on my journal entries, emails, texts, blog posts, photos, and on memory, which we all know can be fallible.

Still, it's important to note that my two children were there. Their sharp memories make them natural and ruthless fact checkers. We agreed on how major happenings unfolded and when we disagreed about minor matters, I relented and documented their version.

For the sake of conciseness, I left out some people and events when including them would not have had any bearing on the outcome of the story. I also recreated dialogue and setting to provide a cohesive narrative.

As best as our collective memory allows, this book is a true account of our experience.

. . . .

Map

. . . .

Map

Inverno
(Winter)

. . . .

A Harrowing Ride

SENHOR JOSÉ JOÃO manoeuvred his black SUV through Lisbon's chaotic traffic. It was mid-January, but the day was warm and bright. The sunlight bounced off the pavement and reflected off the windows of the apartment buildings that filled the hillsides. We had been picked up at the airport and were now being transported to our new home in Costa da Caparica, a coastal beach town about a twenty-minute drive south of the capital.

I had been communicating with Senhor José João over the internet about the house rental, and I felt like I already knew him. When our family spoke about him among ourselves, we referred to him by the anglicized version of his name, Senhor Joe John. Now, here we were, finally meeting him in person. As the only Portuguese speaker in my family, I settled into the front seat of his vehicle and prepared myself to carry out some form of simultaneous translation for the benefit of Eric and Georgia in the back seat.

Joe John exuded energy that my brain noted but could not fully appreciate in my jet-lagged state. He was short and a little stocky with close-cropped greying hair and blue eyes that looked like they were about to burst out of their sockets with enthusiasm. When we'd emerged through the doors into the arrivals lounge at the airport, we looked out and there, in the middle of a sea of faces, was a man waving a placard with my name on it and the message *Welcome to Portugal*.

The sign had seemed unnecessary—we were the only ones fumbling with too many suitcases, knapsacks, camera bags, laptops, and a large dog crate housing a black-and-white, four-year-old Portuguese water dog who was barking wildly.

We introduced ourselves to Joe John and performed the requisite greetings—a handshake (Eric), a kiss on both cheeks (me), and a kiss on one cheek (Georgia)—then walked out to his vehicle.

"Maggie can ride in the back seat," he said. "She's part of the family."

Back in the car, he offered us a bag of oranges and said, "They're at their best right now, have one." Eric and Georgia declined. I felt nauseated from exhaustion, but I thought it would be rude if we all refused, so I smiled and took one, peeled it, and ate it. I was not disappointed. The orange was delicious, so juicy and sweet. But now my fingers were sticky.

Joe John was driving and eating, talking fast, a little jumpy in his seat.

"We've had big storms lately," he said. I started to translate but he kept going. "A couple of days ago, we had floods, even hail!"

"I know," I said. "I heard that on—"

"Wait till we get there. You'll see. The water came over the seawall and flooded the road to the intersection, just down from the house."

"Oh, great! Was there any—"

"There was no damage to the house, and good thing, too."

"Has that—"

"Never happened before, not that I can remember."

I looked to the back seat with a helpless glance at my husband and daughter. Part of me was sorry that I couldn't translate, that they were missing the details, but I was also relieved that I didn't have to think. I sat back, took a deep breath, and tried to relax.

We were about to cross the suspension bridge—the 25th of April Bridge—over the Tagus River. Joe John forced his vehicle into the disorganized lanes, ignoring the beeping horns around us. He was still talking, but I was only half listening now. He didn't seem to notice that I had stopped responding a few kilometres back.

I looked down, way down, to the river and imagined us careening off the bridge, slamming into the water, and drowning. Just to add to my discomfort at that moment, Joe John steered with his knees and rummaged through his bag with his hands. Eventually, he found his sunglasses, put them on, then looked at me, and gave me a broad smile.

Please, please, keep your hands on the wheel, I begged, but just to myself. He grabbed the steering wheel again and kept on talking.

"So, what do you think of Lisbon?" I realized he had asked me a specific question.

"It's stun—"

"So beautiful," he said. "Interesting light, isn't it? Lisbon has beautiful light."

Then he shouted towards the back seat, "Eric! It's Eric, right? Do you like Lisbon?" And then, "I forgot, he doesn't speak Portuguese."

"He understands a little," I said.

Joe John kept going. "You've probably figured out that I am hard of hearing."

"Oh! No, I didn't—"

"I was born with eight per cent hearing. Makes life hard sometimes but I do pretty well."

Mystery solved.

"So, if you need to reach me," he continued, "best to send me an email or a text instead of calling. Except that I can't see very well either." He laughed.

We finally arrived at our destination, and I noticed that my hands were clasped as if in prayer. I was relieved we had arrived safely. Joe

John parked on the street, alongside the house, with the car's right-side wheels up on the sidewalk.

The house stood behind a tall green fence. It was an up-down duplex, and we would have the ground floor. The neighbour's door was around the side, and they had the upstairs apartment. Our front yards were separated by a low stone wall. The house looked like a typical Portuguese house—whitewashed, with large windows and green shutters, and a verandah on the lower floor. We stood around at the gate with our luggage while Joe John sorted out the keys. Maggie had a pee on the grass. We could hear the waves but couldn't quite see the ocean over the seawall at the foot of the street.

"I think there are a few year-round residents nearby," Joe John told us. "I'm not sure. Mostly, it's a summer town."

Inside, the house was cold and dark. Joe John opened the shutters and turned on the lights and kept talking.

"I only help out with the rental process," he said. "The house is owned by a lovely couple, Helena and Zé, whom you'll meet soon, I imagine. My duties end today, but let's not be strangers, okay? We'll keep in touch, and I'd like you to meet my family."

The living room and dining room occupied a large open area. There was a fireplace, and French doors that led to the verandah. On the dining table, there was a bottle of red wine, a box of chocolates, and a cake on a pedestal platter.

"Oh, look what Helena has left for you," he said. "Let's call to thank her."

He dialed a number on his cell phone, had a quick conversation with Helena to say we'd arrived safely, then passed the phone to me. I panicked, not feeling ready to speak Portuguese to a complete stranger, especially on the phone, but I managed a few obrigadas and made it through the call.

Joe John continued the tour around the house and finished off in the kitchen. He showed us how to start the on-demand water heater and the gas stove and made sure Eric and I both knew how to turn on the gas and replace the canister.

I was developing a serious headache. I wanted to either go to sleep or throw up, I wasn't sure which, but I needed silence. I was relieved when the conversation was over and Joe John, friendly as he was, left us so we could settle in on our own.

"If you need anything, just text me, okay?"

We claimed our bedrooms—Eric and I chose the one with the queen-sized bed, and Georgia, the smaller room with the double. The third bedroom, with two single beds, would be for Matt when he arrived later on, in the spring. In the meantime, it would be our guest room. I couldn't wait to lie down. I went into our bedroom, took off my clothes, and slipped between the ironed, lace-trimmed sheets. I don't even remember closing my eyes.

I woke up sometime later, feeling like I had slept for days. Eric was snoring lightly beside me, but I nudged him awake.

"What day is it?" I asked.

"Huh? I don't know. Is it tomorrow?"

It wasn't tomorrow. It was still the same day, nearly eight o'clock in the evening. Outside, it was pouring rain and dark. We both got up and walked through the house, closing the windows, and then we woke Georgia up. We hadn't had a chance to explore the town, didn't know where there was a grocery store, didn't have umbrellas, and couldn't find our raincoats. Had we even brought them?

I scanned the kitchen and found a wicker basket full of potatoes and a large bowl of kiwi fruit. I opened the fridge and saw there was a package of butter, unopened, and a large bottle of beer. An hour later we sat down to our first meal in our new home—mashed potatoes with butter, wine, kiwi to cleanse the palate, and walnut cake and chocolates for dessert. Then we sat on the couch, wrapped in several blankets, and watched the rain for hours.

. . . .

How Did We Get Here?

OUR MONTHS-LONG STAY in Costa da Caparica was a dream come true for me. I have often imagined myself living in a beach house, writing with the sound of the ocean in the background, taking breaks to walk in the sand, perhaps going for a swim, and returning home to a scrumptious meal of fresh fish. Costa seemed the perfect place to live out my fantasy.

The sunny dreams probably have to do with the fact that I live in Vancouver, on the west coast of Canada, where it rains for much of the winter. Rain, showers, drizzle, mist—we have numerous words for moisture that falls from the sky depending on its intensity and duration. It doesn't rain all day, every day, of course; there's always a dry day interspersed, just to keep the gloom from becoming over-whelming. But when I'm listening to the radio and I hear broadcasters complain that they're tired of the rain, I know it's not just me and I'm not imagining it—winter in Vancouver can be hard.

I grew up in Edmonton, Alberta, where the prairie meets the boreal forest and the skies are wide and blue in both summer and winter. The snowy winters can be bitter and cold, but the sun shines often, or at least that's my recollection, and you can always put on a coat and hat and mitts and go outside. And sunglasses. You need sunglasses with all that sun and snow.

No one in my family had ever seen snow until we immigrated to Canada and arrived in Edmonton on an overcast fall day in late September. My uncle picked us up at the airport and drove us to his house in the north end of the city. Large, wet flakes of snow swirled in the air as we drove on wide, empty streets. I was entranced. It was as if the snowflakes were twirling and floating all around our car. My uncle had sponsored us to come to Canada and was intent on giving us the bright side of immigrating during the long drive to his home.

"The snow won't last," he said. "It's not really winter yet."

He was right. By the time we reached his house, the snow had stopped, and there was barely any evidence on the ground that it had snowed at all. But it was cold—a slap in the face for people like us, having just come from a temperate mid-Atlantic island, our hearts and minds still tied to our volcanic landscape. September on the island of São Miguel is a month of sunny, warm days and cool nights. It's a time to enjoy the last few dips in the ocean before the cool fall weather begins.

I was born in Portugal, or more specifically, on São Miguel, the largest island of the Azores. This archipelago is made up of nine islands that stretch out over six hundred kilometres in the middle of the Atlantic Ocean between Lisbon and New York City. Coming to Canada was my parents' choice, but the reality of a new house, new country, and new language was harsh for all of us. I remember it as a difficult time, even though I was young and adaptable.

I was happy when real winter finally started, about a month after we arrived, and the snow accumulated on the ground. I liked the snow. I would shovel it, roll in it, play in it, even eat it. I especially liked the big mounds that formed on either side of the sidewalks after people shovelled. To me, they looked like mountains of icing sugar.

"It's like you were born at the North Pole," my mother would sometimes say to me. "How can you like this snow and cold?"

Central heating was a new concept for all of us, and my mother enjoyed turning up the thermostat and keeping the house warm. I protested.

"It's too hot in here," I would say and then, in later years, I would add with the indignation only a teenager can muster, "You can put on a sweater, Mum, but I can't take any more clothes off."

I didn't mind winter because although it was cold, it was often sunny, and that made me happy. Even today, well into my mid-life, I can feel myself come alive on sunny days and slow down on the dark, rainy days.

After twenty-three years in Edmonton, I moved to Vancouver where I now live. I still miss the Alberta skies, and I also miss the rugged seashore of São Miguel. After an especially long spell of rainy weather in Vancouver, I will sit at my computer and look up flights and the associated costs to go back to "my" island or to Portugal's sunny south coast. I have bookmarked the weather forecast sites for Lisbon, Ponta Delgada, and Faro, in the Algarve (Portugal's southern province), and I check them often to see what the weather is like in the various regions of my other country.

I clearly remember the day when I was doing just that, checking the weather and flight options to Lisbon, when Eric walked in, totally drenched because he'd ridden his bike home from work, and suggested a temporary move to Portugal.

"You'll never guess what," he said as he took off his rain gear, just inside my office door.

"Okay," I said. "What?" I didn't even move my eyes from the screen.

"One of my grad students cited a paper today on computer simulation of wastewater treatment, exactly what I want to work on some more. And guess what? The paper was written by a group from guess where?"

"Chile?" I looked at Eric, then down at the floor where the water draining from his gear had formed a small pool.

"No, guess again."

"Um, Switzerland?"

"Nope. Again."

"Scandinavia? I give up."

"Lisbon. Well, actually, a place called Costa da Caparica, near Lisbon. We've been there before, haven't we? Isn't it that beach town we really liked?"

"Really?" I squealed. "Yes, yes, it is! Wait a minute. Why is there a university in a beach town? That's almost too good to be true."

"It's a campus of NOVA University Lisbon. What would you think about spending a few months there?"

I said "let's go" before I thought much about it. I was jumping up and down with excitement. I remember this because Maggie came barrelling down the stairs and started jumping and growling, thinking it was play time.

There would be lots of planning required. We had left our house for extended periods several times before and each time required a massive amount of work leading up to our actual departure.

Eric is a university professor and is eligible for a one-year sabbatical every seventh year. It is possible to split that up and take six months every fourth year or some other combination—the options are numerous and seemingly extravagant, but there are always big decisions to be made, and a salary cut. How much, exactly, depends on how long one has worked in that seven-year period and the length of the absence. It's significant enough that some professors never go away on sabbatical. Others take every opportunity they've earned. Eric, with prodding provided by me, is in the latter category. We have lived in Auckland and Christchurch in New Zealand, and Toronto and Quebec City in Canada.

Eric is quick to remind me that a sabbatical is a privilege, even with a salary reduction. And it's not a holiday. It's an opportunity, he says, to go somewhere to learn a new skill and then bring the knowledge back to his university. It's a chance to work with different people and live in another part of the world. But it's not a holiday.

It's not a holiday for him, but it is for me. Every time we've gone away, I've either been between jobs, working freelance, or able to take a leave of absence from work. We've always taken our children, of course, and while it does get more difficult as they get older, we've managed to make it work each time with varied degrees of success.

The year we went to Quebec City, we enrolled them in the local francophone school. Georgia was in Grade 5, which was a perfect year for her to learn the intricacies of French grammar (she became fluent in one year), but Matt was in Grade 9, and he was expected to already know those intricacies. His experience was different and more complicated than hers (think Grade 9 math all in French!) but he also learned to speak the language and became nearly fluent that year.

Each time we go away on a sabbatical, we rent out our house in Vancouver to help offset the difference in salary. Each time we come back, there are surprises to deal with. Years ago, we had overzealous plant waterers who didn't notice excess water leaking onto the hardwood floor. The water stains and the damaged wood are barely noticeable under the chair we've placed there now. Then, there was the one couple who kept forgetting the house keys, so they made multiple copies of the front door key and placed them strategically around the garden. We changed the locks when they told us that. And we kept finding old keys around the yard, even a year later. There's been broken crockery, glued casserole dishes (which we don't find out about until we put them in the oven, and they crack again, spilling the contents), and the fancy glassware that we had received as a wedding present that mysteriously disappeared. "I don't remember any glasses like that," the couple said when we asked them. It's a small price to pay for being able to go away, we tell ourselves. But I have shed the odd tear at a favourite something or other that's gone missing or been broken. We've learned to put special things away, but still, strange things happen (three keys hidden in the rhododendron?).

Usually, Eric and I discuss where to go on sabbatical, and we try to compromise. What is the best place to go professionally for him that will be the most interesting for me and the children, since much of the day we spend on our own. We had been chatting off and on about where we'd go this final time (Eric's last sabbatical before retirement), and I had come up with Chile (dreaming of hiking in Patagonia), Switzerland (more hiking), and Portugal because it was always worth a shot. A long shot, usually. I remain fully aware that our decision is about work more than anything else. I can look at it only from my perspective, however, because my knowledge of wastewater treatment process design is limited to non-existent.

On that rainy evening after work, Eric was more exuberant than usual. The soggy bike ride home had not dampened his spirits. His enthusiasm over the possibility of going to Portugal for the last sabbatical was about more than making me happy, I think. He loved the idea too. We were both imagining Costa da Caparica as a sunny, warm place to live for a few months, and we were thinking about the delicious seafood and, of course, the wine. For our children, Portugal was a country that was comfortable and familiar but also foreign enough for them to find it interesting and exciting.

There were serious logistics to figure out this time, even more so than usual. We would be leaving partway through the school year, in January. Georgia would be in Grade 10, and Matt in his second year of university. We also had a dog now and travelling overseas with her would be a new experience for us.

Once my excitement subsided, I started mulling over the possibilities. As we had done before, I would look after the travel arrangements and Eric would look after the academic side of things.

He would contact the professor and research group he wanted to work with in Portugal, arrange for letters from both universities, ensure we had adequate extended medical coverage through his plan at work, and I would look for a place for us to live in Costa da Caparica, put our Vancouver house up for rent, book our flights, and liaise with Georgia's school. We discussed everything together, but some division of labour was necessary to keep us both from becoming overwhelmed.

When I contacted Georgia's school, the administration was perplexed. They had only entertained such a request once before, and on that occasion, the student was gone for the entire school year which, evidently, was easier to arrange than for a student to leave partway through the year. I was undeterred—this was Grade 10 we were talking about; how could it be so complicated? I met with the vice-principal, and he decided he would support the endeavour because, well, the experience was bound to be educational, no? He left the logistical arrangements to me but suggested that Georgia finish the year through the distance education arm of the Vancouver School Board. He added that she would be welcomed back to her school for her Grade 11 year without having to reapply.

Matt's situation was more problematic. He would be starting the second year of his university program in September, and he lived with us at home. If we rented out our house, he would have no place to live. We decided he would live in residence at the university for the academic year and join us in Portugal in May, after he completed his exams. He threw his name into the lottery for residence, and luckily, he was able to secure a spot. He lived in residence in the fall term while we were still in Vancouver, which helped him make the transition to being on his own. We found renters for our house, a family from Sweden who would be on their sabbatical, and the rent would cover both Matt's residence costs and our rental house in Portugal.

But then there was the dog.

The thought of Maggie, our adorable, fluffy dog, travelling to Portugal in the cargo compartment of an airplane for ten hours or more made me shudder, but leaving her in Vancouver with someone else for eight months was out of the question.

After consulting the internet and several books, talking to two veterinarians, to friends with dogs, to friends without dogs, to friends who worked for different airlines, and to people who had travelled with their dogs, we chose an airline that had an excellent reputation for transporting live animals, including horses. It even had a pet hotel at the arrival terminal should pets be required to lay over. I was assured our dog would be treated well and, while the experience would be stressful for her, it was the best option we could think of.

Since we couldn't fly directly to Lisbon, we decided that it would be best for Maggie to fly from Vancouver to Amsterdam on the same flight as Eric. Georgia and I would use our airline points to get to Europe, which meant that we would be taking a very roundabout route and would arrive in Amsterdam several hours after Eric. We would all stay in Amsterdam for a few days so we could explore the city and also give Maggie a rest. Then we would embark on the next leg, a much shorter Amsterdam to Lisbon flight, on the same airline. It was all working out.

. . . .

Passport Woes and Flight Plans

ERIC AND I WERE LYING IN BED, and I was staring at the ceiling.
I could hear Eric's breathing change, and I knew he was falling asleep.
Me? I was having trouble calming my mind. Our life was in transition
and so much uncertainty lay ahead. A few deep breaths. We hadn't
left Vancouver yet, but I was already feeling homesick—which didn't
bode well for the months ahead.

We were staying at our friend Jonny's place because our Swedish
renters needed to move into our house before we were due to leave
Vancouver. Staying in Matt's university residence apartment, which
he shared with five other young men, was not an option. We needed to
impose on friends. But when you are three people and a dog and you
need a place to stay for a week, you need to choose wisely. And then
our friend Jonny offered! He and his son were rattling around in their
large house, he said, and there were a few available bedrooms. They
also welcomed Maggie; how perfect was that? Their house is only a
few blocks from ours, so we were able to stay in our neighbourhood,
meet our tenants, even pick up a few things we'd forgotten to pack. It
had worked out well, until that one night in the bedroom in Jonny's
house. We hadn't pulled the curtains closed all the way, and there was

moonlight streaming into the room. I could see Eric's face beside me, which meant it was a clear night—a rare occurrence in the month of January in Vancouver.

Eric bolted upright.

"Shit," he hissed.

"What? What is it?"

"Shit. Damn. I can't believe it."

That's about as much as Eric ever swears. In our twenty-five years together, I can't say that I remember him ever saying "shit" before.

By this time I was sitting up in bed too, my heart thumping hard in my chest.

"I forgot to apply for a work visa," he said.

Neither of us got much sleep after that, both of us tossing and turning and not wanting to blame the other for the oversight. How could this have happened?

In the chaos of planning and packing, we'd simply forgotten.

Eric would be working in Portugal, though getting paid by his Canadian employer, and we'd be staying longer than three months, so he would need a visa. The rest of us had Portuguese citizenship, so we did not have to make any special arrangements for our extended stay.

I was plagued with images of Georgia and me—the two of us living in Costa on our own for weeks, if not months, before Eric got his visa. And then there was Maggie. She was booked on the same flight as Eric, and she couldn't fly on her own…I had to fight off the urge to dwell on the complications.

The morning after our sleepless night, we headed to the Portuguese Consulate in Vancouver and arrived just as the office opened. With our scheduled departure in a few days, we knew there would be no time to get the visa before we left, but we hoped our plans would somehow be salvageable. We found the staff eager to help us out that morning. Maybe they felt sorry for us when they saw the look of panic and disbelief on our faces.

After some discussion of our predicament, it was agreed that Eric would begin the process for the visa application in Vancouver, gather all the required documents to support his application, and then he could leave as planned and enter Portugal as a visitor. Once the visa was granted, Eric would need to mail his passport back to Vancouver to have the work visa inserted, at which point Matt would need to pick it up and mail it back to us in Portugal. Only then would Eric be able to officially start working. It was an unsettling prospect, but we had no choice. The idea of sending the passport in the mail left us with pits of worry in our guts, but we had to forget about it for the time being or it threatened to ruin the first part of our stay in Portugal.

Eric spent our remaining few days in Vancouver getting a physical at the doctor, applying for security clearance from the Vancouver Police Department, and filling out many forms. It was stressful, but we were grateful that consulate staff had offered an alternative to waiting in Vancouver until the visa was granted.

On the day of our departure, I was a nervous wreck. I repacked my bag several times. I checked my packing list over and over, and I made two last-minute trips to the drugstore. The first to pick up energy bars in case Georgia and I got held up somewhere and had nothing to eat, and the second to buy a small bottle of my favourite shampoo. I don't know why I did this, thinking back, but on that day, it seemed very important to me. I tried to prepare for every eventuality. I mean, what if I couldn't find good shampoo anywhere in Lisbon?

Because Eric's flight left after ours, he drove Georgia and me to the airport to see us off. I was glad not to have to be the one to send off our dog, locked in her crate, to spend the next ten hours in the dark cargo hold of an airplane. Eric wasn't looking forward to it either, but when there's a job to be done, even if it is unpleasant, Eric just does it and usually without complaining. He told me later that, moments before his plane took off, the flight attendant came to his seat and told him that his dog had been loaded onto the plane and had settled nicely. That helped him relax, and he slept most of the way to Amsterdam.

When Georgia and I arrived, I was filled with dread and believed in my heart that Maggie had died mid-flight and that we'd be dealing with grief over a dead dog. I had already decided I would accept all blame because I was the one who had been most eager to embark on this sabbatical, and I had made the arrangements for Maggie. I was envisioning that our first few months in Portugal would be filled with the emptiness of loss. I don't know how I became such a pessimist.

Once inside the terminal at Schiphol Airport, I thought it would be better if Georgia, my daughter of not yet sixteen years of age, heard the news of our dog's death first, then broke it to me, gently. I didn't exactly tell her this, but I conveyed it. Telepathically. I busied myself looking for luggage, rummaging through my purse, gathering documents, and finally, turning on my computer to find the address of the hotel where we were headed for our two-day rest stop before going on to Lisbon.

"Why are you doing this? Dad and Maggie are meeting us," Georgia said, sounding a little exasperated with me. "He knows where we're going; I'm sure he has the address." And then, "You're not afraid that Maggie is dead or anything like that, are you?"

"No, of course not. But I'd like to know where we're going just in case they've gone on without us and decided to wait for us at our hotel," I replied.

"Dad would so not do that, and you know it, Mum," Georgia said.

Once we had our luggage, and I could no longer put off the inevitable, I pushed our trolley full of bags and looked for the exit sign. Then I heard Georgia say, "There she is!"

Beyond the frosted glass, in the arrivals area, I could see the tip of Maggie's tail wagging, and below the pane, I could see her paws. Eric was holding her on-leash, but she started doing her puppy leaps and I could see he was having a hard time controlling her. When she spotted us, she broke free and ran towards us, almost knocking me down. She jumped up on us and ran back to Eric, then back to us. People around us were smiling. It was obvious that she was a very happy dog. And she was very much alive.

We were happy to see Eric too, and I was relieved that he had survived the stress of travelling with our beloved pet. Since his arrival, he had found the storage lockers in the airport where we would leave most of our luggage, bought our train tickets into downtown, and figured out how to get from the train station to our hotel. I could finally relax.

• • •

For the most part, our stay in downtown Amsterdam was relaxing and fun and relatively stress free, except for the fact that there wasn't a square inch of grass anywhere for Maggie to do her business. Why hadn't we thought of that? It became clear to us soon enough why every square of dirt surrounding the trees on the boulevard was full of dog poo. Maybe Maggie was suffering from constipation due to the flight or maybe she just didn't like the new facilities, but our poor dog was unsettled. She eventually figured out that going anywhere was better than nowhere, and she made use of the square of dirt around a tree near our hotel. We felt sorry for her and planned to head to a park the next day for her morning constitutional.

The closest park turned out to be a forty-five-minute walk away and when we got there, there was some grass, much to Maggie's relief, but not a lot. Mostly there were trees and dirt and gravel paths, more canals, and lots of cyclists.

An overnight downpour had given way to a blue sky, and while it was bitingly cold, we were in holiday mode. On our way back, we stopped in at cafés, drank hot chocolate, and sampled stroopwafels. We had to take turns going into the cafés because of Maggie—one of us would wait outside with her while the other two would go in and order, and then we'd switch, because despite all that we'd heard about how dog-friendly every single restaurant in Europe was, we were finding that this was not the case, not here anyway. Most restaurants and stores had a *No Dogs Allowed* sign. At one café, the server told us it would be fine to bring Maggie inside as long as no one complained. We didn't want to open ourselves up to the possibility of being reprimanded, so we opted to continue taking turns. We did the same when we visited the Anne Frank House and the Rijksmuseum, which meant that everything we did took twice as long.

I was less stressed about the flight from Amsterdam to Lisbon since it was much shorter—under three hours—and Maggie had already proven herself resilient. Still, Eric was the one who took her to the live cargo handler and checked her in, while I watched from a distance. Then we all continued through security, onto the plane, and we were soon on our way to Lisbon.

. . . .

Around Town

THE MORNING AFTER OUR ARRIVAL in Costa, the sky was blue
and clear, and I could tell even before I got out of bed that the sun
was shining. We must have been really tired when we went to bed the
night before because we hadn't even thought of drawing the blinds.
On this first morning in Portugal, my head still on the pillow, I felt the
energy of adventure, of newness.

"Are you awake?" I asked Eric beside me.

"Yes, are you?"

"Ha ha. I'm ready to get up, let's go."

I sat up in bed and put my feet on the cold tile floor. Now that was
a familiar sensation. For a split second, I was transported to my childhood home in São Miguel. It had a big kitchen with a green-speckled
tile floor, and I always walked around barefoot, much to my mother's
chagrin. "Put your slippers on; you'll catch a cold," I could almost hear
her saying.

I got out of bed and went into the living room, walked over to the
French doors, and pulled them open. We'd forgotten to draw those
blinds too. I stepped outside on the cement verandah and squinted. It
was so bright. I looked at my watch to check the time—9:07. Was that

Lisbon time? Whatever time zone I was in, my body knew that it was time to get up. I shaded my eyes and looked up to the sky and saw a fine wispy cloud off to the right—over the ocean, I figured.

So this is January, I thought to myself. I felt like I had come home even though we had yet to step out of the house or explore the town. I could hear the ocean, and I could taste the salt in the air. I wanted to run down the street to the beach, meet the waves, and feel the sand squish through my toes, but first things first—I had to get dressed and go into town, find a grocery store, buy coffee, locate a bakery, and get the lay of the land. This was especially important for me as I have to admit to a spatial disorientation that plagues me for several days every time I arrive somewhere new. I needed to get my bearings. We would go to the beach later.

Eric woke Georgia up, and the three of us met in the kitchen. There was nothing for breakfast. We were eager to discover the town, but we were also hungry. We had a few kiwis each, then stepped outside to explore the yard.

A terrace extended from the back half of the house, and a narrow set of concrete steps led up to a rooftop patio. We stood up there, twirled around, and feasted our eyes on the magnificent view. To the west, there was the sand and sea of the beach and the horizon beyond; to the north was an urban park, just behind the house; and to the east, there was a bank of sandy cliffs that bordered the town. We could see the western end of Lisbon and past that, Cascais in the distance. All of this under a glorious blue sky.

From the rooftop, we could also see into the neighbour's yard. We had heard barking but hadn't yet figured out where it was coming from. Now we could see there were two large dogs in the enclosed yard next door. They were both about the size of German shepherds; one had dark, short fur that made it look like a police dog, and the other was sand-coloured and fluffy. There were piles of dog waste dotting the yard and, in the corner nearest our house, there was a small nylon tent but the rain and wind of previous weeks had ripped the material from the poles and exposed the inside. We went back downstairs to see if we could get close to the dogs, but the fence was too high for us to see over it. The dogs seemed curious and came right up to the fence to sniff us. We squeezed a couple of treats between the slats and hoped the owners would clean up the mess and walk their dogs soon.

We left our front yard and headed into town. There were no remnants of yesterday's storm except for the fresh, clean smell in the air that you only get after a big rain washes away days' worth of dust from the pavement. The sunshine flooded our eyes, helping our bodies adjust to our new time zone. No sunglasses for a few days. We'd heard this helps with jet lag.

We found a café and sat at an aluminum table on the patio and watched the town come alive. Between the café and the butcher shop across the narrow street, there was a pop delivery truck and a bread van, both with their motors still running. Dark smoke curled out of the exhaust pipe of the bread van. At that time of the morning, the street seemed reserved for delivery vehicles. Eric and I each ordered a coffee, and Georgia ordered a chocolate milk drink that came in a bottle.

"Hot or cold?" the waiter asked.

"Um, cold?" Georgia answered, and looked around to the other tables, wondering if she'd given the right answer.

The waiter sensed her uncertainty and said, "It's good either way, you just have to choose."

The short cafézinho that Eric and I each got was, well, small. A thick brown liquid with a layer of crema on the top, it looked like a perfect coffee. But after two or three gulps of liquid, the experience was over. We laughed when we finished it, and I made some comment that "going for coffee" was going to be different here than it was back home where you can order a coffee that is medium, large, even extra large, and sip it over a long period of time. These short coffees were just not conducive to lingering at a table for very long, I imagined. Yet, there were other people sitting at tables on the patio, doing just that—lingering. Some sat alone, others with a friend or two. Everyone seemed to be watching the goings-on in the street, looking around, squinting into the sunshine.

We were about to leave when we saw a delivery of pastéis de nata, the ubiquitous, and now famous, Portuguese custard tarts. Two young men made several trips from their van to the coffee shop counter, each time balancing two large trays of tarts, one in each hand.

Our waiter had been standing near our table, leaning against the wall of the shop, also mesmerized by the to-ing and fro-ing of the custard tart delivery men. I half stood out of my chair and asked him, "Can we have three of those," and pointed to the tarts on the counter, inside. He turned to me and snapped, "You want them now, after your coffee?" He might have been genuinely confused, but he startled me.

"Yes, is that all right?" I don't think I said it in a snarky way.

He shrugged and walked away. It wasn't clear exactly where he was going, and I hoped he had decided to bring us the pastry after all, even though it may have been out of the logical Portuguese sequence.

We waited for a while and wondered when or if we'd get our order. Just when we'd given up and thought of moving on, our waiter was back, carrying our tarts on a dish lined with a sheet of wax paper, and placed it in the middle of the table without even looking at us. I wanted some kind of contact, maybe even a smile, but no, with hardly a glance, he took to his post against the wall and went back to watching the delivery trucks on the street. I wanted to tell him that we had moved here, that we'd probably be coming in regularly, that I was Portuguese but now also Canadian, that my family and I were from the west coast of Canada, from Vancouver, did he know it, and yes, it's really, really far away. But I said nothing; I didn't have a chance.

I was disappointed by his indifference. I remembered this feeling from before, from the many visits I'd made to Portugal. Service here was different from service in Canada, or was it? Perhaps my expectations were higher here. On this first day in town, I wanted some connection, even for a second, but I sensed that would be hard to get. I would just have to get used to the lack of response. I always did.

We walked east from the coffee shop and found the central square, a couple of bakeries, several banks, a bank machine, a grocery store called Minipreço, and the farmers' market. There was a shop at the market entrance with a vast assortment of fish on display. There were eels and cuttlefish in separate buckets and squid and octopus sprawled on shelves of ice. There was sole and flounder, grouper, and swordfish, and so many other kinds of fish I couldn't identify. Everything looked like what it really was—dead fish with gleaming skin, and head, eyes, and tail still attached. There were no fillets to be seen, no steaks of anything, just whole fish. The shop smelled strongly of the sea, of fish and salt. I was struck by my desire to buy, cook, and eat, and the realization that I had no idea how to clean most of this fish, or cook it, or even how to eat it.

One of the fishmongers stood at the edge of the shop, looking out onto the square. She was wearing a long, white plastic apron that covered her from chest to ankles. Underneath, she had on a blue fleece sweater, and her jeans were tucked into her rubber boots. She had dark, wavy hair, about chin length, and big, dark eyes. She smiled at me, something I did not expect, especially after the encounter with the waiter at the café earlier in the morning. I smiled back and said, "Bom dia."

She gestured at the bucket of cuttlefish, then picked up an octopus from the ice shelf next to her and offered it to me with a hopeful look on her face. I held up my hand to say no, chuckled, and said, "Obrigada."

We moved on to the Minipreço and stocked up on staples—cheese, a few bananas, oranges, coffee, milk, and yogurt. We also bought cleaning supplies. I'd have to clean our kitchen myself before I felt like

it was really mine. We stopped at a bakery to buy Portuguese buns—
six for less than a euro. They were fresh and crusty, and we started
tearing off pieces as we walked back home. It was not an easy walk;
we stumbled over the cobblestones and gravel, trying to negotiate our
way while wrestling with so many bags. We meandered through the
deserted streets, setting off a chorus of barking dogs. The properties
and houses were large and most of them were shuttered, making us
think they were empty, but almost every house had a dog that threw
itself at the gate or fence as we passed and not in friendly greeting.

At one house, on a corner just a block away from our place, there
was a Rottweiler at the front gate. It barked at us and we went over,
closer to it, wanting to say hello, thinking the poor dog might be
lonely. It growled and bared its teeth, and we knew enough to keep
our distance. His barking became so fierce that I was afraid he'd jump
the fence and maul us. We avoided eye contact and quickened our pace.

The welcome that our own dog provided when we got back home
was in stark contrast. As soon as we approached the gate to the
yard, we could hear Maggie in the house, barking her usual greeting.
She knew it was us. We opened the door and she came running out,
jumping up, her tail wagging wildly. You'd think we'd been gone all
day, but it had just been a couple of hours, if that.

We took our cue from Maggie and decided it was time to go for
a walk and introduce her, and ourselves, to the beach. We put the
groceries away, leashed our dog, and headed down the street. It
was less than a five-minute walk to the beach. A few steps up to the
seawall, and the view was stunning. We were up high, on a walkway
lined with restaurants, bars, and surf shops. Most were closed for the
season. Straight ahead, it was just ocean; left and right, beach as far
as the eye could see. The wind was up, and it whipped wildly around
us, tousling our hair and nipping our earlobes. It wasn't exactly
lounge-on-the-beach weather, but this was a beach all right, and it
was beautiful. This—this small chunk of coastline on the edge of this

small country—was my backyard for the time being. There wasn't another person to be seen anywhere. All I could think was: how could I possibly be so lucky?

. . . .

The First Big Storm

IN THE TWO WEEKS SINCE OUR ARRIVAL, we'd managed to put in place some semblance of a work schedule. Eric and I would start our days with breakfast and coffee either at home or at a nearby café, and Georgia would sleep in and then have breakfast on her own. By nine o'clock or so, we'd all be ready to start our workday. Eric worked from home (until the work visa came through) and Georgia logged on to her online schooling site and chipped away at the British Columbia curriculum for Grade 10. I would take Maggie for a walk on the beach, and we'd often be the only ones there. I liked to start my days like this because we both got some exercise, and the look of the water gave me an indication of the kind of day it would be. If it was grey and still, I knew it would be cold and cloudy. If it was blue and foamy, chances were good that it would turn into a sunny day.

One day, on one of our walks, we reached the parking lot below the seawall and saw garbage everywhere—beer bottles and foam pillows, plastic water bottles, and chunks of wood. Maggie sniffed wildly and pulled on the leash to head to the next clump of trash. My first reaction was to think, there must have been quite the party last night! I started to feel old and cranky, ready to blame young, partying types for the mess. I looked to my right, then to the left, and saw that the cobblestones had been torn up and now lay in heaps on the ground, leaving holes where they had once been. What happened here? I wondered. Some party. Did people pick up cobblestones and chuck them at each other?

I headed to the steps that led to the seawall and saw that they had been closed off with blue police tape. *Polícia Marítima*, it said. Oh no, I thought, my brain still in Vancouver-big-city-mode, there's been a murder! I ducked under the tape and made my way up the steps, tugging at Maggie's leash to make her come with me. She whined.

I was not prepared for the devastation I saw when we got to the top of the steps. The path had been torn up and chunks of asphalt lay strewn about the walkway. Wood siding from the restaurants had been ripped off the walls, metal staircases had been twisted into broken wreckage on the beach below, water bottles and bleach jugs had washed up onshore, and traffic signs had been ripped away and tossed around. Light posts were lying on the ground like logs and numerous chairs were overturned on the sand. I gasped.

Restaurant owners and a few curious types like me stood in awe, mouths gaping. Some people were taking pictures, others were wandering around, but no one was talking to anyone. The sea was calm and bore no evidence of an overnight storm. I walked along the seawall and passed a man standing near one of the restaurants. He was wearing a white apron and looked like he was about to start his day at work, cooking meals. I wanted to say good morning but that seemed inappropriate. Instead, I gestured at the debris around my feet and asked him, "Was this all from the ocean?"

He looked out to the water and squinted, put his cigarette to his mouth, inhaled, and as he let out a whoosh of smoke, he nodded, then looked at me, and raised an eyebrow and said, "Claro." Of course.

After my initial shock, I turned around, went down another set of broken steps and ran all the way home, tripping on Maggie who was jumping and biting at the leash and weaving between my legs. Even her dog's brain must have been wondering what was going on.

I was out of breath when we reached the gate to the house. As I felt for the keys in my pocket, the woman in the yard next door started speaking to me. She was holding a pail and a scrub brush. She had come to check on her property and the dogs, she said. She didn't introduce herself or even start with bom dia, she just started talking as if we'd known each other for years.

"Such an unusual year," she said. "Second time in just a few weeks that the water comes over the wall. Last time, it came to that sign over there," she continued, pointing to the intersection about fifty metres away. "All the restaurants on the seawall were flooded."

"There's so much destruction today," I said. "It's incredible."

"When you live by the sea, you have to learn to live with the sea," she said. "Even when it gets angry."

I had questions for her, wanted her name, wanted to ask about the dogs, who checks on them, who walks them, wanted to tell her who we were, how long we were staying, but I was in a hurry to tell Eric and Georgia about the chaotic mess on the beach. And she had already turned around and kneeled down to scrub the garden stones.

I opened the gate, and Maggie broke loose from the leash and ran up the front steps, jumping, whimpering, and scraping at the door. Eric came to greet us just as I was putting the key into the keyhole.

"You'll never guess what happened," I said. "There's stuff every-where and the asphalt is torn and light posts are down. It's a mess."

"Whoa, what? Slow down. What are you talking about?"

"Yeah, some storm or something. The restaurants are flooded, the cobblestones are all over the place. Come with me, come, come and see. *Georgiaaa*!"

The previous day, we had had lunch at one of the seaside restau-rants. We had sat outside on the patio, and we were enjoying the sun when the server told us we might have to hurry through our meal because the tide was coming in.

"You're kidding, right?" I asked, and laughed.

"You'll get sprayed for sure, or you might get soaked," she said.

We finished eating before high tide and we left, never knowing whether she was telling the truth or exaggerating the risk. The storm must have hit during the night but none of us heard anything.

The three of us headed down the street to the beach, leaving Maggie at home this time.

"You won't believe the damage," I said. My voice was still shaky with disbelief.

By the time we climbed onto the path, it looked as if the entire town had come to the seawall. Proprietors were still standing around, though now they were talking to each other. There was a buzz of unintelligible conversation around us. Some people sat on their haunches and held their heads in their hands, others were looking out to sea, as if in a trance. One man I saw was running his fingers through his hair over and over, no doubt contemplating the amount of work there was to do that day and in the coming days, just to clean up the mess.

We passed a restaurant with a damaged patio and Georgia said, "Hey, we were sitting right there yesterday!" I saw our server, standing with a few others, and she recognized us. She waved and started walking towards us, then quickened her pace as if she wanted to tell us something. We stopped and waited until she caught up. The four of us stood there, shading our eyes and looking out to the ocean.

"See," she said, "I wasn't kidding yesterday. You thought I was, didn't you?"

"It's awful," I said. "What will happen to the restaurants?"

"We'll be closed today, for sure. I don't know what we'll do; the water came in from below, and it seems to be burrowing a tunnel under the building. I don't know what will happen to my job."

"I'm sorry," I said. It was all I could think of saying. She took my elbow in her hand and squeezed my arm with her other hand. I sensed she was saying goodbye but also telling me that we'd all get through this, somehow. I placed my other hand on hers, and we stood there for a brief moment, two strangers in solidarity. Then she went back to the restaurant, and we continued along the seawall.

Our stay in Costa da Caparica was off to a stormy start. I was beginning to realize that living so close to the beach would require constant vigilance—that I'd have to listen to weather reports and look at the tide tables or consider the cycles of the moon and the direction of the wind. It was turning into an unusual winter in Costa, and it would be unusual for us too. Stormy weather was not what I had expected. I hadn't expected ocean waves that would reach six metres or more; I hadn't expected that the sea would be alive and moody; I hadn't expected any of this.

At dinner that evening, we mostly talked about the storm but then I realized I had forgotten to mention to Eric and Georgia that I'd met the neighbour.

"Did you ask the dog's names?" Georgia wanted to know.

"I didn't," I said. "I forgot. I didn't ask her name either or tell her mine. I was distracted by the beach scene, and I wanted to tell you all about it."

"Well, I'm going to name them Dave and Ingrid," Georgia said.

I have no idea where those names came from, but they stuck, and still today, that's how we refer to them. Georgia also named a stray dog on the street Reybeez. This dog had a large tumour on her belly, and she lugged herself around from house to house and yard to yard. It seemed that people left food out for her—containers with leftover pasta, mysterious sauces, and potatoes. She would eat at one of these containers, then lie beside it for a while, then move on to the next container at another neighbour's house, and finally make her way into the yard next door to settle down for the evening. I learned early on that I needed to keep Maggie on a firm and short leash anytime we left our yard. She is a food-motivated dog and would pull forcefully towards these containers, even if they were a block away.

My heart ached when I saw so many dogs around town, clearly homeless, wandering aimlessly and searching for food. Other dogs were behind fences, but the houses looked empty. These were the guard dogs—they lived outside and seemed confined to their yards indefinitely, their sole purpose being to scare away potential intruders.

I looked over at Maggie, lying on the couch near the fireplace. Our beloved house pet was one lucky dog.

. . . .

Portuguese Hospitality

WE NEEDED TO PAY OUR RENT. This thought had been plaguing
me for a few days. We could have gone to the bank machine in the
town centre, but there was a daily limit to how much we could with-
draw. Given that limit, we would have had to make several trips to
obtain the right amount and even then, we'd have cash, and our landlord preferred a bank transfer. Also, our bank in Canada charged us
every time we withdrew money. If we bought a car, we would need
money for that too. Relying solely on our Canadian bank account
was not going to work. We needed a local bank. I thought it would
be straightforward.

Eric and I walked into a random bank in town where we saw a long
queue of very bored-looking people. They looked as if they'd been
there awhile, perhaps most of the morning. We stood around for a
few minutes, and then one man gestured towards a ticket machine—
we needed to take a number. I thanked him, then walked over to
the machine and tried to decipher the instructions. There were
four options and none of them said "open a bank account," so I was
confused. I pressed A and got a number. We waited.

After half an hour, no numbers had been called, and we were getting restless. I was still unsure if I'd picked the right option, so I went up to a teller who was serving someone and interrupted with a polite "excuse me" and asked where I should go to open an account. The teller jutted out her chin to indicate the ticket machine. I showed her that I had one and she said, "Now you wait."

I can't remember how much longer we stood there, but finally Eric said, "Must be because it's getting close to lunch. Let's go home and try again this afternoon or tomorrow."

"But we need money. What are we going to do?"

"We don't need it right this minute. We'll figure it out tomorrow," he said.

We stopped by another bank on the way home and looked inside, only to find another long queue. Yes, it must be the time of day, we agreed.

Shortly after we got home, my phone rang. It was our landlord, Zé, checking in to see how things were going.

"Muito bem," I said. Very well. "We're adjusting, you know. Trying to set up a bank account. Oh, is that why you're calling? We owe you money!"

"No, no, please. I'm just checking in to see how you're doing," he said. "Don't worry about the money. There's no rush. Are you keeping warm enough?"

"Yes, well, most of the time. It's been chilly, though," I replied. "Much cooler than we imagined. But we're fine. We've used the fireplace every night, so it's nice and cozy."

Back in Vancouver, when I was looking for a house to rent in Costa and I found this one, I had called and spoken to Joe John directly. We had agreed on the monthly rent, and then we made arrangements to meet at the airport. That was it. When I asked if he needed a deposit, he had said no and added that we'd look after everything when we got to Portugal. We didn't sign a contract and had no documentation to confirm that we'd made any arrangements at all. I felt uneasy about how casual all of this seemed, but I decided to trust. Eric, on the other hand, was skeptical and often expressed doubt that we'd have a house at all when we arrived.

"I think it's just how things are done," I'd say.

"I understand that. But I'd still feel better if we had something in writing before we moved halfway around the world," he would insist.

"Well, we're talking about Portugal, not Canada, so you're just going to have to get used to the idea that things are different there, and just accept it."

I hated the tension this caused between us and I was surprised how defensive I felt. If I had been honest with myself, I would have admitted that I was a bit worried about the housing arrangements too, but I wasn't prepared to challenge my contact and ask him for things in writing when he hadn't offered. I thought it would be rude.

We all sighed with relief when Joe John met us at the airport. And now here we were—we did have a house to live in, and so far, everything had gone as planned. Except that we had now been here for a couple of weeks and still hadn't paid rent and still couldn't transfer our money. No one seemed worried about this except Eric and me.

After the workday, that evening around six or so, there was a knock on the door. It was Zé. He had become concerned after our earlier conversation when I'd told him we found it chilly. He realized we couldn't buy any wood because we didn't have a car, and he didn't want us to run out, so he was delivering some. He had brought another man to help him, and together they unloaded and stacked one hundred kilograms of wood for us.

"Obrigada," I said.

We enjoyed our evening fires, but at some point the winds picked up, and this affected the draft in the chimney. It got smoky upstairs, and the other tenants complained. Zé's wife Helena called us and asked that we not use the fireplace until they could figure out the problem, or at least have the chimney cleaned.

Later that day, there was another delivery to our house. This time it was a brand-new, large electric heater.

"So you don't get too cold," Zé said.

"Oh my goodness," I said. "Muito obrigada."

He came inside to set up the heater for us and show us how to use it. While he was fiddling with the plastic wrap on the different components, Eric and I were just standing there watching him, and then I blurted out, "I'm sorry, we haven't paid you yet! I'm so embarrassed. But we still haven't been able to open a bank account. The banks are all so busy and different banks keep asking us for all sorts of documents, none of which we have."

"Yes, it's not easy here," Zé said. "Especially because Eric is not getting paid by a Portuguese employer. And you don't have a job."

"But we have money. I mean, Eric is getting paid, but by his university in Canada. It's not like we're asking for a loan. We actually want to bring money into the country!"

Eric stood near me, his arms crossed. I could tell he was trying to follow the discussion, but he couldn't keep up with the fast-flowing Portuguese.

"Listen," Zé said to me. "I have a good friend who is a bank manager. He will walk you through the paperwork. Just let me know when you want to do it and he'll help you. It'll get done, don't worry."

I started to translate for Eric but Zé was moving on to the next item he thought we should discuss. "Now, tell me, are you going to buy a car?"

I explained that we had considered it but decided we would just rent one on the occasional weekend to get out and see some of the countryside.

"No, no, no," he said. "You don't want to do that. It's much better to have one when you want it and then you don't have to plan too far ahead. You need a car to explore this beautiful country."

"Okay," I said. "Eric and I will talk about it again, but we can't even think about buying a car until we've paid you for the rent."

Eric was looking a little bewildered, still unable to follow the conversation. Zé looked at him and said, "Okay, fine?"

Eric shrugged his shoulders and said, "Sure, okay," and we all burst out laughing.

"I know someone," Zé went on, "who can sell you a great car. It's not fancy, but it's mechanically sound. Good price too. Think about it. Let me know, okay?"

Yes, yes, we were nodding, but I was starting to feel dizzy with all that we had to consider.

"We'll need to talk about it a bit more. I'll be in touch soon. Obrigada," I said.

After Zé left, Georgia, Eric, and I stood around the heater as if it were a religious icon, such was the reverence with which we observed it. It hummed but ever so quietly. We closed the doors to the living room to keep the heat in, then sat on the couch, waiting to feel the warmth. Maggie jumped up on my lap and sprawled across both me and Georgia. The heat of her body warmed my legs.

"He has a friend who's a bank manager and he can help us open a bank account," I blurted out.

"Surely that's something we can do ourselves," Eric said. "I don't know, I don't think I want him pulling strings for us. I'd like everything to be above board. Let's try another bank tomorrow."

"I don't think it's pulling strings, just someone who knows what to do and is willing to help us. What do you suggest I tell him, that we don't want any help? That would be rude."

"We'll just let him know when we've done it. That should be fine."

"Oh, and he thinks we should buy a car. And he knows someone who can sell us one."

Silence filled the gulf growing between us. I sensed that Eric wanted to say no bloody way, but I was starting to think that it was a good idea.

"I think we can definitely buy a car ourselves," Eric said. "Should we decide that we want one. This is getting to be too much. We don't even have our money yet."

"I know you're skeptical," I said. "But I don't think there's anything nefarious behind his offers to help. There's nothing in it for him whether we buy a car or not."

Zé seemed nice enough, but our Canadian sensibilities made us suspicious of this level of interest. Eric felt that our affairs, especially anything related to our finances, were private, and he was uneasy discussing them with someone who was essentially a stranger. Since our arrival, both Zé and Joe John had been very attentive, checking in on us, offering help, showing up at our door to say hello.

"I think they're just being kind," I said. "It's the Portuguese way."

Poor Georgia. She didn't want to deal with any of this; she just wanted her parents back. All we seemed to be doing was worrying and arguing or standing in bank lineups.

"When we get all this sorted out, Georgia, we'll start living a normal life, I promise," I said.

"I hate this," she said. "You're both super stressed all the time. I can't wait till we have money. This stresses me out too."

I can't remember how many banks we tried. Not one would allow us to open a bank account. We had no job, according to them, and no lease or contract for our house. One bank manager we met with said she would consider it, but we had to go to City Hall to declare our residency and get a letter from them first, to prove that the house existed.

"Proof that the house exists? Can I just bring you a picture?" I asked. I was not trying to be a smartass; it was a serious question, and I was almost in tears.

"No, that's not how it works. It needs to be a notarized document."

Oh, for fuck's sake, I thought to myself. I was struggling to maintain my composure.

"Let's go to City Hall, Eric," I said and we got up and left her office without saying thank you.

It was a very patient clerk at City Hall who explained to us that I, the Portuguese citizen, needed to get a número de contribuinte, a tax number, before we could do anything that involved money, including getting a bank account. Normally people get this number by having a job, he told us, but he thought I should still be able to get one if I explained our situation. He told us where we could go to get this done, even drew a small map on the back of an envelope for us. I thanked him profusely.

We walked across town to a government office and waited in line for at least another half day, but I got my number. It wasn't even that difficult. I showed my Portuguese identification card, and the clerk asked me a few questions. It was straightforward, and by the time we walked out of there, I felt like I had a new identity. Tax-wise, I existed. Eric wasn't a citizen; he didn't have a job that paid him in euros, didn't even have a tax number, so all of the financial arrangements we made would need to be done in my name only.

"Do you think it will be possible for me to open a bank account now," I had asked the clerk.

"Oh, that I cannot say, minha senhora," he replied. "I don't know exactly how it works at the banks, but I don't see why not."

We had just arrived back home when my cell phone rang. It was Zé's brother, the voice on the other end of the line said. He had a car for us and would we like to see it? If so, Zé could pick us up in fifteen minutes.

When Zé arrived at our door, he said, "Bring your documents. We'll go see my friend at the bank after you see the car."

Zé's brother, the owner of the car, was a mechanic and had a shop in a nearby town. The car he showed us was an older model station wagon that looked to be in perfect shape.

"Oh, I don't know...it may be hard to sell it when we leave," I said to the two men standing there, waiting for our reaction.

As usual, I translated the highlights of the discussion for Eric's benefit. I explained that Zé's brother had offered to buy the car back from us for an agreed price when we were ready to leave. If anything went wrong with the car, mechanically, while we owned it, he would fix it for free. It was a great deal; how could we say no?

"Well, we can't pay for it yet, we don't have our money," Eric said.

"No problem. Take it now, I insist, and pay me when your money arrives," the mechanic said.

"Oh, I don't know about this...we'll need insurance, and..." I said.

"I know someone who can help with that too," Zé assured us.

Outside it was pouring rain. Eric and I exchanged looks of exhaustion. Georgia called us on the cell. "Are you guys ever coming home today? What's happening?"

The grey of the day was closing in around me. If a plane had materialized to take me back to Vancouver at that moment, I would not have hesitated. Eric put his arm around me, squeezed my shoulder, and whispered, "We're going to be fine. You have a contribuinte number." I couldn't help but smile.

Zé led us around town on a few errands, all related to our finances and the car purchase. We went to the bank and met with his friend, the bank manager, who had the paperwork ready for us. An hour later, we had a bank account. We bought the car and agreed to pay for it later, when our money came through from Canada, and then we went to see another of Zé's friends who was an insurance broker. Zé paid our insurance fee, and we walked out of there as legitimate owners of a new-to-us car, complete with Portuguese licence plates and insurance.

We drove home to show Georgia our new purchase and celebrated by driving to the big supermarket in another town to load up with staples. We could finally buy more than a couple of bags of groceries at once. We filled our cart with all the heavy things we'd been missing out on—bottles of wine, milk, canned tomatoes and beans, bags of flour and sugar, and a large package of toilet paper. As we strolled the aisles, Georgia mused out loud about what she'd bake first, and Eric and I chatted, still incredulous at all the generosity we'd been shown that day.

"I guess they were just being kind after all. Zé has been amazing," Eric said.

"He certainly has. It's like the extreme version of Portuguese hospitality. I mean, he knows nothing about us, really."

"I don't think we'd be able to do all of this without his help," Eric conceded.

When we got home, Georgia announced that she was going to make cookies. We had looked for chocolate chips at the supermarket, but unable to find any, we bought a chunk of cooking chocolate instead that we could chop up and use as chocolate chips. There were no cookie sheets in the house, but Georgia improvised by layering a couple of sheets of aluminum foil. The smell of baking filled our house and made us happy. It was starting to feel like home, and perhaps our luck was finally taking a turn.

We had dinner, and chocolate chip cookies and tea for dessert. For the first time since we had arrived, I felt that I could breathe easily.

"I'm still annoyed that we didn't get a bank account on our own," Eric said.

"You're going to have to let that one go," I said. "We have it now and that's the important thing."

Georgia had gone quiet as the talk turned to our finances again, but she offered a remark that seemed to sum things up for me: "Sounds like you just needed help navigating all the bureaucracy," she said. "I'm really glad Zé helped us."

• • •

The first thing I thought about when I woke up the next day was that it was Valentine's Day. It's not traditionally celebrated in Portugal, and even when we're in Vancouver, Eric and I don't really mark the occasion. But I felt like celebrating, and this would be a good excuse.

"It's today?" Eric asked.

"Yes. Let's go have a nice lunch," I suggested.

"Georgia," I called out. "Take a break from schoolwork today. We're going out for lunch."

Zé also owned a restaurant in the nearby town of Cacilhas. He had told us this a few times and suggested we come for lunch or dinner, but we hadn't paid much attention. Or maybe we had but then purposely avoided it because, you know, we might not like the food. But he had done so much for us recently, and I thought it might be a nice gesture if we did go there sometime, and why not today? Eric agreed, and we set out.

As soon as he saw us standing at the door, Zé came to greet us, shook our hands and said, "It's good to see you. I'm so glad you've come."

The restaurant was large, and it was packed with people. There were at least a dozen long tables and several smaller ones, some square, some round, all of them covered in white tablecloths. People were eating and drinking, talking loudly, laughing; some were gesturing with their arms and waving their hands while conversing. I saw some people wearing napkins on their chests, bib-style, so as to eat freely without staining their clothes.

There was a large display case running the width of the room, filled with different types of fish—some with red glistening skin, others with bluish or silvery scales, all of them lying on their sides, one dead eye to the ceiling. There were prawns, crab, clams, and lobster. It was overwhelming to see so many fish that looked just as they do when they get pulled from the water. The aroma of garlic and freshly cooked seafood emanated from the kitchen and surrounded us. And oh, the room was so warm.

Zé was a short, stout man in his late sixties, I guessed, with wavy, white, closely cropped hair. He was always energetic whenever we met, but on that day, he seemed to fly around the room. He greeted people at this table, then at that one, then rushed into the kitchen and back out, whispered to a waiter, then moved on to another table to greet more diners.

"Let me find you a place to sit, please wait just one moment," he said to us and then he was off. He came back a minute later and escorted us to a spot near the kitchen where two men were bringing in a table from the back room. They spread out a white tablecloth, and within seconds, there were three place settings, complete with white linen napkins.

We decided to have a feast. We were due, we thought, especially because we'd managed to survive all the bad weather, because it was Valentine's Day, and because we wanted to give back by patronizing our landlord's business. We ordered arroz de marisco, seafood rice, and a bottle of vinho verde, green wine, as recommended by our charming waiter.

"I'll bring you a few appetizers too," he said, and then he plied us with sausage and fresh buns, warm, runny cheese, and an assortment of olives.

The three of us shared the main dish—a steaming pot full of rice with a wild-looking mixture of lobster claws and crab legs, clams and mussels, and hefty chunks of white fish. It was a lot of food, and I imagined that they gave us an extra-large portion. With the first mouthful, I could detect a perfect blend of garlic, saffron, and cilantro. We ate until we could eat no more, but there was still some left over. When the waiter cleared the table, he lifted the lid off the pot, then looked at us and raised his eyebrow.

"What's the matter?" he said. "Didn't you like it?"

"We loved it but there was so much. And we had all those appe-tizers too."

"Ah, Canadians. You eat so little," he said, looking disappointed.

Saying no to dessert was out of the question after that exchange, so we ordered chocolate mousse to share. Our waiter's disappointment grew.

"All three of you are going to share one dessert?" he said incredu-lously. "But this is not possible!"

It was possible, and we did share, but the waiter laughed at us. Eric and I finished off with the perfect cup of coffee—a small cup half-filled with perfectly brewed espresso. All three of us deemed lunch to have been superb.

"A conta, por favor," Eric motioned to our waiter.

He returned to our table but not with the bill. Instead, he presented us with an assortment of liquor bottles: whisky, port, and the local ginjinha, a sour-cherry liqueur.

"It's on the house," he said. "Courtesy of my patrão."

We were replete but managed to have a shot of the ginjinha each, so as not to appear rude or ungrateful. He suggested Georgia try some as well. "It helps with the digestion. I'm not kidding," he said.

Georgia sipped from my glass and scrunched up her face. "Too strong for me," she said.

Once more, we asked for the bill. After a long wait, Zé came to the table, wished us a Happy Valentine's Day, and said that the lunch was on him.

This meal, this celebration where we'd gone all out was our way of showing him our gratitude. I didn't know whether protesting would be rude. What was the right thing to do at a time like this? I felt myself blush. "Oh no, please, you've done so much for us already," I said.

"I insist," Zé said.

"Muito obrigada," was all we could come up with.

. . . .

A Rainy Day in Lisbon

AAHHH, LISBON. The beauty and charm of this city have inspired songs and poems, novels, and films. Lisbon is often the subject of the bluesy tunes of the fado. Imagine not being able to live in Lisbon, the fadistas lament in their songs.

. . .

One morning I opened the French doors to the patio and saw big patches of blue in the sky. Could it be that the weeks of bad weather had finally come to an end? I noticed a bank of dark clouds in the distance, but from where I stood, that part was easy to ignore. Georgia and I decided to take the bus and spend the day in Lisbon.

We had two options for travel into Lisbon—by bus right from Costa, or by ferry from Cacilhas. I preferred the latter, because there's a certain romance to arriving in a city by boat, but this option was bit more complicated. It meant taking a bus to Cacilhas first and then transferring to the ferry, so we needed to juggle transit schedules and plan accordingly. The bus ride directly from Costa was much more straightforward and took less than an hour. To my mind, it was not quite as magical as going by boat, but it was also enjoyable and the views were spectacular. I especially liked going over the suspension bridge and looking at Lisbon's hillsides with all the white buildings and red tile roofs. Both options into the city required us to connect to the metro to travel into the centre.

Lisbon and Vancouver are similar in size—both cities have a population of around half a million in the city proper and roughly two million in the metropolitan area. The Lisbon Metro system and Vancouver's SkyTrain both serve about half a million riders each day, but Lisbon's system is much older, and the trains are significantly longer than the ones in Vancouver. To accommodate the longer trains, Lisbon's stations are huge, with multiple entrances, numerous turnstiles, and three or more storeys. Art was incorporated into the design of the stations when the metro system was first built in the 1950s, and today, different stations showcase different artists and styles of art, with some even featuring quotes from famous writers and poets. The Parque Station, for example, is decorated in azulejos, Portugal's traditional blue tiles, and includes excerpts from Fernando Pessoa's writing. The station we used most frequently, Baixa-Chiado, is devoted to the minimalist style of the artist Ângelo de Sousa and includes symmetrical bars and geometric designs. Touring the various stations is like visiting several art galleries and museums, and it's all possible for just the price of a transit ticket.

On this particular day, Georgia and I were so sure the good weather had arrived to stay that we left our umbrellas at home. As we rode across the bridge, we talked about what we would do when we got into the city. Georgia wanted to go to the bookstore, and I lobbied for lunch at an outdoor café. Both of us wanted to stroll along the river. When we saw the aqueduct over the roadway ahead, we knew our stop was close, so we rang the bell. We got off the bus and crossed the freeway at the crosswalk to take the metro into the city centre.

As we climbed the last steep flight of stairs out of the Baixa-Chiado metro station in the centre of Lisbon, we caught a glimpse of the sky. In the time that we'd spent underground, the dark clouds had moved in, and now it was pouring. There were small groups of people huddled at the station entrance to wait out the rain, others who scurried to nearby awnings, and some who dashed off down the street, covering the tops of their heads with newspapers or purses. Still others had been more prepared and walked purposefully underneath city-sized umbrellas. Why hadn't we brought ours?

We ducked into A Brasileira, the popular coffee shop in Chiado Square near the metro station. Normally, the outdoor patio would be full of tables and chairs, buskers, tourists, and locals, but right then, it was deserted. The tables and chairs were nowhere to be seen. The umbrellas were folded and leaning against the building, and the cobblestones were glistening. Inside, the coffee shop was crowded like I'd never seen before. All the tables were full, and people stood at the bar, two or three deep, calling out their orders to the servers behind the counter; dishes and cutlery clattered, espresso machines hissed, and bursts of steam puffed from the spouts. The smell of coffee surrounded me. I didn't care if it was raining outside; standing in that café, right at that moment, I felt an overwhelming sense of joy. I ordered a bica and a pastel de nata—a shot of espresso and custard tart. Georgia didn't order anything.

"I don't really want a tart, Mum. I only like them fresh out of the oven," she said. "Besides, I feel like I just finished breakfast."

I tried to make the experience last as long as I could, but I gulped the coffee and ate the tart in three or four bites. I was standing there, claiming barely a few inches of counter space, but I felt like I couldn't linger too long.

Back outside, the rain had stopped, and I posed for a picture next to the bronze sculpture of Fernando Pessoa, Portugal's celebrated twentieth-century poet. He is sitting at a table, wearing his signature hat; his legs are crossed, and his hands are resting on the table as if he's waiting for his coffee. I have dozens of variations of this photo, but I felt like I needed another one. To walk by without taking a picture would be like passing someone I knew on the street and not saying hello.

"Georgia, can you take my picture?" I asked, feeling a bit awkward. Posing for pictures does not come naturally to me.

"Okay, but let's do it quickly," she said. "And, um, you already have a dozen photos right here in this spot."

"I don't have any in the rain," I countered.

Posing for pictures also makes Georgia uncomfortable, even when she's the one behind the camera. "We're not really tourists anymore," she said, but she humoured me and took the photo.

We walked half a block down the hill to our favourite bookstore, Livraria Bertrand, to browse. This bookshop was founded by two brothers from France in 1732 and is now the oldest independent bookshop, not only in Lisbon, but in the world. There's a certificate from Guinness World Records on display inside the door to assure any skeptics.

The books at Bertrand are laid out on shelves and in glass display cases, in a series of rooms with hardwood floors and dark-panelled walls. There are comfortable couches and chairs strategically placed around the store. Georgia gravitated to the English section, and I headed to the room with guidebooks and picture books of Lisbon. It would be easy to spend a few hours in this place, especially on a rainy day. There were others browsing in the store, but the atmosphere was quiet and peaceful, a contrast to the bustle of the coffee shop from where we'd just come. I moved on to the Portuguese literature section after what seemed like an hour but was probably a lot less than that, just as Georgia approached me to say that she was ready to go.

"I think I'm ready for a snack after all," she said, knowing that right next door she could buy pão de queijo, the Brazilian cheese buns made with tapioca flour that have become her favourite snack. She had two of those and a freshly made carrot-orange juice. I had a small bottle of sparkling water and a roll.

"These are so light and fluffy," she said. "Yum."

Navigating the cobblestone streets of Lisbon's hilly neighbour-hoods is a challenge anytime, but it's doubly difficult when they are wet and slippery. Dodging umbrellas is an added hazard, making the simple act of walking an activity requiring concentration and atten-tion. We carried on down the hill, very carefully, to Rossio, the central plaza. Here, there are two large fountains on opposite ends of the square, and the ground is a dizzying array of two-toned cobblestones forming a mosaic. The area is a hive of activity with shops, cafés, bars, and restaurants along the edges of the square. Numerous vendors hawk everything from sunglasses to lottery tickets and hordes of people rush for taxis and buses, dodging motorcycles and mopeds. I noticed smoke swirling from several carts around the plaza. Vendors roasted chestnuts on hot coals, wrapped them in paper flutes, and sold them to passersby for one euro. The characteristic aroma hung in the air around the carts, and the smoke tickled my nostrils. I could almost taste the chestnuts even before eating them. Georgia was hesi-tant to try them, but we shared an order, and she fell in love.

"These are delicious!" She took the paper flute and moved over to a spot against a building so she could peel the chestnuts without having to worry about cars. I was surprised that she liked them; I've always thought they were an acquired taste. She ate several chestnuts, one after another, sometimes popping two into her mouth at once.

"Can I have just one more, maybe?" I asked.

She smiled, being careful to keep her lips closed since her cheeks were full on both sides. She swallowed and laughed, then passed the flute on to me and said, "Okay, if you must."

"Well, we can always buy more," I added.

I had tried chestnuts roasted like this decades before, but I was still startled by how good this first mouthful tasted. The chestnuts were crunchy but dissolved easily in my mouth and had a faint chocolatey flavour that remained on my tongue long after I'd swallowed the last morsel.

"Now *this* is Lisbon in the winter," I said to Georgia, and rattled off a couple of lines from Amália Rodrigues's famous fado, "Cheira a Lisboa."

"Hey, I recognize that tune," Georgia said.

"Yes, well, the lyrics are about exactly what we are doing right here, right now," I said. "Drinking coffee in Rossio and eating roasted chestnuts on a cold day."

We wandered around the square and browsed in shoe stores and jewellery shops. We found ourselves on Rua Augusta, a pedestrian-only street with yet more cafés and restaurants. All the browsing had made me hungry, so I decided to stop at a café for a bolinho de bacalhau, a fried codfish cake, and a rissol de camarão, a small pocket of dough filled with shrimp in a creamy bechamel sauce. Once again, I stood at the counter to eat. There are different prices for menu items at most cafés, depending on where you choose to eat. Standing at the counter is the cheapest option (lingering is discouraged), followed by sitting at an indoor table, and sitting at the outdoor patio is the most expensive option.

Georgia passed on food at this stop too. I knew she was holding out for her favourite, the Padaria Portuguesa on the next street over. This is one of a chain of bakery cafés that we first discovered while exploring the Benfica district a couple of weeks earlier. Georgia ordered a brioche croissant, "the best thing ever," she said, and a slice of salame de chocolate, a rich dessert that looked to me like raw cookie dough rolled in sugar.

We sat at a table, and although I could not eat any more, I had another coffee and an Água das Pedras, naturally carbonated spring water from the northeast of Portugal. On our way out, we bought a loaf of rye bread and a half dozen whole-wheat buns to take home.

The rain had stopped so we meandered along the river for a while, then made our way back to Rossio and up the hill towards Chiado. The sun peeked through the clouds, and it got warm enough that we removed our jackets. We passed a new ice cream shop on Rua Garrett, just before the metro station, and Georgia looked at me with a little twinkle and said, "I still have a bit of room. I should try their pistachio."

Whenever Georgia buys ice cream, she almost always orders the same flavour. This provides her with a good benchmark for comparison purposes, and after taking her first taste of this one, she rolled her eyes back and deemed it the best she'd ever had. I chose a passion fruit sorbet, hoping it would be less filling than the creamy choices. It wasn't lost on me that I'd eaten something at each one of our stops while Georgia had been much more selective.

By the time we were on the bus and heading back over the bridge, the weather had turned miserable again. It was foggy and drizzly, and we could barely see the river below when we crossed the bridge. The bus was full of people heading home from work. We were lucky to get a seat, and we were sitting together too. I was warm and dry and feeling very content. I started dozing, but Georgia nudged me with her elbow and said, "Do you realize we didn't see any of the sights? All we did was eat!"

"You're right," I said, slouching down in my seat and resting my head on her shoulder. "I'm so full."

We got off the bus at the last stop, at the edge of the market in Costa. The rain was pelting once again. Right there on the sidewalk, a few steps from the curb, was a man selling umbrellas. We bought one. It was the end of the day, so our purchase didn't make much sense, but we both felt better having one for the walk home in the downpour. One umbrella wasn't quite big enough for both of us, though, so we still managed to arrive home drenched. Eric opened the front door to greet us and a marvellous aroma from the kitchen followed him and made its way to us in the front yard.

"I thought you might be wet and tired, so I've been working on dinner," Eric said. "A nice penne with tomato sauce and chouriço. I sure hope you're hungry."

. . . .

Planning to Run

ON ONE OF OUR BUS TRIPS into Lisbon, I noticed a video monitor at the front of the bus, near the driver, with rolling ads. I started watching, sometimes becoming mesmerized. At some point, I saw the words *labour strike* and *buses* but that was all I absorbed. I figured that the bus drivers might go on strike, but I didn't know why or when.

A week or so later, Georgia and I were standing in a queue at the bus station in Costa, and I noticed other people in line were restless. Some were sitting on the ground. We waited for a long time. So long that I thought maybe the bus drivers were on strike.

I asked the woman standing in line behind me and she said, yes, today was a day of labour action, but it didn't necessarily mean that there would be no buses, just that the schedule would be disrupted. Bus drivers were limited in how they could protest the fact that their wages had been cut by forty per cent practically overnight. It was part of the crise (pronounced creez) —the economic crisis that was affecting Portugal. Austerity measures such as the severe pay cuts were imposed by the European Union and carried out by the Portuguese government. As this woman explained things to us, it seemed everyone in the queue had an opinion. They got out of line and came to gather around the woman who was talking. There were three or four women and a couple of men, all expressing their opinions with passion, and they were all in agreement. From what I could tell, they supported the bus drivers and others who were experiencing similar pay cuts. The government wanted too much, one woman said. Another woman walked up really close to me and threw both of her arms in the air and said, "Regular people, regular families, are suffering, senhora. It's a travesty." I thought she was going to cry.

This scene was definitely not what Georgia nor I had expected when we set out for the bus stop and our day trip into Lisbon. I had heard about the economic crisis on the news, and I'd overheard conversations in coffee shops, even talked about it a bit with Zé and Helena, but this conversation was different. I saw the despair on people's faces and heard it in the tone of their voices. Georgia understood the gist of the discussion, but mostly she watched in amazement. I sensed that she was perplexed by people speaking so passionately to people they didn't know.

After waiting for an hour and a half, Georgia and I gave up and went home. A few people in line had left before us. I made a mental note to pay closer attention to the news on the bus screens after that.

On another day, back on the bus and heading into Lisbon, I was watching for the aqueduct to make sure we didn't miss our stop. I glimpsed some passing information on the monitor at the front about the Lisbon Mini Marathon in the spring. Was it March? May? I couldn't be sure. Damn, I'd missed it. I was waiting for that same ad to scroll through again when I noticed that Georgia was standing at the back door, ready to get off the bus.

"Mum! Come on! You're not paying attention!" she said in a loud whisper, loud enough that I could hear, two rows of seats away.

I was startled back to the present, grabbed my bag, and rushed to the back door. "That's why we travel so well together, darling. Thanks for looking after me," I said to Georgia as we got off the bus.

We crossed the freeway, and then Georgia said, "We just about missed our stop. What were you reading about this time?"

"I think I saw an ad for a mini marathon and it looked like the route goes over the bridge. Wouldn't that be fun?"

"A marathon, are you kidding?"

"A mini marathon," I corrected her. "The operative word here is 'mini.'"

We walked down the steps to the metro, in unison.

"Well, yeah, it could be fun, I guess. But I'm not a runner, and neither are you."

Georgia was blessed with a practical gene. Being pragmatic is one of her many strengths, being a dreamer is one of mine.

We just missed the train. For a few minutes, we were the only ones on the platform.

"I know. But I could become one. And so could you! Let's do it," I proposed.

"No thanks," she said. "I'm really not into running."

"But it would be fun, G. And we'd have time to train."

"You think? When is it?"

"Um, I'm not sure. I didn't get that information," I conceded.

"How far is it? Marathon sounds far, even with 'mini' in front of it."

"I don't know that either. But we could do it. And we'd get fit!"

The train arrived, and we got on and found a seat, side by side. I nudged her a couple of times, adding, "Let's do it, okay?" She didn't quite agree, but she did say that we should pay attention to the rolling ads on the way home so we'd at least have more information.

A mini marathon, on the 16th of March; 7.8 kilometres. That's pretty mini, I thought. Even I might be able to do that. As soon as we got home, I looked up the website, registered, checked in with Georgia who nodded, albeit reluctantly, and I paid for both of us. We were committed.

Georgia's online Grade 10 curriculum included Physical Education 10, a required course. She had to log hours of activity to fulfill this requirement and this race, and all the training, would be considered course work for her. I thought it was a brilliant idea.

Since our arrival, I had grown concerned about our social isolation, especially Georgia's. We knew so few people. I, at least, could talk to waiters at restaurants or to the vendors at the market, but Eric and Georgia had only me and each other to talk to. I wondered, but only to myself, what impact this seclusion would have on Georgia. I thought that focusing on physical activity, with the added challenge of setting a goal like this, would help her—help us both—feel more connected to our community. If nothing else, I figured it would provide us with some precious mother-daughter bonding time.

We started our training sessions the next day. We decided to follow the schedule that is recommended for beginners who register for the Sun Run back home in Vancouver. A walk-run program that builds stamina over time seemed a good option since neither of us had ever run before.

Following this program also gave us a chance to discover the park behind our house. It was a small urban oasis of green in the middle of town that was flanked by cliffs on one side and sand and sea on the other. In our half hour of walking and running, we covered most of the trails in the park. We knew we were becoming regulars when we started seeing some of the same people, and occasionally one or another would smile and say hello. How our spirits would lift when someone would greet us or tell us to "keep going." This was a new experience for both Georgia and me, to have someone initiate contact with us. It was minimal, but we agreed that it made us feel like we belonged.

Later, when we ran for longer periods, we would take the wooden bridge from the park to the beach and then run along the seawall. This beach extends for more than twenty kilometres to the south so we never did make it all the way to the end—that would have been too far for us—but we would run as far as our training program dictated then walk back home.

It became easier to keep to our schedule when the weather warmed up and the sun came out. A few times we ran in the other direction, to Trafaria, the next town to the north, and had Eric pick us up there and drive us home. On those days we felt especially accomplished.

After each run, I would do a series of stretches in the hopes of preventing injury. I had experienced serious back spasms before, and I wanted to do everything I could to prevent another onset of those. I acknowledged that to start a running program at my age would require more deliberate care and attention to the various aches and pains that might arise.

Once I completed my stretching routine, it was time for lunch— fresh bread, cheese, and a fruit salad with oranges, bananas, and kiwis. When I was growing up, we called fruit salad "titi-fruto." My mother would sprinkle the fruit with cane sugar for extra sweetness or add a splash of port just before serving. Here in Costa, the oranges were especially tasty. I would buy them at the market, and they were so juicy, I could swear they had been picked that morning. Georgia and I would eat our lunch on the front porch, taking in the longed-for sunshine. Those moments felt blissful.

Georgia combined her training runs with yoga. She would take her mat and the laptop up to the rooftop deck and she'd follow a yoga video on YouTube. She preferred to wait until evening and practise under a starry sky.

After dinner one night, I logged on to Facebook and decided to send a message to Beth, the mother of Georgia's friend, Claire. On a whim, I extended an invitation for Claire to come and visit during spring break. After a few days, Beth replied that she and her husband had thought it over and that Claire was keen to accept the invitation.

She would arrive in a few weeks, the day before the Lisbon Mini Marathon.

Georgia, Eric, and I were thrilled. The weather was improving, and we were expecting our first guest. Our life was taking a social turn.

. . . .

Winter Market Days

ONE OF MY FAVOURITE THINGS to do in Costa was to browse at the market. I often went alone, in the morning, while Eric and Georgia did their work at home. I would stop and have a coffee at the counter of one of the coffee shops on the way, and sometimes I'd have a pastel too. I'd go to the bakery to buy a loaf of bread or a few buns, and then head to the market, where I would talk to the vendors and fulfill my need for conversation.

The market in Costa is a large building that reminds me of an airplane hangar, though perhaps it's not quite that big. Inside, it's dark and a little damp, always cool. It's a hub of activity—there are people milling about, talking, examining the produce, and there are delivery people pulling dollies, transporting crates, and others packing and unpacking boxes. Vendors stay close to their tables, arranging and rearranging their produce. A mixture of smells—musty soil or fish or raw meat—swirls in the air, depending on which area of the building you're wandering in. Everywhere, people are talking, discussing, explaining; some are hawking their products. The building is open on both ends so there's a lot of traffic noise, too. I can't imagine that it would be a comfortable place to work. Luckily for the vendors, it closes at 2:00 p.m.

At a small stand right inside the north entrance, a woman sold mostly verduras, or greens. She didn't seem to have much to sell on any given day and what she had always looked a little wilted, but I usually bought something from her—lettuce, if nothing else. She would smile and greet me as I entered the market, and I found it difficult to get past her without buying anything. I would stop to talk to her, and then the woman from the next stall (who had much better-looking produce) would join in our conversation. From her, I'd buy potatoes, kale, carrots, and whatever else looked good. She'd often ask me what I was making for dinner and then throw in a handful of herbs, like parsley or cilantro or rosemary, that she thought would go best with my dinner. No charge. And when I tried to give her extra to cover the herbs, she'd wave her hand wildly and say something like, "Oh please, that's not necessary, they're just herbs."

Farther down, in the fruit stall area, there was the man who sold what I deemed to be the sweetest oranges. I chatted with him often. Once, he told me that he had a cousin who lived near Vancouver somewhere. I asked where because, as I explained, the Portuguese community in Vancouver is quite small and who knows, I might know him. He told me he would check with his wife and tell me next time. But he kept forgetting.

The crisp, peppery smell of citrus in this part of the market often permeated my nostrils and filled my head with memories of my childhood in the Azores. I was in Costa, but my heart was back in my parents' quinta in São Miguel. I remember looking forward to Saturday morning walks to the orchard with my father because it felt like I was going to work with him. We'd come home laden with bags of oranges and lemons and sometimes bananas too, and my mother would promptly make fruit salad.

Here on the mainland, I saw orange trees everywhere—on the road-sides, on the boulevards, in front yards and backyards. Every few days, I'd buy a couple of bags of oranges from my favourite vendor and carry them home, just like I remember doing as a child. I ate oranges with yogurt for breakfast, then again for a midday snack, and for dessert, sliced in rounds, sprinkled with chopped mint and slivered almonds.

Past the fruit stalls was a large, partly closed-off area full of tables with fish and seafood displayed on mounds of ice. Women in oil-cloth aprons called out their catch of the day and competed for customers. I didn't go in there very often because I felt conspicuous in my igno-rance, and I found the noise and activity level disorienting. I was overwhelmed by the immense variety of fish, most of which looked foreign to me, and I was intimidated by these women, all of whom were loud and looked strong and confident. If they told me to buy something, I knew I would, just because I wouldn't know how to say no. I wasn't yet brave enough to buy fish as I had no idea how to clean or cook most of it. I'd sometimes peek in the entrance and then walk away quickly. One day I'll buy fish there, I'd think to myself.

Next to the fish area was an open section with meat of all kinds—poultry, beef, and pork. The butchers were burly men who wore white, blood-smeared, full-body aprons. The smell of raw meat in such large quantities made me gag and feel like my stomach was turning upside down and around, so this was one area I avoided. I chose to buy our meat at the supermarket where it was handled by people behind counters wearing white lab coats, hair nets, and rubber gloves, and where I couldn't detect a meat odour.

I loved wandering around the market, but what I found most relaxing was that I could talk to people, and I didn't have to translate. It was a treat when my brain could operate in just one language. I often wondered about Georgia and Eric—they had no one else to talk to except me, or others through me, and yet they seemed less lonely than I often felt.

One Friday morning, Georgia, having just handed in an English assignment to her teacher via email, decided to take the rest of the day off and come shopping with me. While I enjoyed my solo market trips, I was happy to have company on this one. The sun was shining, and it was as if even the pavement was warming. Birds were flitting about in the trees that dotted the plaza, and people on the streets were almost…smiling. When we walked into the market, the verduras lady at the entrance greeted me with a smile and a wave, just as the vendor behind her called out a "bom dia, minha querida" to me. They all eyed Georgia, no doubt wondering who she was, but they just smiled and no one asked.

"She called you darling," Georgia said.

"It's a term of endearment," I said.

"She must like you."

"Why wouldn't she?" I said, with a broad smile.

As we walked up and down a few of the aisles, most of the vendors had something to say to us, a greeting or a quip, bookended with laughter.

Georgia leaned in to me and said in a loud whisper, "Gee, Mum, you're like a movie star."

We both laughed. For someone so shy, I could tell that the attention made her uncomfortable, but she looked a little bit pleased too. Perhaps she sensed what I, too, was feeling—that we were no longer strangers, and somehow, we'd managed to make inroads into community life in our new town.

We stopped at the fruit stall for oranges and then chose a few bananas and strawberries. The vendor saw me, and almost on cue, slapped his forehead with the palm of his hand and said, "I forgot to ask my wife for the name of the town again."

"It's okay," I said, laughing. "I'll be here for a long time. Tell me next time."

"And who do you have with you today?" the man next to him asked, looking right at Georgia.

"Oh, this is my daughter. Her name is Georgia," I said.

"Your daughter? How nice. She's so branquinha," he said. So white.

"Is your husband a Canadiano?" someone else asked.

"Yes, he is," I answered.

I didn't bother to add that my father had also been very fair, with blue eyes. I often offer that explanation back home when people openly assume that all Portuguese people have dark hair and olive skin, but I am tired of that conversation. And it seemed that the stereotype existed here, too—white skin equals Canadian, olive skin equals Portuguese. I sensed a difference, though. In Canada, this generalization is one of exclusion, a societal message that if my skin is not white, I don't belong, that I must be from somewhere else. Here, I understood his comment to mean that I was "one of them," and it was Georgia who was pegged as a foreigner.

"What was that all about?" Georgia asked me as we moved on from the fruit stall.

"He was remarking that your skin is white. Or fair, I guess," I said.

"He actually said that?"

"Something like that," I said. "I think it was just an observation, but he said it out loud."

"That's so weird."

"It doesn't feel great to have someone comment on your skin colour, does it? I guess that doesn't happen to you very often," I said. "It happens to me at home." And by that I meant in Canada. I was immediately transported to all the times in Vancouver and Edmonton where I'd been described as "not quite white" or "not quite brown," even by people I knew well. Whether white or brown or somewhere in between, I find it difficult to accept that anyone would feel free to comment on skin colour. Even here, in the country of my birth, it seemed that white skin was more desirable and perhaps that was why the man, a bystander I didn't know, had felt he could openly comment on Georgia's fair complexion. Or maybe I was just overly sensitive to the whole issue.

On our way out of the market, I wanted to check out the fish shop facing the square. Georgia took our bags of groceries and went to sit on a nearby bench. This was a much quieter fish-selling area, more like a small shop within the market, and there were no hawkers. The fishmonger, decked out in her oilcloth apron and tall rubber boots, walked out from behind the counter to come and talk to me. She smiled and said, "What do you want to try? Some sole?"

I felt bolder today, maybe because I was shopping with Georgia, and decided that today was the day I'd buy some fish.

"Hmm, I already know how to cook sole, and I know what it tastes like. Can you suggest something else? I'd like to try something new."

"How do you want to cook it?"

"In the oven, I think. And I need it to be easy."

"How about some garoupa? Look, here, it's lovely. Just came in this morning."

I could identify that fish—grouper. The Portuguese name even sounded similar to English. I had never cooked it, though I do remember eating it when my mother or my sisters cooked.

"Great. Is it easy?"

"Super easy," she said.

"No, I'm not kidding. I've never cooked a whole fish like this before. I have no idea what to do. And I don't know how to clean it either."

"No problem. I'll clean it for you. And cooking it is super simple. You place the fish in a baking dish, sprinkle it with coarse salt, garlic, black pepper, and cilantro." As she said this, she rubbed her fingers together to mimic the sprinkling action. Then she continued, "Drizzle with olive oil and maybe a bit of white wine, and that's it."

"How much oil? And how much wine?"

"Not too much. You don't want to poach the fish."

"Okay," I said, feeling unsure.

"It'll be delicious. You can't go wrong," she said. She handed me the bag with the fish in it; I paid, then started to walk away. Then I quickly turned around and asked her, in a half whisper, "At what temperature?"

The three women behind the counter could not contain their laughter. Eventually, one said, "Set the oven at 180 degrees. Bake it for ten-to-fifteen minutes. Don't overcook it!"

As if they were guessing what I would ask next, one of the women said, "Just cut off the head and keep it to make a nice soup tomorrow."

I gave her a thumbs up and a smile along with my "obrigada, senhora."

I went to meet Georgia at the park bench and held up my bag of fish, feeling triumphant.

• • •

My feelings of accomplishment evaporated as soon as I started to prepare dinner. How much olive oil is a "drizzle"? And how much wine is a "bit"? Was I supposed to add the cilantro before or after baking? I winged it, decided that a bit was a splash (of wine) and a drizzle was a zigzag (of olive oil), and I added cilantro before and after baking. The one thing I remembered her saying quite emphatically was to not overcook the fish, so I made sure of that. I removed it from the oven a little before the fifteen-minute mark and checked it. It looked opaque to me, so I decided it was done and not overdone. I transferred it to a platter I had warmed with hot water, surrounded it with steamed potatoes (sprinkled with black pepper and parsley) and took it out to the table much like I've done in the past with birthday cake creations that I've been proud to present. Eric and Georgia had made an elaborate salad with different kinds of lettuce, cucumber, and sweet peppers, and we opened a bottle of wine. Everything about the meal was near perfection, including the fish. Each morsel held together on the fork but dissolved in my mouth, leaving a slightly salty, almost buttery aftertaste on my tongue. There wasn't much meat left over—the fishmonger had picked the perfect size for the three of us. All of us, including Georgia, deemed the fish to be delicious.

I was so pleased the dinner had gone well. It had indeed been simple, and now, I felt emboldened to try other fish. We'd go on to have grouper several more times but also hake and sole, different kinds of mackerel, and a variety of shellfish. The biggest surprise for me was that cooking Portuguese-style was so much easier than I'd previously thought. There aren't a lot of fancy sauces or complicated techniques required, just a few ingredients. Simple cooking allows the flavour of the fish to come through, as long as you don't overcook it!

. . . .

Ashes to Ashes

THE END OF FEBRUARY brought a turn in the weather. We had endured six weeks of wild storms, and now it was as if even Mother Nature had decided we'd had enough. The rain eased, the wind diminished, and the days began to warm. On the first weekend of March, Carnival was in full swing, a reminder for me that Lent, and spring, were not far away. Carnival is not something we celebrate in Vancouver, but here, there was a festive air around town, and it was hard to miss. People walked around dressed up in silly costumes, and restaurants and shops were decorated with streamers and balloons, and many offered special deals.

Carnival refers to those few days of indulgence and excess that precede the fasting and abstinence of Lent, a solemn period of prayer that leads into the celebration of Easter. During Carnival, there are parades and parties with lots of dancing, fatty foods and sweets. This culminates on the Tuesday before Ash Wednesday, the first day of Lent. The cities of Rio de Janeiro, Venice, and New Orleans are famous worldwide for the street parties and festivities of Fat Tuesday, or Mardi Gras.

On São Miguel, the start of Lent is marked, as I remember from childhood, by going to church and receiving ashes on our foreheads. After Mass, my family would have a simple meal, and there would be much discussion about how the adults would fast over the next six weeks until Easter. I was not aware of all the details and requirements, only that pregnant women, older people, and children did not participate in the fasting rituals. For me, it meant we wouldn't be having dessert or sweets for a long time, not until my mother baked the traditional sweet bread, massa sovada, for Easter. On Fridays, my parents would eat very little. My mother would mostly drink tea, but she would allow herself the occasional slice of bread. I still got my three meals.

For Catholics, Lent is a time of repentance for all the things we have done wrong, as well as a time of reflection and reconciliation with God. The ashes are a symbol of death—a reminder that we are all mortals, but also of the death of sin through forgiveness. It's a heavy time, especially for children like me who wanted to understand everything about the grown-up world.

I remember going to Ash Wednesday services with my mother. We'd walk hand-in-hand down the street to our local church that was no more than a hundred metres from our house. Once we walked through the big doors at the front, it was instantly dark and quiet, and I can recall the smell of incense, even to this day. My mother and I would choose our seats, and once she got settled, she'd reach for her purse and take out her handkerchief to wipe off her bright red lipstick. Then she'd take her rosary in her hands and close her eyes and pray until the priest started the Mass. I sat really close to her and watched her lips move, then followed along with her when the lector read the stories from the Bible, and I'd sing the hymns just like she did. I knew all the words.

Near the end of the Mass, we would line up and make our way to the altar to receive the ashes. We knelt along the altar rail and waited while the priest moved from one person to the next, dipped his thumb in a bowl, and marked our foreheads with the sign of the cross. When it was my turn, I could hear him mumble the words, "Remember that you came from dust and to dust you will return. Repent and be saved." It used to scare me to think about turning into dust.

On the way home I'd have so many questions for my mum—"What does that mean, that I came from dust?" and "How long does it take for bones to become dust?" I don't remember how she responded, exactly, but I do remember the sense of comfort I felt when my mother answered my questions. All she had to do was put her arm around my shoulder and I felt protected and safe. Later, when I got ready for bed, I'd tell her that I couldn't get the image of people turning to dust out of my head and that I was afraid. She'd hold me and tell me to pray three Hail Marys, and I'd be sure to fall asleep quickly and have good dreams. "Mary is a mother to everyone; she protects us all," she'd say.

I have never attended a service on Ash Wednesday in Vancouver. The distribution of ashes still happens since it's an important part of the liturgical calendar, but this usually occurs on the Sunday that follows Ash Wednesday. I do go then—I'm still a weekly attendee— but I wipe the smudge of ashes off my forehead before I leave the church and head back into my regular city life. It's unusual to see people walking around with crosses on their foreheads, and I don't want to be one of them. I'm not comfortable with public signs of religion, especially those that set me apart from everyone else in a secular city like Vancouver.

I wondered what Lent would be like in Portugal, a predominantly Catholic country, and if Ash Wednesday would be anything like what I remembered from my childhood. I decided I would go into Lisbon for the day and see if I could arrive in time to attend a church service. Eric and Georgia wanted to come with me as well. I sensed they wanted to support me, but they were also curious to experience this day, this religious tradition, in a culture that was new to them.

We took the metro to the Baixa-Chiado Station in the late morning and checked the schedules at a number of churches in the area. Each church had a service on the hour, every hour in the morning, and then again in the evening, and some had afternoon masses as well. We went for lunch first, then arrived at the Church of the Martyrs on Rua Garrett ten minutes before the start of the first afternoon service. When we walked through the doors, it was dark and cavernous, with a gold-laden altar at the far end. I recognized the smell of the incense immediately. A few people were wandering around—tourists, I presumed, since they were taking pictures of the Gothic columns and the stone statues of saints that lined the walls. We chose to sit in a pew about halfway up the main aisle. There were ten or twenty people sitting already, mostly elderly women. That makes sense, I thought— it is the middle of the afternoon on a weekday. But over the next ten minutes, the church steadily filled, not just with elderly people but also with families, couples, kids and teenagers, men and women, young and old.

The Mass started, and I recognized the tune of the first hymn right away. Half a dozen altar boys processed up the main aisle, followed by the priest who was dressed in the purple vestments symbolic of the Lenten season. He was young and handsome, probably in his thirties, something I noticed right away since most priests in the churches I attend in Vancouver tend to be much older. When he started speaking and welcomed everyone, I noted that his Portuguese, like mine, gave him away as being from elsewhere. He is not Lisbon-born, I thought, though I couldn't place exactly where he might be from. His accent was not from the Azores either, but could it be from Brazil? Angola?

He started the Mass with the sign of the cross and the words of prayer that are the same no matter which Catholic church you go to, anywhere in the world. I slid into a comfort zone. I still knew all the words, not just the responses but the priest's prayers too. How were the Portuguese words still stored in my brain, and how was it that these prayers rolled so easily off my lips, even decades after I last recited them? Eric and Georgia both gave me quizzical looks as if to ask, how do you know what to say? I shrugged my shoulders and smiled a silent "I have no idea." But in my heart, I was transported to our local church in Lagoa, and I was there with my mother. I brought my hand to my lips and wondered if I had refreshed my lipstick after lunch. Like my mother, I own various shades of red, and while I don't wear much makeup, I always put on lipstick before I leave the house. And then my eyes filled, and a tear rolled down my cheek and onto my upper lip. I wiped my face with my hand, then opened my purse to look for a tissue. Of course, I didn't have any. I sniffed, and that was it, tears spilled from both eyes. Eric and Georgia looked puzzled, wondering what on earth I was crying about. I tried to compose myself. I used my sleeve to wipe the tears, and I took a few deep breaths.

I understood that this Mass, these words, were more than a religious rite for me, even more than a cultural tradition—they were an integral part of me, of my childhood, and my upbringing. My own little history was playing out before me, and it was familiar and comfortable. And oh, how I missed my mother.

The reading from the Book of Psalms was even more beautiful in Portuguese than in English, maybe because the psalms are written in verse and Portuguese is such a poetic language. I glanced over at Eric, desperate to share the beauty of what I was hearing, but he didn't return my look. He seemed focused, as if he were trying to discern the odd Portuguese word, and we didn't connect. He was here for his own reasons, and I was alone in mine.

The next reading was from the Gospel of Matthew. I knew these words. I have heard them so many times on Sundays throughout my life, mostly in English. But the message made more of an impression on me today.

Do not let your right hand know what the left is doing; do not be a hypocrite; do not boast or think that you are better than others; do not let others know of your generosity for if you get your reward from others, you will not need it or get it from God. Do good things just because, and offer them to God; don't tell everyone how great you are. Be in relationship with God. My head was whirring with memories of my childhood but also with love for the poetry of this language. The first language I learned to speak.

The priest started the homily and talked about the meaning of fasting during Lent.

Let it not just be about food, he said, *but also refrain from taking part in impure acts. Do not speak ill of your colleague, do not gloat; be at peace, and create a pure heart.*

I leaned over to Eric and tried to do a simultaneous translation, but I was missing so much of what was being said, and I couldn't convey the impact that the priest's words were having on me. Eventually, I stopped. Eric whispered to me that he was having trouble following, and he couldn't really hear me. I'll tell him later, I thought to myself, but I knew that it would be harder once this moment had passed.

The three of us lined up in the aisle to go to the altar for the distribution of ashes. Unlike in Vancouver, there was no order to how people lined up. It wasn't one pew at a time, from front to back. No, here people just swarmed from the back and sides and somehow jostled into position in the lineup. I found it disorienting, and later, both Eric and Georgia would tell me that they had found the chaos unsettling.

We didn't have to kneel at the rail like I remembered doing as a child; we just stood one by one in front of the priest, and he made the sign of the cross on our foreheads. The words he said were the same as I remembered from my childhood, but they no longer scared me.

The priest gave the final blessing, and then he and the altar boys processed out while we sang another familiar hymn. I felt exhausted by all the emotion. I wanted to sit there awhile and listen to the organ, but both Georgia and Eric were making their way to the door so I got up and followed them out.

We walked out into the brightness of mid-afternoon and the bustle of the city.

"Can I wipe these ashes off my forehead?" Georgia asked.

"If you want. I'm keeping mine," I said.

We made our way down the hill, stepping carefully to avoid uneven cobblestones. People passed us going in the opposite direction, many with crosses on their foreheads. No one looked at me or seemed to notice the black smudge on my forehead. It's what is done here on this day, I thought to myself. It's normal, and I don't have to explain it or defend it to anybody.

"Let's go sit down by the river," I suggested. "I need to process."

"What's to process," Eric asked. "We just went to church." I noticed he'd rubbed off his cross. Only a tiny smudge remained.

"I don't know exactly but my heart is so full. It feels like it was way more than just going to church to me."

I sat in the middle, all of us on a cement bench facing the Tagus. No one said anything for a long time. Then I broke the silence.

"I think it was something about the language, the Portuguese. It was so beautiful."

Georgia said she had been able to pick out many of the words. "I recognized the readings, and I understood a lot of what the priest said in his homily," she said. I sensed she was proud of that.

Eric added that he hadn't understood much, but he had been able to follow along since all masses have the same structure. Eric wasn't brought up Catholic, but he has accompanied me whenever I go to a Catholic service. I go with him to the United Church too. Throughout our life together we have managed to honour both of our traditions and alternate our attendance between the two churches.

"There was definitely something about the language for me," I said. "Hearing the prayers, the readings and those hymns, all in Portuguese, brought back so many memories."

"Must have made you think of your mum, eh?" Georgia asked.

"I think that's part of it," I said. I put my arm around her shoulder and gave her a big squeeze. Then I leaned my head on Eric and said, "I know that it can't feel the same for you. So much of this is about my stuff." I got up off the bench and faced them. "But I'm so grateful that you both came with me. And that you try to understand. It means a lot to me."

We held hands and walked down the esplanade to the ferry terminal to make our way back home.

· · · ·

Belonging

IN COSTA, I straddled the two realities of local resident and tourist while not fitting well into either one. When I am in Vancouver, I long for Portugal—to live in a place where I feel understood, where no one asks me where I'm from, or how to spell my name. Adapting to life in Costa gave me that and more. I found that hearing my language everywhere afforded me a sense of comfort and belonging that can be elusive in Canada. In Costa, I knew what was expected of me in different situations, and I eased into the culture. But I had also been frustrated by bureaucracy and my inability to reason my way through the challenges we encountered. How hard did it have to be to open a bank account?

Despite feeling like I had come back home, I found myself missing many aspects of my Canadian life. I missed the order of things—the expectation that there are rules to follow, and if I follow those rules, tasks get done. I missed organized traffic lanes and parking spots and customer service with a smile. I missed my home near the woods; I missed the mountains and the calm ocean in the bay. I missed people patiently waiting their turn.

The Canadian in me had been collecting sales tax receipts for the bigger purchases I'd made so I could claim them at the airport when I left the country to return to Canada. But I'd soon learned that staying in Portugal longer than 180 days classified me as a resident and made me ineligible for a reimbursement. For the time being, I was fully Portuguese.

Most of the merchants in Costa recognized me after a month or two, and some even knew my buying habits. There were the women at the market who offered me menu suggestions, for example, and the woman at the bakery who knew how many buns I'd buy every day, and that I bought a loaf on Fridays for the weekend. She knew that I brought my own bag and turned down the plastic ones. She sometimes laughed and thought that was a little strange. "Too frugal," she said once.

While Portugal is the country of my birth, I've always been a tourist in Lisbon. Costa da Caparica was as new to me when I arrived as it was to my Canadian-born family. There was adventure and discovery for all of us, but for me, also the comfort of home.

"But you're not from there," Matt would remind me when we talked on a video call and I mentioned that I felt so at home in Costa.

He was right, of course. I am from the Azores, a two-hour flight away, but it is still Portugal. My family always had strong ties to the mainland—several of our family members had moved there, my mother went to hairdressing school in Lisbon, and my sister Antónia studied at the University of Lisbon. When we made trips back home from Canada, we spent most of our time on the islands, but we also went to the mainland.

I grew up Portuguese rather than specifically Azorean. We didn't distinguish between the two. My family was never sympathetic to the separatist sentiment in the Azores that wished for the region to govern its own affairs independently from the mainland. When the archipelago became an autonomous region in 1976, it wasn't something that felt meaningful for my family. By then we had lived in Canada for seven years, and we had become used to saying that we were Portuguese. Sometimes we added "from the Azores," but for others as well as for us, the distinction felt unnecessary.

The fact that I grew up in Canada and all my schooling has been in English puts me in the category of "not really Portuguese," according to my children. It is often a topic of conversation around the dinner table. Our discussions go something like this:

"Oh? What's real Portuguese?" I ask.

"Well, you haven't lived in Portugal for a long time, so, I dunno."

"So, are you telling me that if you moved to Thailand now, for example, you'd consider yourself Thai? After how long?"

No reply.

"Would it be different if I had immigrated to Canada when I was fifteen instead of seven? Or if I'd been twenty-five?"

"Oh, whatever, Mum."

Invariably, Eric says something like, "It's whatever you feel that you are." He puts an end to the discussion before it escalates and results in hurt feelings.

And so I continue to wonder, what am I? Where do I belong if I'm born in one place but live in another? Am I from here or from there, from both places or from neither? I had decided that this was a good question to ponder during my time in Costa da Caparica, but even after several months I was no closer to an answer.

• • •

I remember walking along the shore of Lake Athabasca in northeastern Alberta one afternoon, many years ago. I was working for a few days in Fort Chipewyan, or Fort Chip as it is more commonly known. This hamlet is an Indigenous fly-in community near the 60th parallel. It was wintertime—January, February maybe, and cold. I was wearing a down-filled parka zipped up to my chin, and I could feel the wind, sharp against my face. I should have attached my hood, I remember thinking to myself. My lips stung, and my wire-rimmed glasses pressed against two spots on my cheeks, later leaving small burn marks.

I had been in meetings for most of the workday and had maybe one too many cups of coffee. I needed to stretch my legs and get some air, I told my colleague, and I was going for a walk.

"Be careful, it's cold out there," he warned me. "Make it a short one."

I walked down the hill from the lodge where I was staying and out to the lake. I didn't see anyone else around, and the light was fading. That far north, the days are short in winter. A woman walked up behind me and startled me when she spoke. She was elderly, in her eighties perhaps, and she was bundled up in a parka with a hood tightened around her face. I couldn't understand what she was saying.

"I don't speak Cree," I said to her, and I smiled apologetically.

"You Chip?" The area is home to the Athabasca Chipewyan First Nation, the Mikisew Cree First Nation, and the Fort Chipewyan Métis Nation.

"No, I'm from the south," I said to her and wondered if she understood me. Could she be one of the few people who still spoke her Indigenous language and not much English?

"You a school teacher?" she asked.

"No, I work for the government," I said. "Department of Environment."

"Humph," she said, and walked away. She continued along the lakeshore, then headed up the road. Maybe she was going to the grocery store and thought she'd come and check out the new stranger in town.

I felt foreign in Fort Chip and very much like an intruder. The fact that this woman seemed to come out of nowhere and spoke to me in Cree had warmed me. Had she really thought that I belonged there? I didn't get a chance to ask her. I don't think I saw her again. I say that because if I'd seen her somewhere else in town without her parka and hood, I probably wouldn't have recognized her. She would have had to come up to me, and no one did. Why would they? I was only there for a few days.

My brief interaction with the woman at the lake has stayed with me. I think about her once in a while. Why had she thought I was Cree? Was it my olive skin and dark hair? Was it that I dared go down to the lake on such a cold day?

Many years ago, I studied in Thailand for several months and worked in a small village in the interior of the country. It was very hot, and I found it uncomfortable. I decided I would get a haircut. I went to a hair salon with a friend who was able to translate for me, and one of the first things the hairdresser asked me was if my mother or father was Thai.

No, I told her, but why did she ask? She said that I had hair like Thai women. It was dark and silky, and it hung the same way.

"Easy cut," she said and gave me a big smile.

I was told to lie down on a chair that folded out into a bed (because every haircut starts with a massage). One woman massaged my head, another my feet. The stylists giggled because my feet hung over the edge of the chair-bed, and I could rest them against the wall. At five foot seven, I towered over most Thai women I encountered, and they found me amusing.

A few days later I was walking in town, and I got caught in a monsoon. My clothes were soaked. I decided to duck into a shop and buy a dry T-shirt and skirt. The shop worker had to go to the back where they kept the bigger sizes, and still, they were a tight fit.

"You are so tall," she said (through my friend the interpreter). "I thought maybe you were Thai, but you are so tall." She giggled, and then she added, "The skirt is not right. Too short."

"I'll take it anyway," I said. We all laughed.

So I'm not Thai, and I'm not Cree. How is it I can fit in easily in different countries and cultures yet still feel like an outsider in Canada?

When I first arrived in Edmonton, I remember trying to fit in with the other kids at my elementary school. My sense is that I learned English easily, and by the time I was in Miss Lane's Grade 3 class, I was fluent and getting As in spelling. But I was also frequently taunted.

"Go back to Brazil," Roman, my classmate, would say to me whenever he saw me in the halls.

"I'm not from Brazil, you idiot," I'd reply.

"Oh, wherever, just go home. Go back to where you came from."

That would make me so angry, and I didn't have a good comeback for it. I'd feel my nostrils flare with rage, and I'd run home after school, fumble with the key, open the door, slam it behind me, and then stew as I watched *The Flintstones* on TV and waited for my mother to come home from work. As soon as she came in the house, I'd hop into her arms, and she'd hug me, and I'd burst into tears. I would tell her my story, and amid the sobs I'd ask, "How does he know I'm from some-place else?"

"It's nothing to be ashamed of, you know," my mother would say. "He should be so lucky to be from the same beautiful place as you."

Over the years, my classmates got used to the way I looked, and I began to feel like I fit in. But even after high school, and outside the school environment, people questioned me. As I moved around the city, I continued to feel different—a cashier at a store would ask me, "Are you Italian?" or another, "Are you Persian?" Sometimes I would answer, "Why do you ask?"

A cab driver once asked me, "Are you Pakistani?"

He must have caught me on a bad day because I remember ranting, "Do I really look Pakistani to you? Why would you ask me that?"

"I'm sorry," he said. "It's not an insult. The women from Pakistan are beautiful. I know that because that's where I'm from. You could be from the north; people there have light skin, like you."

I didn't get it. Edmonton was my home, but everyone thought I was from somewhere else. And when I travelled somewhere else, no one believed I was Canadian.

When Eric and I got married, we decided to live in Vancouver. It's where we raised our children and where we continue to live today. It's a multicultural city where diversity is celebrated, but even so, I still get asked where I'm from. I have been at social gatherings where people comment on my skin colour, then talk about my being Portuguese as exotic or ethnic. How I've come to dislike those words. They make me feel othered, as if I don't really belong. Will this ever change?

After living in Costa for a few months, it felt like home, but Matt was right—technically, it's not where I'm from, not where I was born. It's not the Azores, not the volcanic landscape I knew in childhood; it's not my island. But over time, I eased into coastal life on the mainland and felt that I could now claim the wide expanse of beach as also my own.

Despite the early challenges of setting up a home in Costa, there was comfort in belonging. And always, there was the language. My language. My accent gave me away as an islander but also as Portuguese. And so, no one asked me where I was really from.

My musings about longing and belonging continue to unsettle me. I worry about the subtle message I send to my family. Do they think I'm just never happy anywhere for very long?

"It's not about happiness or contentment or feeling satisfied," I try to explain. "It's about figuring out where I belong."

They don't challenge me. I know they want to understand me.

I have come to appreciate that I am of two places and of two cultures. And that such is the plight of the immigrant. I am the hyphen between Portuguese and Canadian. The fit will never really be perfect in either place. But is it ever? Even for those who are not immigrants, are they ever fully "at home" in any one place?

• • •

On the west coast of Canada, the arrival of fall signals the beginning of a long season of grey skies and drizzly days. My soul sinks a little with the lack of sunshine, but I've learned to adapt—I cook stews and heavier meals, eat more bread, do less outside, read more. I've noticed that Georgia likes the fall. She perks up when it cools down. The heat of summer drains her energy, she says, and she looks forward to the change of season.

"I love it when it starts to rain," she has told me many times.

Are you kidding me, is all I can think of saying, but I try not to judge. It's for real, she assures me. "I love the cool, drizzly days, especially the quiet that comes after the busy, sunny, active summer."

And then it dawns on me. Perhaps we are most at home in that place where we are born and where we are cared for. Our first homeland must become embedded in our psyche. I realize that not everyone has had a loving upbringing or felt protected in childhood, but in my case, my longing for Portugal was starting to make sense. I refer to Portugal as home because that is where I remember being a child. It's where I was protected and cared for by my parents, where I had no worries or responsibilities.

Once we arrived in Canada, even though I was only seven, I took on responsibility. If my mother was sad or missing her life back home, I kissed her and hugged her and told her that I liked Canada but that if she wanted to go back to Portugal, I would go with her. I helped my father shovel snow in the winter and water the garden in the summer. I wanted to spend time with him so he wouldn't feel lonely. And by the time I was ten or eleven years old, I was translating for my parents. I accompanied them to the bank, to medical appointments, and to parent-teacher interviews. I was more mature than I should have been.

If I think about it in these terms, it makes sense to me that I feel Portuguese. And that even though I have lived in Canada for decades, there are times when I long for my island home in the Azores or the bustle of Lisbon with a nostalgia that would be more understandable if I had just moved to Canada a year or two ago.

For my children, Vancouver is clearly their home. It is where they have grown up and felt protected. While we have lived in a number of different places, our moves have always been temporary. Living in Portugal was significant for me, but in our family's life, it was a short-term dislocation. We all knew we'd be returning to Vancouver, just before the fall rains took hold and our active summer days turned quiet and cool.

I am the daughter of Portuguese parents, and I am the mother of Canadian children. I am the link between the two places and the two cultures, and so I am both Portuguese and Canadian. In some ways, it seems so simple—"it's whatever you feel that you are."

. . . .

A Phone Call from Canada

THE THREE OF US WERE SITTING at the dining room table, working at our respective laptops, clicking away at the keyboards. We had the patio doors wide open, and we could hear the roar of the ocean in the distance. It was a bright day, though still cool, but it felt good to have the windows open and a fresh breeze blowing through the house. Georgia was doing homework for her online courses, I was researching places to take Claire when she visited, and Eric was still working from home. We figured this arrangement would change soon as it would be only a matter of days before Eric received his work visa and would finally be able to go to his office at the university.

A couple of weeks earlier, we had been informed by the Portuguese Consulate in Vancouver that everything was ready and Eric needed to mail his passport to them so they could add the visa. However, while consulate staff could receive mail, they were not able to return it to us by mail. It would have to be picked up by someone, in person. Fortunately, Matt was still in Vancouver, and he would be able to do that for us.

We had gone to the post office in Costa to inquire about sending the passport by courier. When the clerk quoted us the price of just over seventy euros, we opted for the much cheaper but still secure option of registered mail and a seven-to-ten-day delivery period. Matt would then pick up the passport in Vancouver and mail it back to us, by registered mail once again. It was a longer delivery time but we had waited so long already—what was another week or two? It was all working out, and we were beginning to relax. It never occurred to us that we might need to travel out of the country in the meantime.

My cell phone rang. We all stared at it. I'm the only one in my family who normally jumps to answer the phone but even I hesitated. Eric tends to think of the phone as an intrusion and will only answer it if he is not doing anything else (which is hardly ever) and Georgia and Matt, like so many people their age, prefer to text than to talk. At that moment, though, even when we were all keen to speak to people, I'm sure Eric and Georgia would've been quite happy to let the phone ring. I, on the other hand, realized I was thousands of kilometres away from my son and knew I had to answer it.

When it first rang, I remember noticing the floral pattern of the oilcloth on the table, and feeling a current run through my body, all the way to my scalp. Maybe it was dread. Whatever it was, I didn't have enough time to identify it. I shoved my chair back along the floor and leaped up to grab the phone.

"Hello," I said, sounding breathless.

"Hi Es, it's Pete."

"Oh no. Should I get Eric?"

"Yes, please."

Pete is Eric's brother. He doesn't like phones either, so I figured the call had to be important.

Sure enough, the news was that their mother, Addie, who had been ill and living in a care facility for years, had taken a turn for the worse. She'd had a mild cold but now wasn't eating or drinking and wasn't expected to live much longer. At ninety-four, her body might've just decided it was time. She had suffered from Alzheimer's disease for fourteen years and had lost her husband of nearly seventy years just three months before.

Eric paced, phone to one ear, and his hand cupping the other. He was straining to hear Pete over the road noise so I walked over to the patio and closed the doors. Georgia was up and pacing now too, biting her fingernails, her eyes watering.

"Thanks for calling, Pete. Keep us posted, okay? Yeah, let's use video call next time."

Eric hung up the phone and went over to sit on the couch. He leaned forward and held his head in his hands. Georgia and I went to sit on either side of him, both of us instinctively putting our arms around him.

Our family is no stranger to grief. In the last decade, we had provided palliative care at home for my mother and then cared for my father until he died nine months later. Three years after that, my sister Maria died, four months after a diagnosis of metastatic cancer. Our family had been overwhelmed by all the loss. Georgia and Matt, then ten and fourteen, had already had more experience with death in the family than many adults. And then, when we were all starting to feel like we were recovering, Eric's father died. He was ninety-five. That was in December, a few weeks before our move to Portugal.

When Garry died, Matt was in the middle of finals at university. We planned the funeral date around his exam schedule to enable him to attend. It was still tight—he flew from Vancouver to Toronto on an overnight flight, drove to Burlington, slept for a few hours, went to the funeral, and then we had dinner as a family before we drove him back to the airport for his flight home. He landed back in Vancouver just twenty-six hours after he had left, and he wrote an exam later that day.

When someone is in their nineties, death is not unexpected, but it can still be unwelcome. Right then, in the moments following Pete's phone call, being so far away did not feel right. The Atlantic Ocean carved a big gulf between us and the rest of the family. All we wanted to do was go. Go to Canada. Be with family. Huddle together and hold each other up.

"I'm going to have to go to Ontario," Eric said. "I need to be there." His eyes were red and watery, and he had that look of confused despair that comes with the realization that your mother is going to die soon.

"Of course," I said. "I'll make the arrangements."

I was already thinking about logistics and realized that Georgia and I would not be able to go with Eric. Claire would be arriving in a few days for spring break. Maybe I could leave two fifteen-year-olds alone for a few days, but not in a strange country and not when neither could speak Portuguese. At this stage I couldn't ask her not to come, and even if I could, we didn't know anyone who could look after Maggie. I had worked it all through in my head—Eric would be going on his own. I sat down at the computer to look for flights and then remembered that Eric did not have a passport.

I stepped outside onto the patio, out of Eric's earshot, and called Matt. I told him about his grandma, and then I asked about the passport.

"The passport?" There was panic in his voice. "You told me to mail it. I sent it a few days ago."

"I know, I know. Did you get a tracking number?"

I tracked the package and learned that it had left Vancouver and was on its way. All we could do was wait.

Primavera
(Spring)

. . . .

The Lisbon Mini Marathon

IN THE LEAD UP to the Lisbon Mini Marathon, I was uncharacteristically secretive. Aside from Eric and Georgia, I hadn't told anyone about my plans to participate in this event. I don't consider myself to be a very private person; I will normally tell my plans and dreams to anyone who will listen, but I felt differently about this run. I was very invested in it and I somehow felt that if I told too many people, it would not come to pass. Eventually, I mentioned it to Matt back in Vancouver, but I was even hesitant to tell him! Georgia had already mentioned it to him, and she was surprised that I hadn't said anything.

"Well, I don't need to broadcast it," I remember telling her.

"Telling Matt is hardly broadcasting it," she said. "Besides, since when are you so private?"

"Good question," was all I could muster in response.

Joe John texted me several times to encourage us all to register for the run. Because it would be so much fun, he said. Eventually, I admitted to him that Georgia and I were planning to run, and that we had already registered. And I told him that Eric wouldn't be joining us because of a bad knee. He called me on the phone and spoke without taking a breath.

"What do you mean he has a bad knee. He can walk, can't he? This is not just for runners. He can walk the route." Joe John never seemed to have a slow gear. I wondered how he could be so exuberant, all the time.

"I am going to run with my son, but my wife, Rosário, and some friends are walking it. He can walk with them. Tell Eric to come, we want him to come."

"Someone will need to stay home with Maggie," I said, wondering if he could hear me. "And we will also have a guest. A friend of Georgia's is arriving from Canada the day before."

"Okay, okay," he relented. "But you and Georgia, you will run with my son and me, okay? Let's meet at the start line."

"All right, it's a date," I said, but I worried that I wouldn't be able to keep up with them.

When I allowed myself to think about it, I realized I was afraid of failing. What had happened to my easygoing nature, my take-life-in-stride attitude? I had connected my ego to this event, and I wasn't even sure why.

Thinking of myself as unfit feels like an insult to me. It has for as long as I can remember. I associate fitness with strength, and to be unfit feels like weakness and failure. These feelings took me back to my childhood. I remember that my mother always worried about how little I ate. I was a skinny kid, and I didn't want to be. When I was in school, I wanted to play sports, partly to prove that I was strong and capable even if I was thin. I joined the volleyball and basketball teams in junior high, but I played second string, and I was never very good. I joined the track team and played badminton in Grade 10, but I was never the star athlete I dreamed of being. I wanted nothing more than to be muscular and strong and have quadriceps that bulged. I learned in science class that I was more of an ectomorph than the mesomorph

I wanted to be, and it disappointed me. If I can't look muscular, I thought, then I can at least be fit. And thus began my lifelong quest for fitness.

Although we were only doing the mini route, this run felt daunting. I was afraid that I would injure myself or get sick or, I don't know, have a heart attack. I was so sure that something would come up and that my dream would fall apart. The more Georgia and I trained, the more I wanted to do the run, and the more I wanted to do it with her. The thought of running across Lisbon's beautiful suspension bridge filled me with excitement. The idea of doing this with my daughter thrilled me. My deep-seated wish was to bond with my daughter over an athletic pursuit, something I never did with my own mother. My ultimate goal was humble and concrete—I wanted to cross the finish line without collapsing.

The route started at the toll gates on the south side of the 25th of April Bridge. The bridge deck runs just over two kilometres. On the north side, the route looped around a hill and then extended along the river, westward to the town of Belém, at the mouth of the Tagus River—a total of 7.8 kilometres. The half-marathon route (the real event for the serious runners) headed east along the river before it looped around to finish at the same place as the mini route. When I envisioned myself running past the area's historic monuments and statues of explorers and kings, my heart would beat faster, and my hands would get sweaty. I was really looking forward to doing this.

Claire arrived the day before our big race. She and Georgia were eager to catch up on each other's lives, but it was an early night for both of them. Claire was suffering the effects of jet lag, and Georgia wanted to be well rested for our run.

Race day dawned sunny and warm and we were all up early, making it seem like a special occasion from the start. The four of us had breakfast on the deck. I was too nervous to eat but I took small bites of a cheese sandwich and a banana. I knew that it would not be a good idea to run on an empty stomach. Claire stretched out on the lounge chair and squinted in the sunshine. Nothing we said would make her believe how cold and rainy it had been for so many weeks. Maggie had draped herself over Claire's feet, leaving no doubt in our minds that our little canine remembered this dear friend from her Canadian life.

Despite Georgia's cool demeanour, I knew that she was excited about the run too, though maybe not quite as thrilled to be running with her mother as I was to be running with my daughter. Mostly, I was the nervous one, and it was my teenager who reassured me and calmed me down.

"You're going to rock this, Mum," she told me as she passed me in the kitchen when I was making my coffee. She was taking Maggie out for her morning constitutional.

I turned from the kitchen counter to face her.

"But what if I sprain my ankle?"

"Mum! Stop it! This was supposed to be fun, remember?"

We took a few "before" pictures in the front yard and then we headed to the bus stop. There was no need to take bus fare—all runners got free rides on transit that day, as long as they were wearing their race numbers. I took my cell phone; I'd need it to contact Joe John, and then to facilitate meeting up with Claire and Eric once the run was over.

"Sorry to leave you so soon after your arrival, Claire," I called out as Georgia and I walked out the front gate.

"We'll meet you at the finish line," Eric shouted back.

Any trepidation I had felt about not knowing where to go or exactly where the run would start was quickly dispelled when we got off the bus. There was a moving sea of people, all going in the same direction. There was no way we could get lost.

Thousands of people congregated on the south side of the bridge. I saw baseball caps and sun hats, sunglasses, and colourful

T-shirts—neon pink, bright yellow, shocking green. There was loud music that I didn't recognize pounding from speakers, and everywhere we turned, there were groups of people warming up in small clusters.

My cell phone vibrated, and I could see that the call coming in was from Joe John. I answered but I couldn't hear anything he said. He couldn't hear me either, so he texted me his location, and Georgia and I dodged and squeezed around people and made our way to the steel sculpture at the side of the road. I'd never noticed it before, not in all the times we had driven past.

We couldn't see Joe John anywhere, and it seemed futile to even try to find a particular person in this multitude. I'd all but given up when I felt a hand on my shoulder and then a sequence of three hearty slaps on my back, followed by laughter and a big hug. Must he always be so jovial, I thought to myself. I was trying to hide my anxiety but I'm sure it must have shown on my face. We met Joe John's wife Rosário and their friend Margarida, both of whom were walking the route, and we met João, Joe John's son, who would be running with him. We took pictures and had a few laughs, all of which distracted and relaxed me. A short time later, we were shepherded to the start line. I couldn't even see it, there were so many people ahead of us. Georgia fist-bumped me, put her arm around my shoulder, and said, "You know you can do this. Let's go!"

As soon as the starting gun went off, people rushed past us, and we lost sight of our friends in minutes. We didn't see them again for the rest of the day. Georgia and I were on our own.

When we got to the bridge deck, I was already breathing hard. I looked down through the steel grate to the water below, an effort that made me dizzy both with satisfaction and anticipation. People pushed and shoved past us, elbows out, ponytails swinging. My right foot got stepped on at least twice. The continuous stream of moving people unnerved me, and I could feel the blood rushing in my ears. Georgia jogged past me, then turned around and came back, grabbed my arm and said, "Come on, Mum, you can't stop already! We've only gone about a hundred metres."

By the time we got to the halfway point of the bridge, the runners were spreading out. I looked around, took in the view, and relished the sunshine. The dizziness vanished, and I took a few deep breaths. Georgia could have easily dashed ahead, but she stayed close to me.

"Go ahead if you want, we can meet at the finish line," I said.

"No way," she said. "We're doing this together."

On the north side of the river, spectators gathered in clusters on the side of the road and clapped and shouted their encouragement. That made me feel like a real runner, but it was when we passed a water station and I grabbed a water bottle, that I puffed with pride. Both Georgia and I had a hard time throwing our empty bottles on the ground. I couldn't remember the last time I had littered, and it felt wrong. A race volunteer must have noticed our hesitation because she ran up to us and said, "Don't worry, we'll do a massive sweep afterwards. Just throw it on the ground when you're done. Really. Go ahead."

I felt a strange mixture of elation and fatigue as I ran. I took a couple of walk breaks and, at one point, I wondered if I'd be able to finish. In those moments of doubt, Georgia managed to say the right things to keep me going. "Not far now, Mum" or "Look at the balloons! That's the end. We're almost there."

When we crossed the finish line, someone draped a medal around our necks, and then we were mobbed by volunteers offering us give-aways—bananas from Madeira, ice cream cups, milk boxes, and grab bags. It was a chaotic scene. Georgia and I squeezed through groups of people and managed to get away, walked a few minutes to a park nearby, and found an empty bench to sit down. We peeled our bananas, and less than a minute later, Claire and Eric sat down beside us. That they managed to find us felt like a small miracle.

"Congratulations, you two!" Claire said.

Eric flashed me a big smile. "You did it! Good on you."

We lingered in a big hug till Georgia said, "Okay, okay, you two."

Eric put his arm around Georgia and gave her a high five. I wiped tears from my eyes. I was so thrilled to have finished. It hadn't been easy for me but also not as hard as I had feared. Now that it was done, I wondered why I had been so nervous.

"Okay, I'm really happy," I said. Then I turned to Georgia and said, "I'm extra thrilled that I got to do this with you. And I also don't think I could have done it without you. I needed all your encouragement."

"I enjoyed it too, Mum," Georgia said, and gave me a big hug.

The four of us made our way to the Antiga Pastelaria de Belém, a hundred metres or so away, to introduce Claire to Portugal's famous custard tarts. This is where they are made, using a secret recipe, and where customers can try them fresh out of the oven, while the tarts are still warm.

"Oh, my dad told me to be sure to try these," Claire said. "Custard tarts and sardines are the two musts, he said."

"Yes, it's true, but maybe not at the same time," I quipped. I realized that I hadn't seen sardines on the menu anywhere and made a mental note to check the next time we went to a restaurant.

I was surprised that the pastry shop was not busy. We had our choice of tables, and once we settled, we ordered from the server. I looked around and saw people at a few tables, then noticed that I was sitting up straight and smiling. I was still feeling exuberant and proud to be wearing my race number and medal. I was savouring this moment of pride when I realized our tarts and drinks were on the table, and Eric was already sipping his coffee.

Claire sprinkled cinnamon on her tart as we had advised her to do, then she raised the pastel to her lips and bit into the gooey centre. She closed her eyes and took a deep breath. After swallowing the first mouthful, she said, "These are amazing. Totally awesome."

"This is the only way I like these, fresh out of the oven," Georgia said. "You can find them pretty much anywhere, but these are the best ones, right here."

Back at home, I basked in the satisfaction of achievement, and my runner's high stayed with me for days. Both Georgia and I displayed our race numbers and medals on the cork board in the hallway. Every time I looked at them, I felt pleased. And strong. The challenge will be to keep up my running routine, I thought to myself. I think I ran a few more times, both with and without Georgia, but soon enough it got too hot, and we gave up running.

Claire's presence infused our house with a new energy that we all welcomed. After we got home from the run and the pastry shop, Eric volunteered to make dinner. Claire and Georgia offered to help.

Eric suggested I sit in the living room to rest, which I did, lying on the couch with my feet propped up on the coffee table, Maggie's head resting on my thighs. I grabbed my book to read but then tuned in to the noises in the kitchen. I could hear the clanging dishes of meal preparation and young voices mixed with bursts of giggling and laughter and loud chopping. They were making a salad. Georgia was regaling Claire with anecdotes from our trip so far and making suggestions for what she would have to see during her time with us.

"Oh, and we'll have to go to Sintra," Georgia said. "There is this super cool palace there. It has all these colours and turrets, and it's in a really neat town."

"Awesome," I heard Claire say.

It felt good to hear the vocabulary of the young. I looked at the pages of my novel but couldn't concentrate on the words, so I closed the book, and my eyes, and let myself enjoy the energy emanating from the kitchen.

. . . .

Tracking the Passport

ADDIE HALL DIED IN HER SLEEP on Wednesday, March 19.

By the time we got the call from Pete, it was Thursday for us. A heavy silence descended on our house. Georgia, Eric, and I were more gentle with each other that day. I thought of Addie, and I smiled when I realized that throughout the quarter century that I had known her, I had never called her Addie. She was always Mrs. Hall to me, but we had what I considered to be a close relationship. I liked her and I sensed she liked me.

Even though we lived across the country from each other, we visited once or twice a year and we rarely missed our weekly phone conversations. We talked about the weather, of course, and about food. She didn't like cooking, she'd often say, but she was the expert on roast beef and turkey dinners, and I peppered her with questions about traditional English food. I treasure her turkey stuffing recipe to this day, and I still chuckle when I think of her saying, "Yorkshire pudding, oh forget it, so much work."

She told me stories of what it was like to come from a family of thirteen children, how they had left England by boat and arrived in Montreal, then took the train to Toronto. She described her family dinners as loud and chaotic, and told me how she enjoyed her current life that was orderly and quiet. She often reminisced about when the boys, Pete and Eric, were little, about the annual trips to the cottage, the New Year's Eve parties on the block, and the coffee klatches with the other housewives on the street. I often felt that she, as the only female in her little nuclear family, was grateful for daughters-in-law to talk to.

I remember the look of bewilderment in her eyes one day when we were visiting, and she was confused about what to make for dinner. She looked in the fridge, but it was as if she couldn't discern what was in there. I suggested we cook together that day, but it was the first sign I had that all was not right with Addie. It was days before her eightieth birthday, and a few months before her diagnosis of Alzheimer's disease.

Eric's grief was compounded by the anxiety we all felt about his passport. While he called Matt in Vancouver to tell him about his grandmother's death, I tracked the passport online. It had arrived in Lisbon and was to be delivered the next day, Friday. Someone would need to be home and sign for it upon delivery. With this bit of information, Eric and Pete started planning the funeral and decided on the date—the following Wednesday—a full week after Addie had died. I went ahead and booked a flight for Eric for Monday morning, one of the few seats still available that would get him to Ontario before the funeral.

Eric usually makes his own travel arrangements, but I remembered the scattered feeling I had when my mother died, and I wanted to help him. It seemed like a small thing, but I thought if I took care of the logistics, Eric would have the emotional space to think about his mother, to write a eulogy, and to attend to all the work that needs doing in the days following a significant death in the family, even when you are far away.

First thing in the morning on Friday, I logged on to the Correios site to track Eric's package. I was relieved to see that it was on the mail truck and would be delivered that day. I announced the news at breakfast, and we all sighed with relief.

Georgia, Claire, and I were considering the options for the day's outing when Claire said, "Um, can we go back to that pastry place where we went after your run?"

"Of course, that's a great idea. There's quite a bit more to see in that area. There's the monument to the explorers and the Tower of Belém and the Jerónimos Monastery and—"

"But we can go for some tarts, right?" Claire was not going to leave it up to chance.

"Yes, yes, we will most definitely have oven-fresh pastéis today," I assured her.

Eric reminded us that he would need to stay home. He had work to do, the eulogy to write, and he wanted to be around to sign for the passport when it arrived. Since it was still too early for the postman to come, Eric drove us to Trafaria, the next town over from Costa, about ten minutes away, where we hopped on the ferry for the trip across the river to Belém. When the boat was mid-river, we had a good view of the suspension bridge. I thought back to our run and felt residual pride. One day I will do the half marathon, I thought to myself.

We started out at the pastelaria for tarts and coffee (for me) and hot Ucal (for Claire and Georgia), then went to the Tower of Belém and the Jerónimos Monastery, our main tourist stops for the day. We had lunch by the river and wandered around afterwards, taking pictures on the riverside promenade. In our meandering, we discovered an outdoor playground for adults. None of us had seen one of these before. I doubt this playground has made it into any guidebook, yet this was where we spent a large part of the afternoon and where we had the most fun. There were several machines—a rower, a stair climber, and a bench swing—but it was when each of us tried the glider that we couldn't stop laughing. It was like cross-country skiing without skis. I'm not sure we would have lingered here very long if there had been other people around but seeing as we had the playground to ourselves, we could try everything without being too self-conscious. The laughter felt good, and it was a welcome antidote to the sadness and stress of the previous days.

We arrived back home around four o'clock. One look at Eric's face and I could tell he didn't have the passport yet.

"What happened?" I asked, feeling the anxiety rise in my chest. "Where's the passport?"

"Hasn't arrived yet. I've been here all day and I haven't even seen the postman," Eric replied. "I've tracked the package and it looks like it's in the delivery van."

As the afternoon drew to a close, our panic grew. We usually saw the postman around two in the afternoon. When the neighbour upstairs arrived home from work, she came to give us our mail that had been put in her box by mistake. There, among the flyers and junk mail, was a postal delivery card. I read it and let out a gasp when I saw that it said the delivery of a package had been attempted, but since no one was home, we could claim it from the post office on Monday morning. Eric's flight was scheduled to leave early that day, before the post office even opened.

"But Eric was home. I don't understand," I said to her, almost in tears.

"What? What is it, Es?" Eric was desperate to know what was going on. I explained the note to him in English at the same time as the neighbour was speaking to me in Portuguese.

"You know, sometimes the postmen don't feel like walking around with packages, so they just put the cards in our mailboxes and then we have to go pick them up ourselves. I've noticed they're doing that more and more lately. It's terrible," she said.

We didn't have much time to sit around and wonder what happened or why. We had to get to the post office before it closed. I ran inside to grab the car keys, and Eric got in the car. The neighbour opened the gate to let us out of the driveway. At some point I yelled out to Georgia that we were going to look for Eric's passport and would be back soon.

We sped down the narrow streets to the post office and arrived just as the clerk was locking the door. I jumped out of the car and ran up to her. She must have recognized me—I had been in three times the previous week to ship large packages of books to Vancouver. I knocked on the glass door and she unlocked it, smiling. This was unusual; she never smiled. In my past dealings with her, I had found her to be helpful but a little detached and not exactly friendly. At that moment, I was grateful for her smile.

She opened the door to let us in. I explained our situation, the angst obvious from the shaking in my voice.

"It's my husband's mother. She died a couple of days ago, and my husband needs the passport to go to the funeral. He is supposed to leave on Monday morning."

"Oh, my condolences," she said. "But I can't help you here. We don't get the packages until Monday. You'll need to go to the distribution centre, and you'll have to hurry, they close soon."

I could see the sympathy on her face. In Portugal, the death of a mother is one of life's most significant events, especially for a son. I sensed that she understood our anguish.

"Leave your car here and take the shortcut through the park or you won't make it. The traffic is so bad at this time of day."

She drew a map on a small piece of paper and wrote out a few directions, then told us to hurry.

We arrived at the distribution centre—a large, low building with no windows, in the middle of a big parking lot, in the industrial part of town. There were postal vans and trucks of different sizes and shapes along two edges of the lot. It was dark now, and we could see the shiny metal of a large delivery door at the far end of the building. We ran over and Eric pounded on it, but it felt futile. Who would hear us? I pounded too, but when our hands started to burn, we gave up and sat on the stoop, overcome with helplessness.

A few minutes later, the door opened. A woman asked what we were doing there. She was maybe in her early thirties, but her face looked drawn. She had bushy eyebrows and dark circles beneath her tired-looking eyes, and she conveyed a calm, disinterested demeanour. I explained our situation once more. She said that she was very sorry, but she wouldn't be able to help us. The driver was not yet back and sometimes, on the weekends, they just take the undelivered packages home, then straight to the post office on Monday morning.

I pleaded with her. "Can you call the driver? Please?"

"No, I can't. If he's driving, he won't be able to answer, and if he's home already, he'll have turned off his phone."

"Can you not try?" I was starting to sound exasperated. Eric took my arm by the elbow and said, "It's fine, Es, there's not much more we can do. We tried."

We turned and walked away. I couldn't believe it. She stood at the door and watched us, and when we were about to turn the corner, she yelled out, "Wait!" and motioned us to return.

"If you want, you can wait here and see if he comes back. In the meantime, I'll try to raise him on the phone. Please tell your husband that I am very sorry for his mother's death."

"Obrigada," I said, my voice now a strange mixture of frustration and relief. She shut the door and left us sitting on the stoop.

I turned to Eric and asked, "Isn't that what I asked her to do in the first place?"

"I know, I know, but at least there's a bit of hope now," he said, comforting me. It really should have been me comforting him at that particular moment.

"Why does everything have to be so hard here?" I said, and I started to cry.

We must have made quite the sight—two people sitting in the dark, on the loading dock of a warehouse in a big, empty parking lot—me holding my head in my hands, and Eric with his arm around me.

We sat in silence and checked our watches frequently. There was nothing more we could say to each other. After about fifteen long minutes, we saw a small, white van pull into the lot near the service delivery door. A man got out, opened the back door of the van on the driver's side, and grabbed a canvas bag from the back seat. He looked tired. I could almost feel his relief that his workday had come to an end. We greeted him as if he were our long-lost friend. "Hello, hello," we said. He looked surprised to see us, but he kept walking towards the door.

"We're looking for a package. It's my husband's passport, and he needs it because his mother died and he has to go to the funeral and his flight leaves on Monday morning." I was talking fast, desperate to get all the information out before he walked through the big steel door.

"I can't give you anything from my bag. You have to pick it up at the post office on Monday," he said.

My exasperation got the better of me and I blurted out, "Did you not hear me? The package contains the passport that my husband needs to fly on Monday morning. His flight leaves before the post office opens."

He kept walking and finally I shouted, "To go to his mother's funeral!"

Eric took my arm and pulled me close. "You're getting carried away," he whispered in my ear.

I took a deep breath. What I really wanted to do was shout at the postman and call him an idiot for delivering to the wrong address in the first place. He got to the door and turned to face us.

"Sir, with all due respect," I said, more calmly, "you delivered the package to the wrong address. Or maybe you didn't deliver it at all, didn't even come to the door. I know this because my husband was home all day, waiting for you, and didn't even see you, and you put the card in the wrong box." And then I added, "I hope you can understand that my husband needs this package today. Now."

The man ignored me and focused his eyes on Eric, stretched out his hand for a handshake, and said, "My sympathies, sir."

Then, he opened his bag and the first package he removed was Eric's. Just then, the door to the building opened, and the same woman as before stood there, arms crossed.

"So, you know what they're asking for," she said, addressing her colleague as if we were not there. Then she said to Eric, in English, "You need to show identification."

"Yes, of course," Eric said, and pulled out his wallet. He showed her his British Columbia driver's licence.

She turned to me and said in Portuguese, "This is foreign identification. I cannot accept this."

"That's all he has," I said. "He's a foreigner. What would you like to see?"

"I'm going to need to see a passport before I can give your husband this package," she said.

I imagined that she was enjoying this power she had over us at that moment, but she was not showing any glee. She was not acknowledging the ridiculous nature of her request either. Her face showed the same indifference she'd been wearing during our entire exchange.

I can't remember exactly what happened next. All I know is that she must have relented because she allowed Eric to open the package. Then she held out her hand and he gave it to her. She removed the passport, opened it to check the photo and make sure the name matched the one on the envelope, and then said, "Good thing you weren't lying about what was in your package. Safe travels, sir."

When we got home, we opened a bottle of red wine—Tuella, our favourite—grabbed two wine glasses and sat down at the dining room table, suddenly aware that we hadn't said a word to each other all the way home.

Georgia and Claire bounced into the dining room from outside. "That took you a long time," Georgia said. "What are we doing for dinner?"

I wasn't sure I'd be able to convey to Georgia all that we had gone through in the last hour, was not even sure I wanted to. She and Claire had been doing yoga on the rooftop deck and their faces were rosy from the exertion and the fresh air. It was a big contrast to the emotional upheaval we'd just experienced.

"I'm thinking this might be a good night to go to the beach for dinner; how does that sound?"

We walked down the street, Eric and I still not able to summarize our experience.

"It was so complicated, and we just about didn't get the passport," I managed to say.

"Oh, that would have been terrible," Georgia said. "But you got it. That's a relief."

We climbed the stairs to the seawall and picked the fancier of the three restaurants that were open on that warm, spring evening. The waiter came to our table right away with a basket of bread, fresh cheese, and a small bowl of pepper paste to put on the cheese.

"How are you all today? You have a guest!"

"Yes, my daughter's friend, from Canada. Her name is Claire," I said.

"Welcome, Claire," he said, in English. He handed us the English menus and asked me in Portuguese, "What are you in the mood for today, do you think?"

"Oh, we've had quite the day," I said. "I'm so tired, I'm not even sure I can read the words on the menu. What would you recommend?" I asked.

"I'll be right back," he said.

He returned a minute later with a raw fish on a glass platter.

"This is a lovely grouper. Nice size for all of you. Grilled on coals, with steamed potatoes."

"Beautiful," I said. Everyone nodded in agreement. "We'll take it."

Eric ordered a half litre of green wine and the girls decided to have Sumol, Portuguese pop with passion fruit flavouring.

The waiter stepped away to get our drinks and Eric pulled out the passport from the inside breast pocket of his jacket.

"Just so we can have a good look at it," he said.

He handed it to me, then helped himself to some bread and cheese. I turned to the page with the work visa on it and the first thing I noticed was that it would expire two months before our departure date. I didn't say anything, but I felt sick. Eric could fly to Toronto on Monday for his mother's funeral and that was a relief, but our passport woes were not over.

. . . .

Lost in Alfama

ERIC WAS AWAY for just over a week. We filled our days playing tour guide to Claire, but Georgia and I made time in the evenings to connect with each other and touch on our grief. It was difficult to be away from family at this time, but I was also glad for Claire's presence. Georgia's smiles seemed to come alive with the intimacy of friendship, and the fun we had was a welcome distraction.

Claire struck an imposing figure. Even at fifteen years of age, she stood six foot one in flip-flops. She had long, wavy blond hair that she mostly tied up in a bun or a braid, but when she wore her hair loose, she looked like the personification of Rapunzel. When Georgia, Claire, and I went out together, we drew attention because we were all tall, but it was Claire's height, fair skin, and flowing golden locks that pegged us as foreigners. I often caught people staring at her. Sometimes, they would catch me catching them in a prolonged stare. It didn't matter, the Portuguese are not fazed by staring; it's almost a national pastime. It can be a little off-putting for those of us accustomed to a culture where staring is not socially acceptable, and when you're a teenager, I imagine that it would be even more unnerving. I tried to distract Claire and hoped she didn't notice all the looks.

One day, we hopped on the tram, the number twenty-eight that many tourists take to the historic district. We had planned to spend the day in Lisbon, to visit the Castelo de São Jorge and then wander around the maze of streets and alleys of Alfama.

This particular tram ride is highlighted in tourist guidebooks as a must-do when in Lisbon. It winds around several neighbourhoods, including Baixa, Chiado, and Graça, and screeches and rattles its way up the narrow streets of Alfama. It is always crowded—full of not only tourists but also residents of Lisbon, since the trams are an integral part of the transit system. Few other vehicles can manage the steep hills and narrow streets of this area. This is also a very scenic route, affording glorious views from the tops of the hills. There's a sign at the front of the tram, in English, warning of pickpockets, but I've never had any trouble.

Georgia and I got on and sat down in the first row of seats, facing forward. Claire stepped in next and ran her transit card through the machine, setting off a red flashing light and a low alarm that sounded like an ailing foghorn. Her card was out of money. This meant that she would have to pay the fare in cash. She looked over at me to ask how much she needed to pay but the tram driver waved her on. There was a long lineup of people waiting to get on the tram and I could tell that he thought it would be more efficient to let her on for free. I heard him say something to the effect of "pay next time." Claire fumbled around with her purse and looked at Georgia, as if to say, now what do I do?

"It's okay, it's okay, just come in, come, come." I motioned to her. People behind her in line were growing impatient and pushing their way onto the tram. There were no more seats available, so Claire stood near Georgia and me and held on to the bar beside her. An older woman nearby nudged Claire and started talking to her, though I couldn't make out what she was saying. Claire smiled and shrugged her shoulders and said, "I'm sorry, não falo português."

The woman raised her voice and started on a rant as the tram made its way along the tracks. Her voice got louder, and she was gesturing wildly.

"You tourists are ruining life for Lisboetas," she said. Then she added, "You want to buy everything cheap and now you don't even pay to get on the tram."

She went from grumbling to speaking loudly and back to grumbling. I wondered why she was so angry. Claire turned red in the face but said nothing, and I pretended not to understand. People around us went silent and stared at us. I shifted in my seat. Claire gave me one of those what-is-going-on looks.

The woman continued, "You think you can just come to our city and act as if it is yours. Well, you can't."

At this point, the tram screeched to a halt, and the driver got out of his seat, made his way to us, and confronted the woman.

"Senhora, you must stop this. This young woman got on for free because I said she could. She will put money on her card and pay next time. I would do the same for you."

The woman did not back down. "We are suffering through an economic crisis because of people like her."

"Senhora, if you do not stop this, I'm going to have to ask you to leave. Just stop with this nonsense." Then he turned to Claire and said, in English, "Sorry."

It is unusual to see a man admonishing an older woman like this, and equally rare for anyone to make an apology in public to someone much younger. He must have been exasperated and embarrassed. Tourism was becoming an important part of Portugal's recovery from the economic crisis and residents knew they needed to be welcoming to visitors. The driver had stood up for Claire, and I was relieved and grateful.

He got back in his seat and continued up the hill; the woman grumbled some more. A couple of stops later, she got off the tram without saying anything further. Once she was off, Claire took the woman's seat and riders around us visibly relaxed. Some shook their heads and gave disapproving looks at what had just transpired.

Alfama is the area of Lisbon that survived the earthquake of 1755, and thus, it retains the character of the old Lisbon. Like Venice, it's impossible to walk around the area for long without getting lost; it's a maze of streets and alleys. There are grocery stores and souvenir shops and cafés and restaurants. This historic quarter draws thousands of tourists on most days, but it is also a real neighbourhood packed with tenement houses. People sit on their front stoops to converse with each other, shuck corn, or peel potatoes. Sometimes they set up hotplates and barbecues along the pathways and in the miniature plazas—essentially their front yards—to grill sardines. Most streets are so narrow that laundry lines are hung across them from one building to another, high above where tourists wander. I make a point of greeting people as I walk around here. It is my way of acknowledging that I am an intruder in their day-to-day lives. I say hello because I want to be polite but there have been times when this simple gesture has drawn me into conversations. I've even landed an invitation for dinner a few times though I've always declined.

On that day, I was feeling protective of Claire in addition to having the responsibility of being her tour guide. I wanted to show her this part of town—the beautiful views from high up on the hills and some of the out-of-the-way places—and I wanted her to love it. I also knew that I get lost easily, so this was going to be a challenge for me. The streets of Alfama are not laid out in a grid pattern and there are few street signs. I wanted us to spend time in the area, but I did not want to feel the panic of getting lost.

I missed Eric. We had spent so much time together lately that it didn't feel right to be without him. And I felt uneasy about not being with him at this difficult time in his life. I'd also been wondering how Georgia and I would bring closure to our loss given that we couldn't attend Addie's funeral. I felt unsettled but thinking of Eric brought a smile to my lips. We make a good team when we travel. I rely on him to get us where we are going and back again, and he counts on me to speak to people—waiters in restaurants, taxi drivers, bus drivers, and hotel staff. Even when I can't speak the language, I can make myself understood, sometimes resorting to acting out words and questions. And yet, while I like exploring, I do not have a good sense of direction. I'm one of those people who will get off an elevator and turn the wrong way even when I know the building and have used the same elevator numerous times. I think my brain has a spatial recognition problem. When we are somewhere new, Eric is my compass. The deeper we reached into Alfama's back streets, the more I felt his absence.

It was a warm day, and the sun was bright. We strolled and wandered into shops and cafés; we sampled ice cream and pastries and stopped occasionally for a cool drink. At lunch, we happened upon a restaurant tucked away in the corner of a small square. There was a patio with about six tables set with red checkered tablecloths and napkins. The aroma of garlic and fish that emanated from the kitchen was inviting and hard to resist. We claimed the only available table, glad for the large tree next to it that would provide us with much-needed shade. Claire was an adventurous eater and was always willing to try new foods. Georgia's choices were usually limited to a prego, a thin steak sandwich on a bun, with a side of fries, or a grilled cheese, no ham.

"My dad says I need to try sardines," Claire said. "When he was here years ago, he said that was the best meal he had."

"Hmm, I don't see them on the menu. I'll ask the waiter."

"Senhora, it's not the season. You need to wait until the summer when they will be nice and fat. They're at their best in June," the waiter said. I could almost feel his eyes rolling as he had to explain to yet another tourist why there were no sardines on the menu.

"Oh, all right, what would you recommend then," I asked.

"Our special today is a lovely bacalhau à Brás."

"Bacalhau is dried, salted cod," I explained to Claire, "and à Brás means it's mixed with fried potatoes and egg and olives."

"I'll try it," she said.

"I'll have the grilled cheese and fries," Georgia said.

I saw that polvo à lagareiro was on the menu and my eyes widened. I love octopus, although I have had trouble eating it since I learned that they are very intelligent creatures. I hesitated but ordered it. This would be my first time eating octopus since I arrived. The à lagareiro-style means that the octopus (or cod or other fish) is grilled and drenched with olive oil and garlic, topped with cilantro, and accompanied by roast potatoes.

Claire and Georgia ordered a passion fruit drink, and I opted for a glass of red wine.

"But of course," the waiter said, as if he'd known all along that I would have wine. "That will go nicely with your meal."

My octopus dish was perfectly cooked and delicious. Claire declared her bacalhau the best meal she'd ever had. Georgia said her sandwich was fine, but the bread slices were too thick.

"Oh Georgia," I lamented. "You're missing out on one of the best things Portugal has to offer—the lovely food."

"Oh, Mum." She parroted my tone. "Please don't start in on me again. This is what I wanted. I know what I like."

I marvelled at how this small restaurant, with so few tables, one waiter, and probably one cook who doubled as the dishwasher, could serve such exquisite food. We skipped dessert but I ordered a bica, a short espresso, to finish off my meal. We sat there in the warmth of the day, relaxed, and totally content. The waiter walked by with flan pudding for another table, and I said, "Oh, that's my favourite, maybe I'll change my mind and have one."

"I'm sorry, senhora, these are the last two. We've run out."

He served the couple next to us who looked at us apologetically.

As the waiter walked past us again, I asked for the bill. In Portugal, you don't get the bill until you ask for it. Bringing the bill without being asked would be like ushering you out the door, and that would be considered rude.

We left the restaurant and strolled through the convent garden nearby. We wanted to go into the Sé de Lisboa, the Lisbon Cathedral, but it was closed. We wandered through Alfama, and within a few minutes, we were back in the labyrinth of cobblestone alleys and streets.

"How can anyone fit through these doors?" We took a picture of Claire towering over a green door. We giggled.

Georgia was intrigued by some of the houses with beautiful painted tiles. The geometric patterns provided evidence that the Moors once inhabited this area. I was examining various tiles, then looked down the street and realized I had no idea where we were. I felt the heat of anxiety rise in me. I was lost and all I wanted to do was run. I started to fidget and look around, wandering how I could escape.

Georgia noticed my discomfort and reassured me. "It's okay, Mum, we're on a hill. We can always head downhill to the river or uphill to the castle. We can't get super lost."

My daughter knew how to comfort me. I managed to compose myself and relax, but I was ready to get out of there. We ambled up the hill, Georgia leading the way, and ended up by the cathedral again. It was still closed. Several musicians were setting up in the plaza. Georgia and Claire sat on the stone wall, and I went to the coffee stand nearby to buy a mineral water and another coffee. I was still feeling a little shaky and needed to settle my nerves.

When the band started playing, a crowd gathered and people started dancing. One of the guys in the band came and asked Georgia and Claire to dance. I knew they would be too shy, but the guy was not taking no for an answer. He took their arms and brought them near the band, gesturing about their height and smiling and singing. I decided to just watch, but when they tried to sit down and he pulled them back, I stepped in.

"Um, they're with me."

It was all I had to say; he left them alone. He danced his way back to the band, took the tambourine, and started playing. There were so many people dancing now, but we were much too inhibited to join in. We sat on the steps and listened to the music for a while. I sensed that Georgia and Claire would have preferred that I hadn't interfered, but they didn't say anything. Next time, I'll wait until they ask for my help, I thought to myself.

When the band took a break, we headed up to the Castelo for the views and for the thrill of poking around in an old castle. We walked on the narrow parapets of the outer walls and took pictures. The afternoon light on the houses below was warm and flattering—the city looked stunning. Any tension from the band incident earlier had dissipated, and we were enjoying the breeze and the cool shade of the trees in the castle garden.

"I'm sorry about stepping in earlier, you guys. I'm a little embarrassed that I did that," I finally said to them.

"It's fine. He was a bit of a pain," Georgia said.

"I'm sure you could've handled yourselves, and I guess I prevented that. I'm sorry."

"I really didn't want to dance," Claire said.

Later, in the evening and back at home, the girls were playing cards in the living room when I decided to start on dinner. I peeled potatoes and cut up kale for the traditional caldo verde, which Claire had yet to try. I could hear them laughing and talking about how they almost ended up dancing in the street.

I set the table—fresh bread, olives, and cheese—and then I brought out the soup, piping hot, with a few rounds of chouriço floating on the top of each dish.

"I love this," Claire said. "It's the best soup I've ever had."

Georgia enjoyed the caldo verde too. She even had seconds.

My phone rang and I excused myself from the table. It was Eric calling.

"I thought you might just be arriving home from a day of exploring so I wanted to touch base and say goodnight." He sounded tired, his voice a bit muffled.

"How are you? How are things there?"

"Okay. Just sad. You know how it is. I wish you were here. Matt's here now so that's been good."

Georgia joined me on the couch and asked for the phone. "I'd like to say goodnight to Dad too."

After the call, Georgia and I had a quick hug, then rejoined Claire at the table and opened a package of cookies for dessert. We played cards until we had trouble keeping our eyes open.

. . . .

Fado Concert

THE END OF MARCH brought the end of spring break in Canada and the end of Claire's visit in Portugal. Eric returned from Ontario the day after Claire left, and I expected life would return to normal as we knew it. When I looked at the calendar and saw that we had six weeks of back-to-back visitors coming up, I realized there would be no back to normal—we were about to enter a very busy social period. I had longed for warm weather and friends to talk to for so long, and I was excited about hosting people, but I also felt an immediate pang of loss. Our quiet life would soon be behind us and, while there had been many lonely evenings, we had eased into a groove that had been rewarding in its own way. We had gelled as a family. We played cards and board games, practised speaking Portuguese with my impromptu lessons, and watched British comedies on television. In hindsight, it had been lovely.

I flipped through the newspaper while I sat at the coffee bar enjoying a bica one morning and noticed an ad for a concert featuring Carlos do Carmo. He is a much-loved fado singer and one of my long-time favourites. I made a mental note and logged on to my computer as soon as I got home, to look for tickets.

Amália Rodrigues—known in Portugal simply as Amália—is the most famous fadista of all time. Traditionally, fado was sung by women. But as the genre evolved, many men began to sing it too, and Carlos do Carmo has become one of the best-known male singers of the fado.

I met Amália and Carlos do Carmo at concerts in Edmonton in the 1980s. My sister Antónia knew them both personally from her time in Lisbon and arranged for them to come to Canada for concerts. I remember well what a thrill it was for my parents to meet both of these icons from their homeland. We had dinner with Amália at a restaurant, and I swear my mother was as excited about this as I imagine one would be meeting royalty or a president or prime minister, perhaps even more so. I don't remember much about the dinner, but we have a photo of my mother sitting with Amália, and the framed print became one of my mother's prized possessions. When Amália died, Portugal declared an official mourning period of three days.

This concert, a celebration of Carlos do Carmo's fifty-year career, was a big deal for me.

"We're going to see Carlos do Carmo, I'm so excited," I told the taxi driver who was dropping us off near the Coliseu dos Recreios in Lisbon on the night of the concert.

"Oh, he's passé," he replied. "He's had centre stage for too long."

"My parents loved him. And I do too. I saw him live in Canada."

"Ah, you're an emigrant. People who leave always like the old ones. But for us, here, there are so many new voices. It's time for him to move over and give others a chance."

I felt deflated but undeterred. I did not translate this exchange for Eric or Georgia. They had tuned out and were looking out the window at nighttime Lisbon. This concert had been my idea, and I had been playing it up for days, building the anticipation. I did not want our enthusiasm to come crashing down before we even entered the building.

The area around the venue was bustling. It was as crowded as the after-work rush hour in downtown Vancouver, maybe even busier than that. Where was everyone going? And what kind of concert doesn't even start until 9:30 at night, I wondered. I figured it would be a short concert. Don't people have to go to bed so they can get up in the morning?

When we found our seats, I realized why our tickets had been pricey. We had a theatre box very near the stage. We would have a great view. However, there were two rows of three seats in this box, and ours was the second row. I imagined tall people sitting in front of us, completely blocking our view, a thought that made me grumpy.

"Argh! These are lousy seats. And they were expensive. Someone is going to sit in front of me, I just know it, and I won't be able to see a thing," I grumbled to Eric.

"Well, we will still hear the music," he said. "It's still worth being here."

As I expected, within a few minutes, a man came in and sat directly in front of me. I gave Eric one of my looks, meaning that the concert hadn't even started, and I was already disappointed.

Georgia was sitting at the end of our row, next to Eric, and I imagined she was preparing herself for what would be a boring show for her—traditional music by musicians and singers she didn't know, singing words she didn't understand, to melodies she wouldn't recognize.

Whatever it was I said to Eric next (I was probably still grumbling about how I wouldn't be able to see anything) seemed to give the man in the box permission to start a conversation with us. He turned around and said, "You speak English? Are you visiting Lisboa?"

"Yes. We are from Canada," I said. "But I am Portuguese—from São Miguel, so Lisbon is a little bit new to us."

As I explained, he leaned in and seemed to become intrigued by our situation.

"How interesting. I would love to show you my Lisboa," he said. "I have a boat and I'd like to take you out on it. Up the river or down the coast. It's so beautiful and you really need to see the city and all this area from the water."

The lights dimmed and the show was about to start.

"Here, here, you take the front row. My companions are not coming, so I'll just stand," the man said, and then insisted when I initially declined.

"Obrigada," I said, feeling sheepish for my earlier thoughts.

Before I had a chance to translate for Eric, the man was ushering us all to the front row, and the audience started clapping. The announcer entered stage left and walked up to the microphone to welcome everyone.

As we were shuffling seats, the man whispered to me, "Let me give you my phone number so we can be in touch. Where's your phone?"

I didn't want to miss one minute of the show, so I handed him my phone and said, "Do you mind doing it?"

He took my phone, put on his reading glasses, and added his name and number into my contacts.

Carlos do Carmo sang a few solos, but mostly he sang duets with his protegés—seven in total—men and women I assumed were the up-and-coming new voices the taxi driver had told me about. But there was also Mariza, one of the most famous contemporary fadistas, and my current favourite. I was thrilled with the program. Most of the tunes were familiar to me, and I sang along with the audience to a few of the songs.

"What's this one about?" Eric asked.

Eric is familiar with fado. We listen to it at home, but I always assume that he can't quite grasp the feeling that comes with lyrics about love and loss. Every time I try to translate, I can't convey the emotion, and he ends up looking at me blankly.

"Isn't it beautiful?" I'll ask, feeling emotional. And he'll answer with something like "I'll have to look for the English lyrics on the internet so I can really understand."

"Just let yourself be moved by the music; don't worry too much about the words," I'll blurt out with an irritated tone. It's a scene that's repeated so many times when we listen at home. But this, this was different. The combination of the audience singing along, the beautiful stage, the variety of singers, the fadistas' elaborate dresses and makeup—everything—added to the dramatic feel. Even Georgia was mesmerized—her eyes focused on the stage and a faint smile on her lips. She tapped her foot to a few of the more upbeat numbers.

At intermission, I turned to see where our new friend was standing, and he was gone. I stood up to stretch, we all did, but we stayed in the box. None of us felt like dealing with the crowd in the foyer or contending with lineups at the bar.

"Where did he go?" I asked Eric.

"I don't know. Bathroom?"

"Gosh, he's been gone a long time," I said. I started to worry that I had said something that offended him. But what?

Just as the lights dimmed for the second part of the show, the man came back. He handed me a CD and said, "Here. You and your husband can take this home as a souvenir of this beautiful evening."

"Oh my goodness, thank you so much. That's very kind of you," I said. I tried to picture a similar scene at a concert back home in Vancouver. Would this kind of thing happen? Do strangers even talk to each other at concerts? I couldn't really imagine it.

After the show, when we shook hands and kissed on both cheeks to say goodbye, he held my hand for an extra second, shook it firmly, and said, "Call me. Don't forget."

"Okay," I said. "But you'll have to remember who I am."

"Of course I'll remember," he said, then turned and walked away, putting his hands in the pockets of his overcoat. "Adeus."

I knew I would be too shy to phone him.

I tried to get Eric to call a few days later. "You call him. You're so much better at this kind of stuff than I am," I said.

"I'm not going to call him. Most of the conversation was with you! Besides, have you forgotten? I don't speak Portuguese."

We argued back and forth like this for a while. I can laugh about it now, but at the time it wasn't funny.

"It's not appropriate for me to call. What if his wife answers?"

"Just tell her who you are."

"I can't do it," I said.

"Well, then don't." Things always seem so simple for Eric.

"But it'll be rude if I don't call." I was beating myself up for not having given him my number instead. It would have been so much easier to have left it for him to call us.

A week later, I called. There was no answer. I called again a few days later but didn't leave a message.

I don't remember this man's name anymore. When I recall the details of that evening, I think about fado and emotion and beautiful songs but also about this wonderful man and how generous and polite he was.

When we left the theatre that night, it was close to midnight. Outside, the street was as busy then as it had been at nine o'clock. Waiters at several restaurants were setting up more tables outside for people who wanted to have dinner after the show. Ice cream shops and cafés were open, and the benches in the plaza were all occupied. I could hear faint music in the distance.

"Ah, I love this country," I said. "It's so lively. I mean, it's so late, and look how many people are out."

"It does seem to be a culture made specifically for night owls like you," Eric said.

"Yeah, next time you have a dinner party back home in Vancouver, tell your guests to come at 10:00 p.m. and see what they say," Georgia added.

We all had a good chuckle at that idea as we made our way to the ferry terminal.

· · · ·

25th of April

WITH CARNIVAL, LENT, AND EASTER CELEBRATIONS now behind us, it was time to focus on the next holiday. The 25th of April is Portugal's national holiday commemorating the Carnation Revolution, the end of a decades-long dictatorship and the beginning of democracy. This year marked the fortieth anniversary—festivities had been going on during the entire month of April and would culminate on the twenty-fifth.

Throughout Lisbon, large, outdoor photo exhibits depicted events leading up to and including the coup. Many of the photos featured the Captains of April—the group of officers who, along with their leader Salgueiro Maia, are credited with planning and starting the revolution. We toured the exhibits and examined the photographs and their descriptions, trying to learn as much as we could about this historic day. Eric and Georgia asked me numerous questions about Portuguese politics, and I had to admit that I didn't know very much, so we turned to books. We bought everything we could find, in Portuguese and in English, including coffee-table books. I felt the enormity of this day and all the history it carried.

My memories of Salazar and the dictatorship are few and faint, and since we were already in Canada when the revolution occurred in 1974, I hadn't learned the details of how the coup had transpired. This was a good opportunity for Eric, Georgia, and me to discover this part of Portuguese history together.

My recollection is that our life in the Azores was comfortable. I never felt that we were poor, although my mother would later tell me that she and my father were always scrimping and saving, and they sometimes worried about having enough for us to live comfortably. But I believe that my parents made the move across the ocean not solely for financial reasons, but also to provide their daughters with better educational opportunities.

My sister Antónia had left for university in Lisbon in the late 1960s. I don't know how my parents supported her on their working-class incomes. They must have known that it would not have been possible to do the same for my sister Maria and me. At the time, there was the added complication of a regime that actively stifled the press and discouraged higher education. While Antónia was at school in Lisbon, she often spoke of her fear of the PIDE, the secret police, and told us that as a student she felt especially vulnerable.

The promise of adventure probably also played a role in my parents' decision to emigrate.

"Let's go see what it's like in Canada," I can remember them saying. And then: "We can always come back if it doesn't work out." It was the thing to do then, to go to North America and build a better life.

When I was a child, my parents spoke of the importance of schooling and higher education, and they wished they could have studied more. They each completed primary school, which was the average in the Azores in those days, and my mother went on to obtain a teaching certificate and teach elementary school for several years. Both my mother and father were avid readers and regretted their lack of opportunity. They must have decided early on in their life together that they would do whatever it took for their daughters to go to university.

When my uncle—my mother's brother, the one who had emigrated more than a decade prior—said that there was a university right in his hometown of Edmonton, and that he could sponsor us, my parents began talking seriously about moving to Canada. They reasoned that their daughters wouldn't have to live away from home to attend university, and that it was normal for students to work in the summers to help with their education so it would be much more affordable. I can't even begin to imagine the enormity of such a move. It was hard enough for me to settle in Portugal now, even temporarily, and I am fluent in Portuguese. What must it have been like for my parents to move their family to another country when they didn't even speak the language? I wish they were still alive because I would ask them for all the details. "Why, exactly, did you do it?" and "How hard was it, really?"

I remember both my mother and father being unsure about voting in elections in Canada after they became Canadian citizens, and that they were not comfortable putting signs on our lawn to let everyone know which party they supported. Portugal had been a dictatorship for more than forty years, which meant that neither of my parents had ever voted in free elections until they became Canadian citizens. No wonder they were skeptical. I can only imagine that democracy takes some getting used to.

One of the first vacations I remember after we moved to Canada was a trip back to Lisbon to visit Antónia, who was still in university. It was a chaotic time in the country but especially in the capital. One day, a bomb went off in the military quarter near her shared house, where we were also staying. After a loud bang, the windows in the house shook and the power went out. Antónia was late getting home that day and my mother was frantic. She lit a candle and prayed to Mary, on her knees, then she brought out the rosary for us to pray together. Partway through that prayer, Antónia walked in and said she'd been caught up in a student demonstration down the Avenida, the main street into Lisbon's central square. Soon after that, my parents sponsored her to join us, and she continued her studies in Edmonton. In Canada, she became known as Toni.

When we heard the revolution in Lisbon had been successful, my family was cautiously optimistic. My young mind was relieved that everything would change and people would be free. I began telling everyone at school that I was a socialist. I was twelve years old. Not many of my friends were interested in discussing democracy but I enjoyed my new identity as being "into politics."

The revolution brought a few tangible changes that were significant for me. The name of the street that we had lived on in São Miguel was changed from Rua da Republica to Rua 25 de Abril, and the suspension bridge in Lisbon that had been named after Salazar became the 25th of April Bridge. After five years in Canada, my family felt settled in our new country and my parents decided not to return to Portugal, but we remained strongly tied to our family and friends there, and my parents kept up with current events in our other country.

Prior to the revolution, Portugal had been at war, protecting its colonies in Africa: Angola, Mozambique, and Guinea-Bissau. These wars were costly both financially and in the number of lives lost. It is difficult to fight in several countries at the same time when you have a population of only nine million. The losses were huge on all sides. Tens of thousands of soldiers and civilians died; many were tortured, others disappeared. The Portuguese were also growing tired of sending their sons to fight in Africa, to countries most had never been to and never planned to visit. Still, the government hung on, refusing to give up control. At the time, the ties to the colonies were so strong that Angola and Mozambique were considered provinces of Portugal! Eventually, support diminished, even within the army, and soldiers began to plot a revolution.

In the early hours of April 25, 1974, a group of mid-level officers, led by Salgueiro Maia, overthrew the government. The troops had discussed plans for a revolt, but nothing was finalized until the last minute. It was agreed that two songs would be broadcast on the radio and used as signals—"E Depois do Adeus" ("And After the Farewell") would confirm that the plan would go ahead, and José Afonso's "Grândola Vila Morena" would be the signal to put the plan into action.

Tanks rolled down the streets towards the government offices in Praça do Comercio, the large plaza near the Tagus River.

Marcelo Caetano, who had become prime minister after António Salazar died, learned of the planned coup and tried to rally support from the military, but many refused and instead followed Maia. Caetano realized the inevitable and retreated to the national police barracks up the hill at Largo do Carmo. When the rebel tanks reached the Largo, Caetano surrendered. He was delivered to the Lisbon airport, and from there, given free passage to Brazil.

There are at least two explanations of how the coup became known as the Carnation Revolution. One is that when it became public that the government had been overthrown, citizens poured onto the streets in celebration. Flower vendors began distributing red carnations and people waved them high to show solidarity. Another explanation is that one flower vendor, Celeste Caeiro, offered a carnation to a soldier and placed it in the muzzle of his gun to discourage shooting, and many others followed suit. Whichever version is correct, the red carnation has been adopted as the symbol of the revolution.

• • •

Eric and his brother Pete had spent the week following their mother's funeral together, during which I imagined there was talk of visiting us in Costa. Pete had never been to Portugal, so this would be a vacation and also an opportunity to enjoy some family time with us.

He arrived in the late afternoon of April 24th. We thought he might be too tired to accompany us on an evening expedition into Lisbon to join in the fortieth anniversary festivities. We suggested he stay home to get to sleep early, but he insisted. "I'll come," he said. "I don't want to miss out."

It made sense; he only had six days and probably wanted to pack in as much as possible. Sleep would come later. But he underestimated the effects of jet lag.

We drove to Cacilhas and took the ferry across to Lisbon. From the river, the city looked stunning, as usual, with its twinkling lights filling the hillsides. It's a short trip, ten minutes at the most, but every time I'm on this ferry, I breathe in deeply and allow myself to become mesmerized by the beauty. I don't ever want to take this view for granted. I wondered what it was like for Pete. I wanted to nudge him and ask him if he noticed, if he found it beautiful, but I held back my enthusiasm. All four of us were silent as we looked out the window, and I like to imagine we were all equally awestruck.

We docked on the north side, and hundreds of people poured out of the old boat onto the riverside walkway that leads into one of the city's main squares, Terreiro do Paço, also known as Praça do Comercio. Lisbon had come alive for the evening and was even busier than usual. Restaurants and patios were full, and cafés and food stalls were open and doing brisk business. We showed Pete some of the sights—Rua Augusta, Rossio, the train station—and we stopped for ice cream, but mostly we just walked. We bought red carnations and pinned them on our lapels.

At one point, I noticed that Pete was fading. He was pale and his eyes looked like he'd been up for too long. He was lagging and took every opportunity to sit on a bench or lean against a wall. I was feeling bad for keeping him up after a long flight just so we could walk some more. It was a chilly evening, and we still had another hour or so to wait before the song "Grândola Vila Morena" would be played on the loudspeakers. I was determined to be in Lisbon at midnight to mark the start of the celebration, but I was also worried that Pete would pass out. Eric must have been concerned too, or he read the worry on my face, because he suggested that we leave.

"We're not even sure where the song will be playing or what will happen or even if we'll be able to hear it. Why don't we just go home," Eric said.

We decided to go. I understood why, and agreed it was for the best, but I felt like crying, such was my disappointment. At the terminal, while we waited for the ferry, I promised myself that I'd come back to Lisbon for the fiftieth anniversary, and I would stay right in the city, and I would stay out past midnight.

The next morning, our carnations were looking droopy, but we left them on our jackets anyway. We had a relaxing coffee with breakfast on our deck and then strolled on the beach. Most businesses in town were closed except for a few restaurants. Since it was a special day, we decided to have lunch at Cabrinha again. We were becoming regulars. Since that first time on Valentine's Day, we had gone several more times for lunch and twice for dinner.

As usual, the restaurant was packed. Our waiter this time was an older man we didn't know, who looked frazzled and distracted when he took our order. He seemed to reserve most of his attention for the couple at the table next to us, so much so that I decided they must be famous and wished I knew who they were.

At our table, Eric explained the menu to Pete, and I tried to discuss with Georgia what the three of us would share. On previous occasions, we had found that the portions were so large that a meal for two was plenty for the three of us. But this also meant that we had to agree on what to order. I sensed that Georgia was silently hoping we would choose something she liked, something without a head and eyes staring back at her from the plate. I knew that she liked the seafood rice casserole, so instead of negotiating, we went ahead and ordered our usual, arroz de marisco. Georgia could pick out the seafood she liked and she loved rice. It was always a good bet, and even though I wanted to branch out and try something different, we resorted to this familiar dish. Pete ordered baked cod, which was served on a platter, surrounded by potatoes.

I became intrigued with the couple sitting at the next table, the ones garnering the attention of our waiter. The woman was older, perhaps in her mid-sixties, with silver, perfectly coiffed hair. I thought she was beautiful. The man was sitting on the same side as I was, so I couldn't get a good look at him without making it obvious that I was checking him out.

The woman looked at me a lot. I had become used to this; people did like to stare. Sometimes, I tried to stare back and added a smile. Most people didn't return the smile, and they would eventually look away but only when they felt like it. This woman didn't look away. She didn't outright smile either, but there was a kindness in her eyes, a curiosity, as if she were interested in us. And she *almost* smiled back.

I don't remember who started talking to whom first, but before I knew it, all six of us at our two tables were chatting away, or rather, they were talking and asking questions and I was translating to my tablemates, answering questions, making small talk, laughing. I felt courageous and asked them what they were eating because it looked so good, and I'd like to try something different next time, I said.

"We usually have the arroz de marisco too," she said, "but today we wanted to try something different. This is called trilogia."

That made sense to me. It looked like there were three different kinds of seafood: a white fish, clams, and lobster. The man took a chunk from his plate and plunked it on mine. "Try it," he said. "It's amazing."

I didn't mention that I had chunks of that same fish in my seafood rice casserole. He must have seen the look on my face because he said, "It's different from yours. Different sauce."

I picked it up with my fork and popped it into my mouth, feeling somewhat reluctant but hoping it wasn't obvious.

"Curry?" I asked.

"Yes. It's good, isn't it?"

"Delicious." I licked my lips.

I turned my attention back to my table companions, but it was clear that our new friends were more interested in talking to us than to each other.

"It's my birthday today," the woman said.

I had a brief flash of culture shock just then. How different an experience this was for me compared to going out for dinner back home in Vancouver. Would anyone ever turn to someone at the next table to say that it was their birthday? In my Canadian life, I've learned that celebrations like birthdays are private. In Portugal, that sense of privacy is different, and this woman, and this situation, seemed a perfect example. I wondered to myself how old she might be, she was so beautiful, but I didn't ask. That would be crossing a line in both cultures.

"I'm seventy-one today, and I believe in celebrating that," the woman said, almost in response to my thoughts. "After lunch, we'll go for a walk, just the two of us, then tonight we'll have dinner with the family."

"Really? You'll be able to eat another meal after this?" I asked.

"Of course. Food is glorious, and we love it, don't we, amor?" she said, as she turned to face her husband again.

"We do," he said. "Our three children and four grandchildren will all come over, and we'll have a wonderful celebration. Again."

Our conversation continued. Pete was still dissecting his fish very carefully so as not to ingest any bones, and Georgia was picking through the casserole with her fork, removing anything she didn't recognize, as well as any onions. I began to tell our new friends about our family, and how we had ended up living in Portugal for several months. I explained that our son was in university back home and would be joining us in May when his term was finished, that our family celebrations seemed incomplete without him, and that we had a celebration of our own going on right then too—my brother-in-law was visiting from Toronto.

"Have you ever been there?" I asked.

"Not to Canada," they said. "But we have been to New York, once."

They asked if Pete lived alone, which I interpreted as them asking why he was travelling without his family.

"It's a quick trip for him," I said. "Just six days to visit us and see a bit of Lisbon."

"Oh, but that's not enough! You need more time!"

They said this just as dessert was brought to our tables. Eric and I had finally dared to order what is on nearly every menu but we'd never had the nerve to try—baba de camelo or, in a literal translation, camel's drool. This is a rich pudding made with condensed milk, egg yolks, and sugar. Every time we've seen anyone have it, they close their eyes and make "mmm" sounds. Today, we would try it. Georgia and Pete opted out of dessert, which did not sit well with our new friends.

When the drool was delivered to our table, the man looked at Pete and Georgia and almost shrieked, "What? No dessert?"

Then he looked at me and said, "You did not order the molatof? It's the specialty here." Molatof is another dessert we had seen many times on menus. It is essentially meringue topped with caramel sauce.

Before I had a chance to answer, the man stretched out his arm and hovered a forkful above my plate. "Here, try mine."

"No, no, it's okay, I'll order it next time," I said. But it was too late, he dropped it onto my dessert dish, and there it sat, perfectly formed, not losing its shape.

"Try it. Do you like it?"

"Oh yes, it's amazing."

That's all it took. He signalled our waiter and ordered molatofs, all around, for our table. One for each of us. "It's on me," he said.

The restaurant was quieter now. Some people had finished and left, and the servers were cleaning tables. Zé came to our table with several bottles of liquor. There was port, as well as ginjinha, and Ballantine's Scotch whisky.

"Ah, so my favourite tenants have met my dear friends," he said, sitting down with us. "Let's celebrate that."

"Oh, I don't think I can eat another bite or drink anything else," I said.

"Nonsense, this helps with digestion. Which one would you like?"

"All right then, port," I said, knowing that refusing would be futile and rude. Eric chose ginjinha. Even Georgia was encouraged to try the port.

"It's our national pride," he said.

Pete chose the scotch and, with the first sip, looked like he had found a long lost love. "I don't think I've had scotch since I was in my twenties," he said.

I shouldn't have been surprised then, when we stopped at the supermarket for groceries later in the evening and Pete bought himself a bottle of Ballantine's.

. . .

We headed out into the sunshine after our meal and walked towards the bustle of the ferry terminal to head into Lisbon. I was quietly scheming to keep the tradition of long, languorous lunches when we got back to our regular lives in Vancouver. Maybe for special occasions, I thought. I certainly couldn't do it every week. I was also thinking about how I had eaten too much, downed more alcohol than usual, had not one but two desserts, and I was feeling warm and sleepy. Until I got on the ferry—the hard chairs, the engine noise, and the occasional whiff of diesel were enough to jolt me out of my sleepy reverie.

Lisbon was still in party mode. The sun had warmed the day and throngs filled the streets, patios, and restaurants. Near the Avenida, we encountered a political march unlike anything I'd seen before. There must have been fifty thousand people, maybe more. It seemed to be mostly labour unions from what I could tell. They held banners and placards with union slogans but there were also flags for various political parties, including the Communist Party. Marchers chanted and sang, fists punching the air up high. There were red carnations everywhere—painted on signs, pinned on lapels, and bunched in bouquets. People watching at the side of the road waved single flowers in the air and threw them at the marchers. They chanted slogans about the economic crisis, about poor working conditions and corruption. I didn't know the words to any of the chants or songs, but the tunes were catchy, and I found myself humming along.

I was struck that all the marchers felt it important to be out parading on that day. These were not just young radicals but all kinds of people: grandmothers carrying babies in their arms, elderly people who could barely walk, some using walkers and canes, and young men and women. I wanted to throw carnations too and raise my fist in the air, but I couldn't bring myself to do it, not even in solidarity. These people felt like my people and this country felt like my country, but this was not my fight nor my celebration. My family had left Portugal. We had not witnessed the revolution first-hand. And now I was back, but I had not been subjected to tough economic sanctions. Despite my desire to participate, I remained a bystander and an observer.

In our own version of a political pilgrimage, we walked up the hill to Largo do Carmo. This was where it had all ended, forty years before. Portuguese flags and red carnations were everywhere—decorating balconies and doorways, in planter boxes and vases throughout the square, and at a memorial to honour the four people who had died as a result of the coup.

Although the Carnation Revolution is often referred to as a bloodless coup, there were, in fact, four deaths (some say more; I've heard up to seven). There are conflicting accounts of just how these deaths occurred—some say the people were killed when the police fired shots from inside their barracks, others that they were run over accidentally by a tank—but the army managed to secure the government's defeat without firing one single shot.

It was good to see the dead remembered; they are not often mentioned. The memorial was set up in the middle of the square, surrounded by hundreds of red carnations and a plaque.

Eric was fascinated by the photo exhibits, and he went from one to another, matching them to the scenery around him. Georgia and I fixated on the expressions of the people in the photographs. All of us wondered where so many carnations came from. It was not hard to see that they are at the peak of their season in April.

Back at home, we had soup and bread for dinner. Pete got to taste the traditional caldo verde, though I hadn't made it fresh that day. My mother would have frowned at the idea of me serving reheated soup on a special day. I thought of our friends from lunch having another elaborate, full meal in the evening. Our dinner was not elegant, but it was all we needed. After our soup, Pete brought out the Ballantine's. We toasted Salgueiro Maia and the revolutionaries and raised our glasses to Portugal's forty years of freedom.

. . . .

Reflections on Duality

"BEFORE YOU START FRYING FISH, close all the doors to the bedrooms and closets and open the windows," my mother would say. "You don't want your clothes smelling like fried fish."

I'm not sure that my mother enjoyed cooking all that much. She often talked about how much work it was and how she didn't find it all that exciting because she had to do it every single day. And she loved going out to dinner. But whenever she cooked a Portuguese dish, she'd call me over to the stove to teach me and give me pointers. "There are certain things every Portuguese homemaker needs to know how to do," she'd say.

"Yes, Mum, next time. Not now, okay?" That was my usual response. I wasn't that interested in learning how to clean fish or how to make octopus stew when I was a teenager.

Now I wish I had paid more attention. I'll stand over a chunk of dried salt cod on the counter and wonder how long to soak it for, exactly, and how many times to change the water. Or I'll stare at a whole mackerel that I'm about to bake and ponder whether I should add wine or bake it dry, add cilantro or just parsley.

I feel closest to my mother when I'm in the kitchen preparing a meal. I can almost hear her voice and see her smile. She's telling me what to do, of course, but now I'm listening and welcoming her instructions.

Life as a Portuguese-born teenager living in Canada in a traditional Portuguese immigrant family had its drawbacks. I wasn't allowed to date boys without a chaperone. Under any circumstances. Try explaining that to a guy you have a crush on in high school.

I wasn't allowed to go out much with girlfriends either. "Packs of girls roaming around at night get up to no good," my mother would say. And I was definitely not allowed to go on sleepovers. "Your friends can come sleep here if they want" was a common refrain at our house. Sometimes they did, but with the understanding that there would be no reciprocity. By contrast, my Portuguese friends lived by rules that were similar to mine, and we understood each other.

I was one of those immigrant kids who went to language school after regular school twice a week and on Saturday mornings. I danced in the folklore group too, and we practised at least once a week, more often if there was a show coming up. We attended dances and festas, and we went on field trips organized by the Portuguese community. As immigrant families, we had brought our customs with us, and we assumed that nothing back home changed. When I hung out with my Portuguese friends, life was easy and uncomplicated. It was in school with my Canadian friends that my two worlds collided.

In junior high (Grades 7 to 9 in Alberta), my school held an annual winter retreat at a nearby lake. The first year, my parents would not sign the permission slip, and I did not go. The following year, the school counsellor came to our house for a meeting with my parents. She told them that she would personally supervise me and make sure I stayed safe and out of trouble. My mother said she trusted me, that she knew I wouldn't get into trouble, but she was afraid of lakes, especially in the winter, and feared that I would fall through the ice and drown.

I remember that my sister Maria walked in on the conversation and the counsellor asked if Maria could come as a chaperone. My parents thought that was a brilliant solution. Maria, at ten years my senior, would keep me safe even if the teachers, counsellors, and other parent chaperones could not. Maria was not thrilled at the idea, but somehow, she was talked into it and we both went on the school trip.

When we arrived at the camp, I found out that one of the planned activities was cross-country skiing on the lake. I told my teacher that I wasn't feeling well and wouldn't be joining the group. The counsellor came to see me in the cabin and said that she would ski with me, and we would stay near the shore, and she assured me nothing would happen, that I would not fall in, and that she would explain everything to my parents. Even Maria agreed with the plan. But I said no; I had promised my parents I wouldn't go on the lake, and I intended to keep my word. Maria and I stayed in the cabin and played cards while everyone went out skiing. My friends believed that I was sick and were glad that my sister would be staying with me. That night I cried myself to sleep on the top bunk.

While I lived in my parents' home I had an eleven o'clock curfew, even into my late twenties, and I wasn't allowed to move out on my own. I rebelled against my parents' rules, but I never won. Our arguments never lasted long; I didn't like being in conflict with them, and I didn't want to be estranged from them. Some of my Portuguese friends had made choices their parents didn't approve of—they went out with their boyfriends, or they moved out after high school—and they no longer had relationships with their families. I knew I didn't want that. I managed to find a balance between fitting in with my peer group and maintaining a close connection with my parents, but it was a delicate dance. I remember it as being a stressful time.

In my second year of university, I joined an outdoor club and went camping, canoeing, and hiking with friends. I had always been drawn to nature and to outdoor pursuits and this was one way of developing my skills. For some reason, that was okay with my parents, perhaps because it was all lumped in as part of my university education. Or maybe they decided to loosen the grip once I turned twenty. After I graduated, my first job was six hours away, in Lethbridge, Alberta.

"Esmeralda, why do you have to go so far away? Aren't there any jobs here in Edmonton?" my mother asked me one day, as I was packing for my big move.

"Ma, I have to go where the jobs are, and I have no experience, so I can't really be choosy. I'm lucky to get a job. Besides, I won't be that far away—it's only a six-hour drive."

"Minha Nossa Senhora," my mother mumbled. She always prayed to Mary when she was worried. Then she turned to me and said, "We came all the way to Canada so you girls wouldn't have to go away to university, and now you go away to work because you went to university."

I felt a lump of guilt lodge in my throat. I didn't dare tell my mother that most of the jobs I had applied for were out of town. They were the most appealing to me, probably because I imagined myself living in my own place. In my family, there were only two acceptable reasons to move out of your parents' house, no matter what your age—marriage, or a really good job in another city. I didn't want to ruffle feathers and I didn't want to lose my family, but I did want my own apartment, so I left town.

The job in Lethbridge was a temporary position, and when it ended, Maria and I went on a big trip together. We travelled for two and a half months in Brazil, spending six weeks of that time in Rio de Janeiro to meet and get to know the Brazilian side of our family. We visited with our Aunt Teresa, our mother's sister, as well as lots of cousins, more distant relatives, and many of their friends. I was taken with my auntie, who I thought was a spitting image of my mother. They shared so many similar gestures and the same love of laughter. I lapped up all the stories she told of her relationship with my mother and of life in the Azores before she emigrated. Maria and I both eased into our Brazilian family's life as if we'd all known each other all our lives.

Soon after returning to Edmonton, I lucked into an outdoor summer job that took me away from home once again. This time, I would be a leader of a Junior Forest Ranger Camp for young women, sixteen to eighteen years old, who were considering a career in forestry. Our camp was situated along the Sheep River, in the foothills of the Rocky Mountains in southern Alberta. We cleared trails and felled (small!) trees, built fences, repaired footbridges, and counted bighorn sheep for a scientific study. I was there for about six weeks and, given that I had been travelling before that, it had been a while since I had spent much time with my family. I invited my parents to come and visit me and much to my surprise, my mother said yes. She didn't even ask many questions. My father said maybe next time.

I drove into Calgary to buy supplies for our camp, then picked up my mother at the Greyhound bus station in my work truck. She laughed out loud when she tried getting into the passenger seat and needed me to give her a boost from behind. We headed south and west, through Black Diamond, Turner Valley, past the Sandy McNabb Recreation Area, and onto a gravel road.

"Where in the world are you taking me?"

There was a hint of panic in my mother's voice, almost as if she wanted me to turn the truck around and take her right back to the bus station and the noise of the city.

"I told you we'd be out in the sticks, Mum."

I sensed that she was nervous but also excited about this adventure that she was embarking on—a weekend in the real outdoors—with her daughter as a guide, no less.

My mother met all the young women over dinner, sitting at a long picnic table. They loved her—how could they not? She was outgoing and charming, and she had an infectious laugh. She told stories in her broken English that sometimes were hard to decipher, but she did it with such enthusiasm that we were captivated. She told jokes that she translated from Portuguese, which made no sense in English. She asked numerous questions and showed interest in everyone and everything in these surroundings that were so foreign to her.

Later that night, we were sitting around the campfire and my mother turned to me and said, "How ever did you turn out this way? You seem so sure of yourself out here. We never even took you camping."

My mother slept in the cook's trailer, sharing a room with Janice, the camp cook. She was thrilled that there was a bathroom in the trailer, and she wouldn't have to make her way to the outhouse during the night. I slept in my fireline tent on a bed of boughs, cushioned with a thin air mattress. Shortly after midnight, I woke up to go to the outhouse and saw that the light was still on in the trailer, my mother and Janice probably chatting like two schoolgirls on a sleepover.

My mother was an artist, among many other things, but she did not consider herself one. She painted magnificently though, and that weekend, she gave me a tour of the mountain camp I was living in through a painter's eyes.

"I love all the different hues of green," she told me. "I don't think I've ever seen so many. And that sky is so blue." She looked around her with awe. "The mountains are very close, so big and jagged. I wish I'd brought my paints. I'd love to paint them."

I introduced her to the outdoor experience and fed nature to her on a platter.

"Look over there, Mum," I said when she came with me in the morning to check for supplies at a trailhead. "There's the biggest ram in the area. His name is Fifty-Six. It's very special to see him; isn't he beautiful?"

I pointed out a waterfall, then a mountain goat trail. My mother looked enchanted, and she wished, out loud, several times, that my father had come too.

That afternoon, I took our group to the creek so we could wash up. It was a swift running stream but with big flat slabs of rock here and there where we could lie and soak up the sun or sit and dangle our feet in the water. Some of the rocks were naturally arranged in semicircles, forming small pools where we could sit and feel the water rush by on either side. The girls scattered up the creek in twos and threes, and I went from one group to another offering a few drops of biodegradable soap for our weekly cleansing routine. I noticed my mother sitting on one of the big slabs with several girls around her, fussing over her and washing her hair. Her laughter echoed from the canyon walls, and it made us all laugh, too. I returned to my lookout spot on the shore and scouted for bears.

"Be sure to tell me if there's any men coming too," my mother hollered.

I told her there was no one around for miles in any direction, that we were alone. I don't know why she was so concerned; she was fully decked out in her very conservative swimsuit. It covered her, neck to knee, and had a flared skirt, falling from her hips.

More than a decade later, my mother still referred to that weekend as one of the best trips she'd ever taken.

When I found my first permanent job, a government job, it was back in Edmonton. I was twenty-six years old. I moved home again and returned to a life of curfews, lots of questions, and parental hypervigilance.

During those years, I remember being more concerned with fitting into Canadian culture than I was with maintaining ties to my Portuguese heritage. I lived with my parents, but I balked at their strict, conservative rules. I found freedom in nature, and my identity was closely tied to the outdoors. I went hiking and paddling as often as my job would allow, with short trips to the mountains at least two weekends out of four. In my mind, I was Canadian, and I didn't have much desire to return to Portugal, not even for a visit. My parents, however, always talked about going back. They went for long visits and when they returned, they'd start planning their next trip. My sisters and I admitted to each other that we felt hurt when our parents decided to celebrate their fiftieth wedding anniversary in São Miguel with their extended family instead of with us, in Canada.

My parents often travelled in May to attend the Festa do Senhor Santo Cristo, an annual religious festival honouring the patron saint of the island. I would call my mother twice, on consecutive weekends, to wish her a happy Mother's Day because Portugal and Canada celebrated on different days. During those conversations, she'd sound nostalgic, saying she wished she could be with us in Canada, and she'd complain about the cobblestone streets on the island and how her heels would get stuck between the stones.

"I don't get it, Mum...when you're here you always want to be there, and when you're there you want to be here," I remember saying to her several times. And then I'd follow that with "why don't you just decide on one or the other?"

I don't remember how she'd respond to that, and I shudder to think about how impatient I was with her when she expressed her feelings of longing. Things were so clear to me then—I lived in the present, and I believed all the saudade was a waste of energy.

When Eric and I went to Portugal on our honeymoon, he fell in love with my other country. We spent two weeks in Lisbon and the Algarve and then two weeks in São Miguel.

"I had no idea it was so beautiful here," he said, marvelling at the green rolling hills and the dark lava rock of my home island. We would walk along the Avenida in the evenings, then have dinner at a seaside restaurant. "I don't know how your parents could have ever left this place," he said on more than one occasion.

Since we'd met, Eric had taken an interest in all things Portuguese— food, music, wine, and the island life that my mother described to him each time they had a conversation. He accepted the unspoken rules in my family, even my curfew, which was still set at eleven o'clock even though I was, by then, twenty-eight years old and engaged to be married.

Eric and I had met through work, but we lived a country apart—I lived in Edmonton, and he lived in Hamilton, Ontario. Our dates consisted of meeting in Winnipeg for a weekend, kayaking in Mexico, and cross-country skiing in Banff. My parents did not seem to have a problem with me travelling, but when I was home in Edmonton and living in their house, I lived by their rules. When Eric flew to Edmonton to see me, I'd pick him up at the airport and we'd have dinner together, and then I would drive him to his hotel before I rushed home to arrive well ahead of the appointed time. Anyone who puts up with that, I thought to myself, makes for good marriage material.

It was when I married Eric and wove myself into his Canadian family that my Portuguese side emerged again. When I met his parents for the first time, at their house for dinner, I was astonished that there were families who really did sit down for a pre-dinner drink by the fire and talk, one at a time, to each other. Eric's mother brought out dinner, neatly plated, and it was all over in less than an hour. There were no clanging pots in the kitchen, no one getting up and down to check on, and bring out, the next course, no chatting over cheese and port wine late into the evening.

Eric says he discovered that garlic came in cloves when he met me. "I thought it was a powder," he'll say with a wink. He became a fan of Portuguese food early on in our relationship.

I don't know when he realized that adopting Portuguese customs would mean that his in-laws would eventually move in with us, but he took that in stride, even encouraged it, and helped look after my parents as they grew older and more frail.

When my mother started palliative care in our home, Eric did everything around the house in addition to working full-time, so as to free me up to spend time with my mother. And when she died, Eric cried and said, "I'm so glad we were able to care for her here."

My father, amid his tears, thanked Eric for allowing her to die peacefully in our home. "She hated hospitals," he explained.

I don't know when I started becoming my mother, when the nostalgia and the longing started to set in. Throughout my life—even during my teenage years when I negotiated my parents' old-fashioned rules—my mother and I maintained a close relationship. I cherished her. But I told myself that if I ever became a mother, I wouldn't expect my children to hold the same traditional values. I would not establish an eleven o'clock curfew or discourage them from moving out on their own. I would also not feel so much saudade. I would live in Canada and be fully Canadian.

Sometime after my children were born, though, I became determined to teach them our Portuguese ways. I cooked Portuguese food, and I tried to teach them to speak Portuguese. I put up signs with translations for numerous objects around the house such as table, chair, fridge, bed. There were so many sticky notes in different colours that at times it looked like we had miniature prayer flags hung up in various places. I asked my parents to speak to the children in Portuguese so they could tune their ears to the rhythm of our language. We took trips back "home," both to the Azores and to the mainland.

As they got older, my more traditional values began to emerge. I might even have spoken the phrase "packs of young people, roaming the streets, up to no good" at some point. I once heard one of my teenagers mumbling something like "I wish you weren't such a Portuguese mother," and my nieces called our home "the house of rules."

Somewhere along the road of parenthood, I started to experience what I remember my mother voicing—the longing to be in our other country. That feeling has stayed with me. I openly admit to saudade now, and I feel the duality of my heritage. When I am in Canada, I feel Portuguese, and when I am in Portugal, I feel Canadian. My children probably wish I would stop longing and just decide once and for all where I want to be. Growing up and growing older has made me realize that it's not so simple. My identity is not clearly one or the other, but rather, both; my values are grounded in not one but two cultures. I wish I could sit across the table from my mother now and tell her that I understood the duality she felt. I would give her a hug and say, "Agora compreendo."

. . . .

Our Guests

I STOOD IN THE SHOWER and let the hot water run over me. I
mentally walked through my day—go to the market, buy fish, come
home, clean the house, do the laundry, hang up the laundry, drive to
the airport, pick up guests, come home, walk to the beach with guests,
come home, start dinner. Phew. Eric often worked from home and
Georgia interspersed doing her online schoolwork with walking
Maggie and going into town with me to buy groceries. She helped me
clean up but preparing for guests was largely my job—and this kind of
mental preparation in the shower happened often.

In the months leading up to our departure for Lisbon, I had invited
numerous people to visit us in Portugal. If I ran into someone on the
street, even someone I hadn't seen in months, I'd tell them we were
moving to Portugal for a while and then add, "You should come visit."
At one point I remember Eric telling me to be careful, that if everyone
I invited showed up, we wouldn't have any time on our own.

"It's part of my strategy," I assured him. "If you invite ten people,
one will come."

"Just be sure to leave some time for us to be there on our own, and
maybe do some travelling," he said.

Sure enough, once spring arrived, we had a steady stream of visitors. There were six sets of overnight guests over an eight-week period. In addition, several friends from Vancouver came to Lisbon for conferences and although they didn't stay with us, we met for dinner at restaurants or enjoyed nights of fado at various clubs.

Our visitors included family members, friends, a new colleague of mine that I didn't know very well, and her husband, whom I had never met. There were friends of my late sister Maria who had become my friends, and our neighbours from Vancouver. This intense period of hosting took its toll on the introverts in my family and, if I am honest with myself, it impacted me too. For a few weeks, I ran on autopilot—cooking, cleaning, doing laundry—and thought of little else. But there was something about all of us being able to sit down and converse with our friends, in English, that was easy and comfortable. I felt more relaxed when I wasn't in translation mode, and I didn't have to worry about making sure that Eric and Georgia felt included in conversations. In English, at least, they could look after themselves.

Despite all the work involved, I enjoy hosting people in my home and cooking for them. It brings me so much pleasure. Cooking breakfast is especially gratifying. I am not a big breakfast eater, but I like slow, meandering mornings, when I can chat with friends over coffee and fresh bread, pick at fruit, or devour pancakes or waffles. The extrovert in me loves to socialize and the Portuguese in me likes to do that over food. I can stay at a table for hours after lunch or dinner, talking, talking, or over breakfast until there is nothing left to say and you have no choice but to carry on with the day. But I've also never had so many guests over such a short period of time.

• • •

When spring arrived, I felt grateful that the weather was conducive to hanging laundry on the line to dry. Since we did not have a dryer, it took careful planning to ensure we had clean bed linens for our guests. There were a few times when it was close—would the sheets dry in time for the new set of guests who would be arriving soon?

I remember one day when I went to collect the sheets from the clothesline up on the rooftop deck and found bird droppings on the fitted sheet. What are the odds of that, I thought to myself, and looked up to the sky, half expecting the culprit to be hovering above, looking down, and laughing at me. I gathered the sheet and ran downstairs to put it in the washing machine again. In less than an hour it was up on the line once more and I made a quick calculation—yes, there would be time for it to dry before I had to make the bed again. I hung it up under that cloudless sky and squinted. This time it was the only item on the line. I looked over to the beach and heard the roar of the waves. Although the weather was calm, the surf was pounding. The tide was coming in.

Just before we headed to the airport to pick up Judy and Louise, I ran up to the deck, hoping to collect the sheet and make the bed before Eric and I had to leave. Could it be that the same bird had come back? Impossible, isn't it? Yet, there it was again, another stain, almost in the same place as before. This time it looked smeared, and I could make out berry seeds in it. This bird has the runs, I thought. Is there anything one can do at a time like that but laugh?

I put the sheet back in the washing machine, set the short cycle again, and we left. I wondered what we would do if we were not able to dry the sheet before nightfall. I called Georgia from the airport and reminded her to check the washing machine and hang up the sheet once the cycle had finished. I suggested that this time it would be a good idea to drape it over the drying rack and place it in the front yard.

"Make sure no birds fly overhead, okay?"

"Are you serious, Mum? How can I do that?" she replied.

I don't know if people ever noticed all that we had to do to prepare for their arrival. It shouldn't be noticeable, should it? I didn't enjoy doing the laundry, although each time I brought clothes in from the line, I felt a wave of satisfaction. This has all dried without using any energy, I would think to myself, feeling proud, as if I had accomplished something grand and line-drying had been a choice. Truth is, I hadn't seen a dryer anywhere, not in anyone's home, not even in a store. This was in stark contrast to my life back home in Vancouver where, technically, clotheslines aren't even allowed in the city. There, I dry my laundry on racks, outside on sunny days and inside during most of the winter, but in a pinch I can always use the dryer—a big dryer. Our family prides itself on being energy conscious but I'd already seen how much less consumptive our life in Portugal was by comparison. The size of appliances was most startling—they were so much smaller in Portugal.

I loved cooking for our guests, especially their first dinner with us. If they arrived late in the evening, I would make soup that I would serve with the day's bread, or I would have a cake or loaf ready for snacking. For their first real meal with us, I usually served fish. This would require a trip to the market to see what the fishers had brought in that day.

I had learned to check the eyes of the fish and smell the skin for freshness, but really, it was all fresh by my standards. For the fishmonger, fresh meant that it had arrived in the last couple of hours. For me, fresh meant within a couple of days and the fish still smelled like fish. It was easier to tell if the shellfish was fresh—the clams were closed and heaped in giant mounds, the crabs milled about in buckets, and the lobsters raised their claws and snapped at the air. All of this I was used to seeing, except for the eels. I could barely look at the bucket of eels slithering around, all snake-like. It sometimes caused me an actual physical reaction, a gagging of sorts, and I'd have to look away. The fishmonger challenged me more than once to buy some and make eel stew—ensopado de enguias.

"Not yet," I said, every single time. Then she'd laugh.

I was glad to have taken on this interest in cooking fish. It allowed me to develop a relationship with the fishmongers at the market and the vendors who would often suggest something for my dinner, then spell out the instructions on how to prepare it. I thought of it as an art form, the way they could imagine a meal for me and then suggest recipes, just like that. They weren't really recipes—more like add some of this and a bit of that, this herb if you have some, serve with boiled potatoes drizzled with olive oil, that kind of thing. Their suggestions made my mouth water. Cooking fish the way these women suggested was simple and always tasty. The fact that the next time they saw me they'd ask how it turned out made me think that I was more than just a regular customer. We had developed a kind of friendship.

I had started with fish that was easier to cook—grouper and sole— then graduated to other kinds of fish: hake, squid, even salted cod, and later, to seafood. I was squeamish at first—holding, cutting, and cooking fish that looked like actual fish was a little unnerving. It looked much more like an animal to me than the sterile, cellophane-wrapped packages of fillets I bought at home in Vancouver. Here, there was no getting away from the fact that I was eating something that was once alive and free, swimming in the ocean. It gave me pause, both as I cooked and when I ate, and I was grateful for so much bounty from the sea.

For Pete's first dinner with us, I baked a grouper. He enjoyed it so much that I made it once again before he left—so, yes, we had it twice in six days! When he got back to Burlington, he looked for grouper in the supermarkets and brought one home to cook for his family.

"It was okay," he said, "but not nearly as good as what I had at your place."

For Nancy, my new friend I'd met at work in Vancouver, and her husband Nick, I made breaded sole. I had cooked sole fillets fairly often at home, but this time the fish looked like an actual fish, with skin and fins still attached, and I had to fillet it myself. Sole was easy to cook, and I wanted something tried and true. I didn't know this couple well, and I didn't want to try out a new recipe on them.

Dinner was delicious and my recollection is that we sat at the table for a long time and the conversation went late into the evening. It was the only time I cooked for them—they arrived with a list of places they wanted to see before heading north to Porto, and their days were full of sightseeing. Sometimes a day or two went by when we barely saw each other. They'd leave before we got up and come back after we'd gone to bed.

One morning, I was preparing my own breakfast, and they were getting ready to leave the house. Nancy complained of sore feet.

"It's strange," she said. "I'm used to walking a lot. Maybe it's the cobblestones? I should have brought my other walking shoes."

I could relate. I'd been wearing flip-flops since the sun started shining consistently in March, and I hadn't put on closed-toe shoes even for the long days of traipsing through Lisbon's hilly, cobblestone streets. I had sore feet too.

"Soak them in Epsom salts," I suggested, but she never found the time.

Their departure day sneaked up quickly, and I was on to cleaning and doing laundry for Judy and Louise, the next visitors in the queue. They arrived in the afternoon, after the bird-poop-on-the-bedsheet drama, so I was too tired to cook anything elaborate for dinner. We went out for dinner at one of the restaurants on the beach.

Judy had been my sister Maria's friend. They had worked for the same airline and they used to travel together frequently. I knew Judy well, but mostly by association, and after Maria's death, I made a commitment to stay in touch. She must have as well because we have maintained our connection over the years. Louise also worked for the same airline and also knew Maria, but she and I had only met once before, briefly.

Over dinner, Louise kept looking at me across the table and finally said, "You look so much like Maria, it's uncanny."

It took only seconds for the tears to trickle from my eyes. I loved that I looked like Maria, and I appreciated this opportunity to talk about her.

"Aw, thank you, Louise. Thank you for saying that."

"Oh, I don't want to make you sad," she said, noticing my tears.

"It's fine. Of course I'm sad. I wish so much that she could be here with us. But failing that, talking about Maria makes me feel good. I like to remember her. I like others to remember her too, so thank you."

An awkward silence followed. It surprises me how uncomfortable it can be to talk openly about grief. In the few weeks after Maria's death, I received a lot of support from her friends and from mine. I was invited to dinners and walks, and everyone seemed to understand my need to talk about Maria. It's in the months and years that follow that grief becomes a more lonely experience, or at least it has for me. Eventually, people stop mentioning the dead person's name. Life happens and there is much to talk about, or maybe people are afraid of making me sad, as if I'll only think about her if they say her name. Truth is, I am sad that I've lost my sister and, whether we talk about her or not, I think of her many times every single day. And so, through the years, not hearing her voice, not even hearing her name, is what makes me even sadder.

I looked over at Georgia who was now also teary. We smiled at each other.

"Well, we all know that if Maria were here, we'd probably be laughing about something," I said.

So much saudade.

We sniffled, and then Eric raised a glass and we toasted to Maria's memory. She was the reason we all knew each other and the reason we were sitting together around this table.

• • •

One day, I bought pescadinha, a variety of hake. When I prepared it for frying, I deemed it the slimiest fish I had ever handled. It required me to concentrate on the cooked version of the fish, which I have loved since I was a child, and not on the slippery, slimy skin. I fried each fish individually and carefully, and while it was still in the pan, I tucked the tail in its mouth, just as the fishmonger had instructed me. Dinner was delicious that evening, and the hake tasted just as I remembered from my childhood. Georgia loved it, and Eric said it was so good, we'd have to have it again, perhaps with our next guests. I was happy and relieved—it made my perseverance with the slimy skin worthwhile. We took pictures because it was such an odd-looking fish and sent them to Matt in Vancouver. He wrote back to say that it looked like we were eating baby dragons.

I was raised to eat all kinds of food. I don't remember being made to stay at the table until I'd finished my meals, but I also don't remember turning anything down. For years, my favourite dish was fried liver, the way my mother made it. I also liked chicken livers, and rice casserole with gizzards. When my mother roasted a whole chicken, the heart was a special treat for me. And while I can still hear my mother's refrain that I was too thin and didn't eat enough, I remember enjoying my food, and that has turned into a lifetime love of cooking and eating.

Cooking for my friends in Vancouver is, however, not always an easy task. Several of my friends are vegetarians and some are vegan, others have a myriad of sensitivities and preferences, which makes it impossible to have them all over for dinner at the same time. I have risen to the challenge on several occasions, but the effort required is significant, and most of the time it's easier to go out or arrange a potluck. Some friends have come for dinner but brought their own meal.

I remember my father once giving a friend of mine a hard time because she wouldn't eat a muffin I had just taken out of the oven while she was over for a visit. My father, at eighty-six, with his broken English, sounded exasperated when he looked at her and said, "Why?" I interjected and explained to him in Portuguese that my friend did not eat eggs. My father could not understand. If you weren't allergic, you ate it, that's all there was to it.

With an upbringing like that, it's no wonder I ate everything my mother cooked, even the things I didn't particularly like—I remember eating lung stew, and tripe and beans, not my favourites at age nine, twelve, or fifteen. Later, as an older teen, I did experiment with being vegetarian for a year, followed by a few months of gluten-free and dairy-free eating. That was hard. I bought my own groceries and cooked my own food. My parents thought I'd lost my mind. But they eased up on me and hoped I'd grow out of these "phases."

It would be hard to be a committed vegetarian if you were visiting Portugal. You would need to eat a lot of grilled cheese sandwiches, I think. And what would you do if you were also gluten- or dairy-free? I imagine it's possible, and new restaurants are popping up all the time, but it wouldn't be easy. Meat or fish take centre stage in the Portuguese diet. And then there's the bread. There's always bread.

On our previous visits to Portugal, we had already noticed that vegetables were largely absent from most restaurant menus. A side salad accompanied most dishes, but it was simple and minuscule. This time, we knew enough to expect a protein-rich diet, so we planned to buy our vegetables at the market and cook them ourselves. A friend of mine in São Miguel once said to me, "Of course we eat vegetables. We know we have to, so we purée them and make soup." I started making soups for dinner too, but we would also have salad with it. And bread, of course. I thought of this as a happy marriage between my Portuguese and Canadian cooking habits.

One day at the market, I saw that my favourite vendor was selling baby spinach. Mounds of it. She must have sensed my elation because she asked me why I was so happy.

"Look at this spinach, it's so beautiful!" I said.

"Yes. Are you taking some today?"

I asked her to fill a bag.

"That's a lot of spinach. What are you going to do with it?"

I explained that I would be making spinach salad and then proceeded to describe it, and give her a verbal recipe of my own, finally. Usually, it was the vendors telling me what and how to cook. I'd become a bit concerned that they might think I was hopeless in the kitchen and didn't know how to cook at all.

After my elaborate description of my spinach salad, she asked me if I was going to cook it or eat it raw.

"Eat it raw, claro," I said. "It's a salad."

She wrinkled her nose in disapproval and then started laughing. She laughed hard. Then she went and told the vendor beside her. They both laughed. They shook their heads and gestured with their hands— no, no, that's not good.

"You don't like my idea?" I asked. "What would you do with it then?"

"Look at these beautiful, young shoots," one of them said. "They would make a lovely, creamy soup."

"Ah, okay. Maybe I'll do that tomorrow. But I'm looking forward to my salad today."

"Well, at least take some nice fresh bread to have with your salad," she called after me when I wandered over to the next stall to buy potatoes.

While I like to think that I eat almost everything, I still could not bring myself to try the enguias. I remember eating moray eel as a child when my mother made it and I loved it, but these small eels squirming around in buckets still made my stomach lurch.

"No, not yet. Maybe never, you know," I said to the fishmonger once again. She had been looking at me and smiling hopefully as I came up to her stall.

"Ah, you're so Canadian," she said. "Wait until you've been here a little longer, you'll forget how to be squeamish. The stew is delicious. Really."

On another trip to the market, I was with my friend Jennifer from Vancouver. I steered us away from the bucket of eels but made sure she had a good look at the large variety of fish available. It had become a source of pride for me. I could now name many different types of fish. Pick one out and I could probably figure out how best to cook it. I kept asking Jennifer what she'd like for dinner, but she would just shrug her shoulders and say, "Whatever you decide."

Jennifer's visit was split into two—first she came on her own for a few days so we could catch up on each other's lives and she could adjust to the time difference. We took long walks on different beaches and in parks and sat in coffee shops in Costa. She was keeping Lisbon for later, when she would return with her partner Mack, after their trip together to Spain.

When she and Mack came back for part two of her visit, we had our big dinner together, all of us around the table. At some point, Mack mentioned that Spain had been hard for Jennifer because she was vegetarian.

"Vegetarian?" I screeched. "Since when? And why didn't I know that?"

"Well, I'm not really. I just prefer to eat vegetables, if I have a choice."

"Why didn't you tell me? And here I was showing you all the fish at the market..."

"Yeah, I found that a little difficult," she said.

"I had no idea. I'm sorry."

"For me, it's about my love of animals," she said.

"I get that," was all I could say.

An awkward silence followed, and I was relieved that we had skipped the eels on our market trip.

I knew I had disappointed the fishmonger when I went to say goodbye to her before our return to Canada.

"You never tried the eel stew," she said.

"No. No, I didn't," I said. "Next time!"

I walked away and wondered what my father would have thought about that.

. . . .

Matt's Arrival

WOULD HE REMEMBER to bring the bags of chocolate chips, our important mail, a recent newspaper, the magazines we'd all ordered? Would Maggie remember him? Would he like Costa? So many questions.

We were all excited to see Matt after these four months and happy to be getting our hands on the treasures from home he'd be bringing with him—if he had remembered to pack them, that is.

Matt's arrival in Costa came towards the end of our hosting season and marked our gathering together again as a family of four. We had all missed him. Saudade. I didn't spend much time thinking about what it might be like for him. He had spent his first year away from home, living in a flat with five roommates, entrenched in university life, and now that had all come to an end and he was flying halfway around the world to come live with his parents again, in a place he didn't know, in a country where he couldn't speak the language.

Our experience at the airport was what it usually was—long. We could see on the monitors that the plane had arrived, but passengers had yet to come through the doors. I imagined how long the lineup was at the customs and immigration counter and I worried about Matt. Would he be given a hard time? Would he have all his papers in order? This was his first time on an international flight on his own—and yes, he was nineteen, an adult, and able to handle it—but this was also my first time experiencing my son travelling this far, alone. Surely it was harder on me than it was on him.

I had last heard from him when he changed planes in Frankfurt. I knew he was safe, and would be fine, but I still felt unsettled. I looked over at Eric to see if he might be feeling the same, but no, he was leaning against a post, looking like he was about to doze off. He looked more relaxed than I felt.

I remember my mother being overprotective and overanxious, and I must have inherited that gene. And yet she survived my youth and my travels, all in the days before cell phones. I don't know how she did it.

I have, on occasion, overheard both Matt and Georgia admit to their friends that I am overprotective and then add, "She's Portuguese," as if that alone would make a plausible explanation. They have bought into the stereotype of the Portuguese mother as one who worries excessively about the well-being of her children. I know my own mother was always commenting on the fact that I did not eat enough, ever, did not wear enough warm clothes in winter, did not call or visit her enough, but aren't all mothers like that? I don't think it's because I'm Portuguese, though being from an immigrant family probably has something to do with it. Absence and worry are embedded in my bones. I react by hanging on to my family. I just have to remember to release the grip before they feel the need to break free.

I don't like to consider myself overprotective, though I do acknowledge that I have an almost insatiable need to be reassured that my children are safe. It's not my fault. I blame my mother. Or my children. They are invariably ready to take the next step towards independence before I'm ready to grant it. They were ready to walk to school by themselves before I was ready to let them go, ready to take a city bus, drive the car, go hiking, climb a rock face, snowboard a black diamond run—all the milestones. I'm forever trying to catch up.

There was a big crowd waiting in the arrivals lounge—families waiting for their family members, tour guides waiting for their groups, business people in suits waiting for colleagues. I got restless and went to the bookstore to browse, then to the coffee counter for an espresso and a pastry. I kept my eye on the door and the ramp. Finally, out came Matt, rolling a cart with his huge suitcase, backpack, and big coat. He didn't look thrilled. The first thing he said to me was, "I haven't slept at all since I left Vancouver."

I could relate. Like Matt, I never sleep on planes, and it takes me a long time to adjust to a new time zone. We took turns giving him hugs and I noticed that I had to reach up on my tiptoes to put my arms around him. How much had he grown in the last few months? As if one hug at a time were not enough, the three of us closed in around him for a group hug. Matt smiled but I could see the exhaustion on his face. His eyes looked drawn.

"Where's Maggie? Did she come too?" he asked, as we walked out to the car.

"No, we left her at home. Good thing too, we've been waiting for you for a long time."

"Yeah, the lineup was long. And it took forever to get my bag. I can't wait to get home," he said.

I noted, but just to myself, that he had referred to our place, a house he had never seen, as home. It made me realize that home for him must be where we are all together, and I smiled contentedly. Maybe I am a quintessential Portuguese mother after all.

He got to our house and said he liked it, that it was closer to the beach than he'd imagined. Once inside, Maggie jumped all over him so that he had to sit down on the couch to say a proper hello to her. And then he went to his room and flopped on the bed and fell asleep for a couple of hours.

• • •

I wasn't sure how to pick the right time to tell Matt that we would be travelling in a few days and spending his birthday (and mine, two days later) at someone else's home, with people he didn't know. Eric and Georgia were both apprehensive about our upcoming weekend in Aldeia, but they had at least had time to get used to the idea.

Zé and Helena had been talking to us for some time about their summer home near Serra da Estrela, the mountainous region in the interior, and how much they wanted to show us that part of the country. It was their idea of paradise and I felt honoured that they wanted to share it with us, but I never imagined that it would actually happen. Zé was always at the restaurant and weekends were his busiest time. I knew that the food service industry is hard on staff and owners alike, and time off is hard to come by. I chalked it up to good intentions only. But a couple of weeks before Matt's arrival, Zé told us that he'd managed to arrange for a weekend away in May. When he told me the date, I was crestfallen. The weekend in the mountains would coincide with both my birthday and Matt's. And while the destination would be magnificent and the company enjoyable, no one would be able to speak to anyone except through me. After weeks of hosting English-speaking guests, I wasn't eager to return to my role as simultaneous translator. It was exhausting when I did that for a single evening, never mind a whole day or weekend.

I couldn't say no, of course. That would have been ungrateful and rude. Eric and I really enjoyed spending time with Zé and his family, but I knew it would be hard on Matt and Georgia.

There was no good time to tell Matt. I waited until the next day, at lunch.

"You're going to make me spend my twentieth birthday with people I don't know and can't even talk to? I can't believe you'd do that."

"I know. I'm sorry. I didn't have a choice on the date, though. We can celebrate our birthdays afterwards when we come back. What do you think about that?"

"Thanks a lot" was all he said in response.

He was tired and jet-lagged. He moped around the house. I assumed his mood was related to our upcoming trip, but it didn't occur to me that he might also be missing his life back home.

On a walk through the centre of town, he looked unimpressed, and I was becoming exasperated. I felt bad for him but also for Georgia, who had been looking forward to seeing her brother. Soon, I felt bad for all of us. This family reunion wasn't working out very well so far. And then I did the unimaginable. I told him to "snap out of it." I caught myself just as I said it, but it was too late; the words hung in the air. He grumbled something back at me, but I don't even remember what he said. I was already wallowing in regret.

When we got home, I apologized. Georgia baked chocolate chip cookies. Matt slept. I leafed through my new literary magazines and Eric read the *Globe and Mail*. Matt had remembered all the goodies we'd requested from home. I opened *Prism International*'s Love issue and saw that my friend Karen had a story in it. I had asked Matt to pick up a copy for me at a bookstore and he told me later that he'd been embarrassed to buy it, that he hoped I appreciated his effort.

Matt had less than a week to adjust to life in Costa before we left on our weekend trip. Every day, I could see he was settling in more and more. He looked less tired and was more engaged with our family life and with Maggie. I could see it was taking some time to get used to living with his parents again, to an eight-hour time difference, and to a town that was completely unfamiliar to him.

"I'm taking Maggie for a walk. Would you like to come?" I asked Matt and Georgia one morning. Eric had gone to work at the university and would be away until late afternoon. I was relieved when they both said yes.

It's amazing how a walk on a beach can heal the soul. We walked with Maggie to the end of the road, climbed the stairs, and strolled along the seaside path until it ended. We continued along the hard-packed sand at the water's edge. It was a sunny day, and the water was shimmering. We squinted, even with our sunglasses on.

"Feels like summer," Matt said.

I felt a rush of joy—summer is Matt's favourite season.

Maggie jumped in and out of the surf, chased her ball, dug holes, and caught the frisbee we tossed high in the air. Farther down the beach, we decided to go swimming. We stripped down to our bathing suits and walked in after Maggie, very carefully. It was cold. We were doing well for braving the waves in May. At first, it felt as if the cold constricted my lungs, but it didn't take long to get used to the water temperature. Matt and Georgia were bobbing in the waves, both smiling broadly. We played with Maggie until the cold set in and we were shivering. We got out but somewhat reluctantly. It had been so much fun. Back on the beach, the sand felt warm on our feet, but we were relieved to wrap ourselves with the dry fluffy towels I'd thrown into my backpack. When I grabbed my bag, I noticed my fingertips had a bluish tinge. On the way back, Matt and Maggie chased each other in spurts, and Georgia and I followed. Matt seemed happy, finally, and our dog looked ecstatic to have him back with her.

We arrived home feeling salty and tired. Eric had returned early from work and had stopped at the bakery to pick up pastries. We sat down to hot tea and pastéis de nata. Matt ate at least three, and at one point said, "Yup, I could get used to this."

Then it was time to pack for our weekend in the mountains.

. . . .

A Weekend in Aldeia

WE ARRANGED TO MEET in the traffic circle near Cacilhas.

"In the traffic circle?" I asked, probably sounding exactly like I felt—confused and bewildered. I was on the phone with Zé, and even after all this time in Costa, I still felt added stress talking on the phone in Portuguese.

"Yes. Meet us there, and then you can follow us north and out of town. It'll be easier that way." Zé sounded very confident in this plan so I didn't question him, but inside I worried, and the tension showed on my face and in the way I spoke.

"How can you meet someone in a traffic circle?" I asked Eric after I'd hung up. I noticed that my voice was screeching.

"I don't know, but don't worry about it. I'm sure it'll become clear when we get there."

"A traffic circle! I'm so glad I'm not driving. Are you okay with this?" I asked.

"We'll figure it out. We can always keep going around in circles until we know what to do."

We laughed, but I was nervous. I had not yet willed myself to drive in Lisbon. I was comfortable driving a vehicle with a manual transmission, that wasn't the problem, but the traffic overwhelmed me. And drivers honked their horns a lot. Eric was able to ignore other drivers' reactions to his mistakes, but the thought of someone honking at me, or worse, yelling and shaking a fist, terrified me. I suppose if I had been alone or if Eric had been unwilling to drive, I'd have needed to muster the courage. But as it turned out, Eric didn't mind driving, and I didn't mind not driving. It worked—we were a team. But in this instance, I feared the worst. We wouldn't be able to meet our landlord and his family; we wouldn't know how to get to their summer house in the mountains; we'd get lost and never find them; we'd be stranded in a strange place, and the entire weekend would be a bust.

"We have their cell number. Please don't worry." Eric tried to reassure me.

Already, this trip was a hard sell for Matt and Georgia. And it was Matt's twentieth birthday. I don't know what he would have chosen to do to celebrate his special day. I didn't ask, and he never said. This was what we were doing.

"Promise me that you won't tell them it's my birthday," Matt asked me when he had agreed to come.

"Of course," I said.

I knew that people gushing over him with well wishes would be stressful and embarrassing for him.

"I can't even spend the day with Maggie," he said.

I felt bad on so many levels. In addition to the birthday, we'd be leaving Maggie with a stranger. I'd asked our friend Pedro for a recommendation for a dog-sitter, and he had suggested someone he knew well. Maggie would be fine, but we were reluctant to leave her. It's only for three days, I kept telling myself.

On the morning of the day we left, we woke Matt up with a rendition of "Happy Birthday" and gave him his gifts. We finished packing and then got in the car and started our adventure. Nothing else was said about his birthday for the rest of the day. It was what Matt wanted, but I felt torn. I was wedged between two realities—my wish as a mother and my duty as a grateful guest. I knew it would be rude not to accept the invitation from Zé. Having accepted it, I also knew that my (and our) role was to show our gratitude and genuinely enjoy all the kindness that would be bestowed on us. But I also knew my family and their need for quiet time alone, even on a weekend trip where the hosts would outnumber us. The attention would be all on us—it's just the way it is with Portuguese hospitality. And while we were all grateful, this would make the introverts in my family uncomfortable. Eric has learned to adjust to an extroverted world, and he'd be fine, I knew that, but it would be different for Matt and Georgia. They were not used to having to step up and do the culturally appropriate thing while putting their own needs aside. They would need to engage and mingle, and I knew that would be tough for them. Perhaps that level of social finesse comes with maturity, or maybe it is strictly a cultural expectation, I don't know.

We got to the traffic circle at the time we had arranged, still not sure how our meeting would work. As it turned out, there was a stopping zone off to one side of the circle. I spotted Zé's white sedan. They must have been watching carefully for us because as we came around the circle, they signalled out of the waiting zone and merged into our lane of traffic, just ahead of our car. It was easy. We followed them through Lisbon and out of the city onto a quiet highway.

It was difficult to keep their car in our sight; they were travelling a lot faster than we could or wanted to. It was a hot day and since we didn't have air conditioning in our car, all the windows were open. We felt every bump in the road and the noise of the wind made for a tiring ride. We pulled over near Coimbra at a gas station, used the bathroom, and bought some water. When we were about to get back in our car, Zé told us that we'd be going with him in his car for the rest of the trip, and his family would be riding in our car. They were used to the heat, he said, and we weren't, so it made more sense for us to ride in the sedan, in air-conditioned comfort.

"I'm sorry, I can't agree to that. That's just too much," I said. I gave Eric a quick translation of the plan and he chimed in with me and said, "Oh no, no, no."

"It's all decided. That's what we're doing," Zé said.

His brother-in-law, Armando, got into the driver's seat of our car, stretched his arm out the window and said, "Please. I need your key."

Armando's wife, Odete, sat in front with him. Helena and her daughter, Rita, sat in the back. Off they went in the car and there we were with no choice but to ride in cool comfort.

"Please don't worry about it. It's what we want to do for you," Zé said. And then he added, "Your son likes history, right?"

I nodded.

"Well, our next stop will be Conimbriga, the Roman ruins. I think you'll all like it but it's a special stop for him. The others will go ahead to open up the house and get dinner ready."

I knew then that it was time to stop contesting their plans. Everything would go more smoothly if we just accepted that this weekend would be an expression of their hospitality. Our job was to relax and enjoy it.

He was right about Conimbriga—we all loved it. The site comprised an ancient walled town (one wall ran about a kilometre and a half) in various levels of excavation. The dig had revealed a stadium and a church, ancient spas and aqueducts, gardens, and houses. It was the largest Roman settlement in Portugal and archaeologists estimate that, so far, only around ten per cent has been excavated.

We took pictures and followed along on the map and brochures to learn about this site we'd had no idea existed. While it may be in guidebooks, it would not have caught our attention and we would have missed it completely had it not been for Zé. I was eager for Matt to enjoy the trip and kept asking him if he was impressed.

"Yes, Mum," he'd say. I sensed from the number of pictures he was taking that he really was enjoying this wonder. The rest of us were intrigued with this find too, and grateful to be walking among these ruins and taking a break from sitting in the car. I was especially taken with the tile work and allowed myself to become mesmerized by the patterns.

The remainder of our trip to the small village where our hosts had their house was a confusing myriad of secondary highways and rural roads, some looking more like tracks in fields than actual roads. Zé's offer to drive made sense to me now—the route was so convoluted we would never have found our way, even with the help of a GPS.

We arrived at the house at sunset.

"You can settle in. We'll have dinner later, and tomorrow we can start exploring, how does that sound?" Zé beamed. I could tell he was excited to show us this part of the country, their family's idea of paradise.

The house was a large, whitewashed, detached building with a Tudor-like front. Inside, it had the now-familiar high ceilings and large rooms filled with dark wood furniture. We settled into our rooms. I washed my face and had a short rest before heading back downstairs to offer my help preparing dinner (none was required) while the others replenished their energy with an hour or so of solitude.

Later, as the women continued to work on dinner, the men took us to the basement of the house to show us around the family "museum." We descended a stone stairwell and stepped into what can only be described as a cave. There were stone walls and low ceilings and rooms filled with old tools and farm implements, all displayed as if in an actual museum. The family had also kept (or collected from others) wine-making equipment and an impressive array of old photographs. Each item had a story, which Zé and Armando took turns recounting. It was an impressive collection, and it became clear to us that the family had a long history in this area.

Dinner was a remarkable spread: a creamy salt codfish casserole—bacalhau com natas—which we all devoured, not aware that it was only the first course. There was salad and rice pilaf, beef kebabs that I didn't have room for, but which made Matt, our family's biggest meat eater, smile broadly, and a strawberry tart for dessert. After accepting a second helping of dessert, Matt leaned over to me and whispered that this was the best birthday meal he'd ever had.

The entire weekend was a sightseeing extravaganza topped with exquisite food and delicious wine. Imagine your own private tour, led by a local guide with vast knowledge of the area's history, geography, architecture, and natural environment. Looking back now, I wonder how we had time to see and do so much in just a weekend.

We put on a lot of miles on the first touring day. We covered much of the area's hills and valleys, towns and hamlets, parks and natural areas. We walked in the patchy snow on the ski slopes of Serra da Estrela, stopped in cheese shops and coffee bars, then visited a trout farm in Manteigas, where we also stopped at a small family-run restaurant inside someone's house. Before committing to ordering lunch, Zé asked the server if there was chanfana.

"Of course," he replied.

"What is that? I've never heard of it," I said, as we took our seats at a large table.

"It's goat."

"Is it a specialty of the area?" I wanted to know.

"Oh yes. And it's not just goat, but slow-cooked goat. It is very special."

We were presented with the usual bread, fresh from the oven, with butter, accompanied by local olives and cold cuts and sausage. Then the servers brought several bowls of salad and steamed vegetables and finally, the chanfana. The thick, soupy stew contained chunks of meat that dissolved easily in the mouth and perfectly cooked potatoes. Oh, and of course, there was red wine.

After lunch, I was ready for a nap, but none of us even dozed as we drove through the scenic Vale do Zêzere. No one wanted to miss a thing. We stopped at hilltop castles to stretch our legs and explore the ruins, but when we arrived at the cliff's edge viewpoint in Corcorinho, I felt dizzy from the harrowing drive.

"That was a white-knuckle drive for me," I whispered to Georgia.

"I was really glad to be in the back seat!" she admitted.

It was hard to imagine that I would ever eat again after that lunch but by the time we arrived back at the house, preparations were underway for a barbecue dinner of ribs and sausages. Helena and Odete were putting together the marinade, a crispy green salad, and another strawberry dessert. Matt and Georgia were delighted and hungry because apparently the idea of slow-cooked goat had not been a big selling point for either of them.

Sunday was a slower day. We started later and toured at a more relaxed pace. The isolated village of Piodão, a collection of houses perched precariously on a mountainside in the Serra do Açor, was a highlight for all of us. The unique homes are made entirely of slate. Their blue doors, window frames, and shutters make them exceptionally picturesque. Set against the lush green of the forest, they are a photographer's dream. As if knowing that their homes are a magnet for photographers, the nearly two hundred year-round residents arrange hanging baskets and pots of cascading flowers on their decks and doorways, adding to the charm. I could have stayed there all day. We wandered the steep, twisting streets and navigated uneven and narrow stone steps, cameras at the ready.

We headed back to the house to explore the local area. This tiny settlement, which the family refers to simply as Aldeia, lies at the bottom of a valley lined with terraces and rough stone walls. Almost every building had vines and trailing flowers in vibrant shades of pink, lilac, red, and deep purple. Nearby, on the Nabão River, residents have blocked off a small tributary, forming a praia fluvial, a swimming beach. In summer, it is a major attraction for residents of the town and the surrounding area. Odete, who admitted to preferring beach to forest, said that it is this little swimming area that keeps her coming back year after year. "It's paradise," she said. It was easy for me to imagine soaking here in the summer when the pool area is in full operation and the banks of the river are lined with cafés and fruit stands.

We stopped at the family's orchard, where the kiwi plants were described as Armando's pride. It made sense now why there was such a big basket of kiwis at the house in Costa when we first arrived. It had been another detail to welcome us to Portugal. We sat on a patio and had cold drinks and fruit and marvelled at the variety of trees. Then we headed back to the house for a rest. Dinner would be on the early side as we still had the drive back to Lisbon in the evening.

Helena took me aside and asked me if there was anything the "children" wouldn't eat.

"No, of course not. They eat everything," I responded.

This was only partly true. Matt was a voracious eater and enjoyed everything, especially if it was protein-based. Georgia, on the other hand, was much more selective. I knew she probably wouldn't like what was served, but I hoped she would eat at least a little bit. I knew she wouldn't starve, and when we got back home to our place, she'd probably have a big bowl of plain pasta.

We sat around the large outdoor table for our last big meal. The patio was filled with flowers growing along the wall and spilling out onto the street. The side and back yards were terraced and shaded by an almost impenetrable roof of grape vines. The fragrance of the flowers mixed with the garlic from the kitchen. I breathed in deeply and prepared myself for the delicious food and for another round of simultaneous translation.

Someone would say something in Portuguese, and I would translate into English, then Eric would respond or say something in English, and I would translate into Portuguese. Then a few moments of silence before another exchange began. Once in a while someone would notice that Matt or Georgia hadn't said anything for some time, and they would direct a question specifically at one or the other. They could understand the questions in Portuguese but would invariably respond with one-word answers, most commonly sim or não. I wished they would volunteer a sentence or two, but not even I could draw more out of them.

After soup and appetizers, Odete brought out a large platter of cuttlefish grilled in their ink. Visually, it was stunning—heaps of tender white tubes of fish surrounded by smashed potatoes in garlic and olive oil—but none of us knew how to even begin eating it. The tubes looked familiar, like squid, which we were more used to eating, but seeing the innards and the ink right there on the plate was new to us. Georgia tried to eat around the grainy innards, and Matt ate more carbs than I had ever seen him eat. Eric and I both loved the flavour but it was a different experience to deal with the dark ink. Dessert was a trifle, and for us coffee drinkers, there was strong espresso.

After our meal, the family got busy packing up the house. They wouldn't be back for another month or so, in the heat of full-on summer. It didn't take us long to pack our bags, then we sat on the patio and waited for our hosts. The drive back was less harried—it's always the way, isn't it?—when the stress of the unknown is replaced with the familiar.

We debriefed over pasta, at home, just the four of us. It had been a tiring weekend but all of us, even Matt, had enjoyed ourselves. And Eric and I marvelled yet again at the hospitality and generosity of our hosts.

. . . .

Haircut

IT HAD BEEN TWO YEARS since Matt's previous visit to Portugal and he remembered Lisbon well, but we had discovered so much this time and we were eager to show him our favourite spots. We decided to go into the city together for a day of sightseeing. We parked our car in Cacilhas and took the ferry across the river.

I never tire of this trip; it is so beautiful. As you come to the middle of the river, Lisbon's whitewashed buildings with their red-tiled roofs look to be rising from the water in the distance. My eyes are drawn to the spires of cathedrals, the domes of churches, and the jagged outline of the Castelo de São Jorge up on the hill to the right. During the day, the sunlight bounces off the buildings, giving the city an almost heavenly glow; at night, a million lights dot the hillsides.

As we neared the shore, the ferry's engine reversed to slow the boat, producing a long guttural groan so powerful that I felt the floor vibrate below my feet. There was a lurch, then the steel hull slide-tackled the dock, the impact buffered by the rubber tires hanging over the side of the pier. The *Campolide* passenger ferry had arrived at the terminal in Cais do Sodré.

We joined others at the exit and waited for the signal that it was safe to leave. The creaky joints of the dock squeaked and squealed, and the water of the river lapped below. The rubber edge of the passenger ramp had barely touched the dock when the thundering began. Hundreds of passengers spilled out of the vessel's two doors. Some hurried past us, elbows out; others sauntered and were in no rush. Still others negotiated the walkway slowly, with canes or crutches. A cyclist wheeled her fancy bike.

Stomp, stomp—the footsteps sounded rhythmic and heavy on the metal grate. Voices and laughter melded into a constant hum. I could hear people speaking Portuguese, English, French, and German, maybe Dutch.

We spent the morning pounding the cobblestones—we walked up the hill to Chiado, the plaza named after the poet whose statue dominates the small square. We watched the buskers and took a photo with the bronze statue of Fernando Pessoa yet again (for Matt's benefit).

Lisbon is a city of literature. While Pessoa is perhaps the best-known Portuguese writer and poet of the twentieth century, writing in various genres under dozens of heteronyms, the surrounding area celebrates other literary icons as well. In the square across the street, there is a tall monument to Luís Vaz de Camões, the sixteenth-century poet who penned the epic poem *The Lusiads* and is considered Portugal's Shakespeare. A block or two south on the Rua do Alecrim, there is a statue dedicated to *The Maias*, the novel written by Eça de Queiroz that is set largely in Chiado. Elsewhere in the city, there's a sculpture of beloved poet Sophia de Mello Breyner Andresen in the terrace of the Miradouro da Graça, and near Alfama, the Casa dos Bicos celebrates Nobel laureate José Saramago. There are numerous laneways and streets named after writers as well. We walked down one of those, Rua Garrett (for poet, writer, playright, and journalist João Baptista da Silva Leitão de Almeida Garrett), to the famous Livraria Bertrand for a quick browse. Matt took a picture of the framed

Guinness World Records certificate posted at the door. We headed down the cobblestone hill to Rossio to the two baroque mermaid fountains that flank the monument to Dom Pedro IV, Portugal's king, who became Brazil's first emperor shortly after he ascended the throne. The bronze statue sits atop a ten-metre stone pillar in Lisbon's famous central square. More photos.

We meandered along a few streets, and I realized we were largely retracing the steps Georgia and I had taken on our expedition into Lisbon on that rainy day, months back. We made sure to stop at some of the same cafés and shops so Matt could try our favourite foods. We walked down Rua Augusta, the pedestrian-only street, and Matt took numerous photos of the imposing archway at the end of the street that frames another monument to yet another king, and looks like the Arc de Triomphe in Paris. Later during his visit, Matt would take the elevator to the top of the archway and take photos of the street from above.

We stopped occasionally for coffee or juice, and sometimes, a pastel de nata. Matt needed to snack frequently. He sampled savoury foods like bolinhos de bacalhau and rissois de camarão and combined them with pastries and sweet treats. He seemed to inhale it all—he ate fast and with enthusiasm. It reminded me what it's like to live with a young man with a healthy appetite. I had missed him.

We wandered for several hours, first along the river then up to Alfama, ducking into churches and gardens and feasting our eyes from various viewpoints near the Castelo de São Jorge.

We stopped for a late lunch at one of those places we deemed a perfect "hole in the wall." From the street, I noticed a few tables set with white tablecloths, sparkling glasses, and small, flowery centrepieces. Once I opened the door to step inside, the aroma of peppery herbs mixed with sweet onion and a hint of garlic rushed out to greet us.

Eric, Georgia, and I opted for a light meal, just caldo verde accompanied by bread, cheese, and olives. Matt had the special of the day—bacalhau à Brás, the creamy codfish casserole with egg, olives, and crispy fried potatoes. It was a warm enough day to warrant a nice cold beer; Georgia was the only one who opted for água com gás, fresca, meaning carbonated water, cold, from the fridge. This often got us strange looks. Once, I asked a waiter why, and he said it was because cold water with your meal slows your digestion. Here, as in other places, I noted that an eight-ounce glass of beer cost less than a small bottle of mineral water. Apparently, cold beer does not slow one's digestion!

Over coffee, I broke our satisfied post-meal silence with "Well, what do you think I should do with my hair?" And then: "Should I get it cut short or leave it on the long side or what?"

After lunch, I would be going for a haircut. That was the primary reason for my trip into Lisbon that day, but then we had all decided to combine it with sightseeing and turn it into a family outing.

My family was probably tired of questions about my hair, and they knew that there was no right answer. There were a few grumbles from Matt and Georgia, something like, "Oh Mum, whatever you like," and then encouraging words from Eric that whatever I did would look nice because it always did. I interpreted this to mean that I was on my own; they were not going to suggest anything.

We headed to Avenida da Liberdade, in the business and fancy shopping district, where the salon was located. Eric, Matt, and Georgia left me at the door and walked up to Parque Eduardo VII at the top of the hill for more views of the city before they picked me up an hour or so later.

It had been more than six months since I had sat in a stylist's chair. Eric had found a barber in Costa and had already gone several times, but I kept putting off getting my hair cut. When I'm somewhere new, the task of finding a stylist is daunting. I had been very methodical about the process this time. I consulted Google and made a list of five or six salons that came up when I searched for "best hair salons in Lisbon." Then, I looked them up on a map to see where in the city they were. I wanted to go somewhere familiar, probably downtown, where I thought I was more likely to get a good technical cut, not too conservative, maybe even a little funky.

I narrowed the top five to two, based on location.

I called the first place and made an appointment. The receptionist was friendly and helpful, and my recollection is that we had a rather long conversation about who would be best to cut my hair. I remember her asking whether my hair was straight or curly, what length it was, how much did I want to cut, and would I be wanting anything else, like possibly a manicure or a pedicure. Just before I hung up, I remembered to ask the price. While I don't remember the exact amount, I remember thinking that this one haircut was going to cost me more than a year's worth of cuts back home. I couldn't do it. But instead of saying no thanks, I asked if they accepted Visa.

"Claro," she had said. "Of course."

This meant that I had to call back a few minutes later to cancel.

"I'm sorry," I said. "It's way more than I'm willing to pay for a haircut. I can't do it. I'm really sorry I wasted your time."

"No problem at all," she said, still with the same upbeat tone she had used in our previous conversation. "Thank you for letting us know."

I moved on to the second salon, located a few doors down. This time I asked about the price first. The receptionist gave me a few options, all reasonable, then offered me a cut with the "art director" for an extra ten euros.

I said, "Sure, that would be great."

She said, "I'll book you in with Pee Wee."

Pee Wee. I stopped myself from judging and felt reassured that someone with such a name would certainly give me a funky cut. How could they not?

The salon was in an older character building, on the second floor. As I went up the stairs, I realized that I was nervous. I relaxed as soon as I opened the door. It was as if I were walking into an oasis of calm. There was dark wood cabinetry and shelving, long silky curtains, leather furniture, and tasteful arrangements of fresh flowers on end tables.

I waited for a few minutes, not long, and could hear the receptionist speaking perfect English on the telephone with various callers. Then Pee Wee came to the waiting room and called my name. I don't know what I was expecting from someone with such a name, but I was almost disappointed that he looked like a regular guy. He was younger than I was, I figured, but not by much. The only thing I noticed about him was his heavy, square, black-rimmed glasses, which I thought fit his title of art director.

He asked me what I wanted done to my hair, and I responded with a rough translation of "wash-and-wear hair, a good cut that I don't have to fuss with, but not too boring." We discussed options and then he took me to the sink for a shampoo.

I wondered about Pee Wee's accent. He spoke Portuguese fluently, but the accent was not local. I wanted to ask where he was from but didn't feel I could. I loathe this question myself, and always wonder what prompts people to want to know such things. I was having this inner struggle when, back in the stylist's chair at the mirror, I mentioned that I was from Canada.

"Oh, I wouldn't have guessed that, not with your name. It's so Portuguese." He said this in English, with a heavy British accent.

He explained that he was from London and had been living in Portugal for nearly twenty-five years, since he had married his Portuguese girlfriend. They had three children and had decided to make Portugal their home. We chatted for the next hour as if we had known each other for years. We both eased into the comfort of a conversation in English.

Pee Wee cut and scrunched my hair, ran his fingers through it, and measured both sides against my chin. He explained that he "took it up a bit" and "took some weight off" to increase the movement and give me a lighter look.

"I think you'll find it very versatile. And it'll grow out well," he said.

When I stepped outside, back onto the Avenida, I squinted. It was late afternoon, but the sun was still bright. It took me a moment before I saw my family sitting on a garden bench a few metres away, on the boulevard. I walked over to them and gave them a big smile. The kids said something to the effect that my hair didn't look much different, just shorter, and Eric said it looked very nice. They raved about the view from the top of the hill and said we'd have to set aside a day to go back to the park up there, that I shouldn't miss it.

We took the subway for a couple of stops to Cais do Sodré then boarded the ferry and headed back across the river. I caught my reflection in the window of the boat and saw the outline of my new hairstyle. I shook my head back and forth a bit to feel the lightness. I smiled.

It was just after six in the evening, and we were caught in the rush-hour commute. The ferry was packed. We landed on the south side, and once again, passengers spilled out onto the walkway. Behind us, there was a metal-on-metal sound like a drawn-out, shrill cry. I turned and watched the crew manoeuvre the ropes and ramps, getting ready for the next sailing.

Outside the station gate, hawkers' voices rose in the open space.

"Dois kilos, um euro; dois kilos, um euro." The temporary market stalls were set up for rush hour and sellers were doing a brisk business. I surveyed the cherries. Two kilos for a euro seemed awfully cheap.

"São nacionais!" another seller bellowed. There were still some local strawberries available.

"Figos do Algarve." The plump figs from the south of the country looked like they would be juicy. I wanted some of those.

I stood still, trying to discern which prices went with which produce. There were at least a dozen sellers—women, men, young boys, and some girls—all at their makeshift stalls, selling, selling. Fruit. Vegetables. Bread. I was hungry, and the food looked irresistible. I looked for Eric and the kids in the crowd, but it was impossible to have any conversation. I tried to ask with my eyes, raising my eyebrows, if they wanted anything, but I couldn't discern their responses in the chaos. I saw Georgia shrug her shoulders hopefully, but Matt and Eric were crossing the street to the square, away from the bustle.

I took out a five-euro bill and moved from stall to stall, looking, choosing, buying. In the end, I left with two kilos of cherries, a loaf of bread, and a bag of figs. And I had change left over.

We were eager to get home because Maggie had been alone for a long time. I was also looking forward to sitting down with everyone and debriefing our big day.

As soon as Eric opened the door, Maggie ran out to greet us, her tail wagging wildly. I was still in the kitchen putting down my bags of fruit when I saw that everyone else had scurried into their respective bedrooms and shut their doors behind them. I was left standing there, wondering what had just happened. And then I knew. They needed alone time to replenish their energy. I, on the other hand, was looking forward to more contact when we got home—more meaningful contact—a summary of the day and a review of the highlights. I knew I'd have to wait.

I sat in the living room and looked around. How long would they need, I wondered. Should I take Maggie for a walk? Should I read my book? I made myself a cup of tea and called my sister in Vancouver. It would be mid-morning for her, and I'd be disturbing her workday, but I did it anyway. We had a long chat. Just as I was saying goodbye to her, Eric emerged from the bedroom.

"Sorry, I just needed to recharge," he said.

"I figured. No problem."

We started preparing dinner. Sometime later, Matt came to ask what we were cooking. Georgia joined us just as we sat at the table for dinner. Given enough time, everyone eventually emerged, but I imagined that the next day would be a quiet one, with everyone working on their own projects. I would read and walk and go to the market. I would get my necessary dose of talking there.

We all went for an extra-long walk on the beach that evening with Maggie. We felt bad that she'd been cooped up for so much of the day. We walked at the edge of the water where the sand was cold, and it soothed our feet after all the walking we had done that day.

The next morning, I picked up the Portuguese newspaper to read while I was having a coffee by myself at the coffee bar on the beach. The cover story was about the Rolling Stones concert the night before, at the Rock in Rio Festival. One of the highlights of the show had been a number with Bruce Springsteen, who had surprised the band when he joined them on stage. Apparently, Springsteen's daughter was living in Lisbon and his visit to her coincided with the Stones concert.

The article went on to say that Springsteen had been spotted on Lisbon streets in the days leading up to the festival. He had been photographed along the Avenida after having gone for a haircut on the day of the show. I put a few clues together and figured he must have had his hair cut at the salon I had originally called to make an appointment—the expensive one. If the article was right on the timing, had I kept my original appointment, Bruce Springsteen and I could have had our hair cut at about the same time. Now that might have been worth the hefty price. I would remember this, years later, as a missed opportunity.

I folded the newspaper, gave my head a little shake, and smiled. I was still happy with my haircut.

. . . .

World Cup Friendly

WE WERE CARRIED ALONG in a sea of people making their way from the train station to the stadium. Eric had dropped us off at Cacilhas, and we'd caught the boat across the river and then the train to the suburb of Belém. The Portuguese national team was playing Greece in a "friendly" before the run-up to the World Cup, and both Matt and I were eager to cheer on our team even if this game didn't really count.

"I don't mind that it's only a friendly," Matt said. "You know I've always dreamed of watching the national team. I can't believe we're actually doing this."

His voice had a higher pitch, and his words vibrated in the space between us.

Matt hadn't always been a fan of Team Portugal. When he was five years old, we spent three months living on São Miguel on Matt's first trip to the country. As a quiet child who could not understand any Portuguese, he was easily overwhelmed by loud family gatherings, and frustrated with all the head-patting, cheek-pinching, and incessant kissing required every time we said hello or goodbye to people.

"I don't like your country," he told me on more than one occasion. "I'm not Portuguese and I never will be."

Even though he was only five, his words stung, and I could feel my chin tremble during his outbursts. Eric comforted me and assured me that his attitude would change as he matured and as we visited Portugal more often.

Soon after that summer, Matt discovered soccer. He started by watching games on television with my father, then asked to attend soccer camps, and eventually, he joined the neighbourhood league. He was hooked.

My father's favourite Lisbon team, Benfica, became Matt's favourite team, and both of them would cheer on the national team during the European Championship and World Cup tournaments like two buddies sitting at a sports bar. Not long after, Matt became an expert on all things related to Portuguese soccer, memorizing statistics and following his favourite players in league play. The next time we visited Portugal, he was nine years old. He spent his allowance that he had saved on an (imitation) soccer jersey of his then-favourite player, Luís Figo. He also tolerated the kiss-on-the-cheek greetings and learned a few words of Portuguese.

Tonight's game was an opportunity for Matt to see the national team in action. I was looking forward to the soccer too, but I was mostly thrilled to be sharing this moment with my son.

Buying the tickets online had been daunting. It was a complicated process and seemed so sketchy that I had my doubts whether we'd ever see the tickets. They were also expensive for us, so we opted for just the two of us to go.

As we walked to the stadium, Matt explained that Estádio Nacional dated back to the days of Salazar and was inaugurated in 1944. It is an austere stadium in the middle of a large park with few amenities nearby.

"This is where the Portuguese Cup is usually held," Matt said. "It's old, but I'm still really excited to see it."

The long walk from the train station in Belém with thousands of others helped to build the excitement. The road was lined with food trucks and souvenir shops selling T-shirts and hats and soccer para-phernalia. We scarfed down a bifana, a pork sandwich (Matt had two), and I bought a bottle of water.

"The seating capacity is thirty-nine thousand." Matt was still reeling off facts. "I wonder if it will be full."

The lineup to enter the stadium was long. Security guards were searching all bags and purses. When it came to my turn, my purse checked out, but I had to turn in the cap to my water bottle. I gave the security guard a quizzical look and he explained that this makes it impossible to throw a bottle in a fit of frustration. I gulped and wondered just what kind of event we had signed up for.

Once inside the stadium, police and security were everywhere. I finally understood that going to a soccer game in Europe is not like going to a soccer game in Canada. People are passionate here, and they are especially passionate about soccer. These guards would help keep the peace.

Luckily, this was a friendly, but it was also Portugal's opportunity to redeem itself after losing to Greece in the Euro 2004 Final, a game that had been played in Lisbon. Tonight's game was taking place ten years later, but the memory of that loss was still fresh.

We found our seats, and minutes later, we stood to sing the national anthem. I felt tears come to my eyes and I looked over at Matt, who was singing along. He's not yet fluent in Portuguese, but he has known every word of the national anthem since he was a toddler. I thought of my father, and how much he would have loved to have shared this experience with us.

Our seats were down low, near one end of the field, but we had a perfect view of all the players as they filed past us. When Matt's favou-rite player, Cristiano Ronaldo, waved to the crowd, we cheered so loudly that I feared I'd lose my voice.

"Wow, he's so tall," I said to Matt.

I thought back to my days growing up in São Miguel and how seriously my father took soccer. The radio broadcast of the weekly game on Sundays usually took place during our family mealtime. We were not allowed to talk so that my father could hear the commentator. I believe this was at the root of my father's favourite saying, "Quando se come não se fala," which translates roughly to "no talking during meals."

If his team was losing, he'd be particularly attentive; we weren't allowed to even whisper. Cheering for another team was not allowed. My sister Toni was an avid fan of Lisbon's other team, Sporting, perhaps just to be contrary or to spite our father, I don't know, but discussions about soccer could be very tense in our family.

If my father's team lost, he'd sulk and give us all the silent treatment for several days. It's no wonder that my mother hated soccer. She was relieved when we came to Canada and we couldn't get the Portuguese soccer broadcast on the radio. In those days, European soccer matches were not televised except for the odd game during international tournaments. My father developed a love for hockey, out of necessity more than anything else, and the Edmonton Oilers became his team. He still followed European soccer, though, and kept up to date by reading the Portuguese newspaper and corresponding with his friends in São Miguel.

In his later years, my father mellowed. After my mother died, he continued to live in our house and as we spent more time together, our relationship deepened. We talked about so many things—children and family, our culture, and of course, sports. I suppose it helped that I liked watching soccer and hockey and that we cheered for the same teams. I have never developed quite the same passion as my father, though. When my team loses, my disillusionment is short-lived.

Portugal and Greece played a defensive game this time and both Matt and I were disappointed with the scoreless draw, but we were still glad to be part of the crowd that evening. During half-time, the announcer had called out that there were 33,566 people in attendance—nearly a full house. That number, I joked, could not possibly include all the security guards. They were easily spotted with their fluorescent vests, and we had estimated there was one for every ten spectators, which was probably only a slight exaggeration. What was more perplexing was how the guards stood, facing the crowd, even as we cheered over what was happening on the field. It must have taken a lot for them not to turn their heads, not even for a split second. Surely the security guards were also soccer fans?

On our way home, the train station was packed but the queue was moving quickly. We followed the crowd and as we neared the front of the line, we noticed a commotion. It was hard to see what was happening but then we saw someone jump the gate and physically pry open the doors that swing open and shut at the turnstile. A young woman had managed to get her head stuck in the fare gate. Matt and I looked at each other in both horror and disbelief. How was this possible? Someone would have to be walking with their head far in front of their body! We still haven't figured out how it happened, but we were impressed by how quickly people jumped in to help. And the man who pried the gate open must have been running on adrenaline. Opening those gates would have taken a Herculean effort.

The woman's head was freed, and everyone cheered. She did not seem hurt and walked away looking more embarrassed than anything. We waited on the platform with thousands of others for nearly an hour before we managed to hop on a train. We rode to Cais do Sodré and then caught the ferry back to Cacilhas, where Eric picked us up by car.

The soccer game that night might have been an indication of what was to come in the World Cup tournament. Portugal lost 4–0 to Germany in Brazil and drew 2–2 with the US and failed to advance to the quarter-final round. It was a huge disappointment. However, two years later, many of the same players, including Ronaldo, would go on to lift the European Championship trophy in the 2016 Final, which was held in France. This earned Matt some bragging rights among his friends, and Portugal fans around the world beamed with pride—the win had been a huge upset over France, who had been favoured to take the championship.

It has been interesting watching Matt develop an interest in sports and figure out his allegiances. Perhaps out of loyalty to his grandfather, Benfica is still his team. And his connection to his Portuguese roots means he will always cheer for Portugal. Until perhaps, the day when Portugal plays Canada in the World Cup.

. . . .

Border Services 1

I WAS STILL ENJOYING MY NEW HAIRCUT, and I felt relieved that I would look presentable for our interview at the SEF. This is the Serviço de Estrangeiros e Fronteiras, the Immigration and Borders Service, in Setúbal, where we needed to go to have Eric's work visa extended.

It had all sounded so easy when Eric had contacted the consulate in Vancouver. He was informed that just before his visa expired in mid-June, he was to contact the SEF and request an extension. It seemed straightforward and we thought there would be no problem. It was only a simple matter of getting the date changed, we had been assured. But it wasn't proving to be that simple, and now here we were, preparing for an official interview with a border services agent.

There's something about meeting with customs and immigration officials that makes my stomach tighten. It reminds me of the times I have been taken aside and questioned, or had my bags searched at security checkpoints at airports. I often seem to be selected for random searches. I've resigned myself to this—it's more annoying than maddening, but still, I feel tense every time I arrive in a new country. It's as if my anxiety sets off inaudible alarm bells and it takes longer for me to get processed than others I travel with, even members of my own family.

This visit to SEF had nothing to do with me, but I was feeling enough stress for both of us. I had probably been clenching my jaw all night because I'd woken up with a headache and my teeth hurt. I skipped breakfast and opted for coffee only, to settle my nerves. If Eric was denied an extension, we would have to leave the country. Where would we go?

"Better bring your letter of invitation from the university here in Portugal, Eric, just in case," I called out. I was in the bedroom getting dressed, and Eric was in the kitchen preparing his breakfast. I was aiming for a professional look. I dressed in black pants and a jacket.

"I think you should dress nicely," I said, coming into the dining room. "Not a suit, necessarily, but no jeans, okay?"

"Fine, but why are you all dressed up? I'm the one being interviewed."

"Well, I imagine we'll be going in together and we have to make a good impression," I said.

The last time I had been to Setúbal was on a previous visit to Lisbon, two years before, with friends of my sister Toni. I was in the city to attend the Disquiet Literary Program, and I had a few days to myself before it started. My sister had contacted her friend Eduardo, and he and his partner had picked me up in Lisbon and taken me for a tour of their favourite spots down the coast, including the beach at Sesimbra. On the way, we had stopped in Setúbal for chocos fritos, fried cuttlefish, a delicacy of the region and Eduardo's favourite dish. Other than that, what I knew of the region was that it produced a nice red wine that we had been buying at the grocery store for the last few weeks. We had not been to Setúbal on this visit yet. We planned our day around the SEF appointment, and we were looking forward to having lunch at a seaside restaurant. I told Eric he had to try the fried cuttlefish.

The SEF office was on the main floor of a three- or four-storey pink building that had massive green doors and iron railings on the upstairs verandahs. Farther down the street, we could see outdoor cafés, shops, and a small plaza. Hanging baskets added colour to the balconies and flowers trailed from window boxes, which made the building, and the whole area, look quaint and welcoming.

When we walked in, we were greeted by a security guard who asked us the reason for our visit. I told him we were there for an amendment to my husband's work visa, and he directed us to the receptionist, who crossed Eric's name off the list, gave us a ticket with a number on it, and told us to sit and wait until the number was called. The waiting room was filled with rows of chairs, all facing a large monitor which indicated the numbers being served. The room was packed, and everyone was watching the screen with blank stares. It was hard to find an empty chair, but we craned our necks to scan the room and found two chairs together in the middle of one of the rows.

"Com licença, com licença," I said, as Eric and I slipped through the row, disturbing five or six people before we got to our chairs. We sat on the edge of our seats and waited, thinking we'd be there for only a few minutes, but our appointment time passed, and we were still waiting. I noticed that I was slouching. Eric was dozing off. It was hot in the room and most people looked like they'd been there for a long time. The woman beside me dabbed her forehead with a handkerchief and sighed. Others fanned themselves with sheets of paper.

I don't know exactly how much time passed but I'd finished two chapters in my book when our number showed up on the screen. We jumped up but it took us a few seconds to get past the people in our row and over to the aisle. We weren't fast enough because a woman came to the front of the room and called out Eric's name twice.

Eric raised his hand in a wave, but as we both made our way forward, the security guard stopped me.

"Where are you going? Who are you?"

"Oh, my name is Esmeralda. My husband has an appointment and I'm going in with him."

"No, you're not. You're not allowed," he said. "The appointments are only for the person being interviewed."

"But I'm his interpreter. He doesn't speak Portuguese," I explained.

"We don't need you. Our officers speak English."

"Oh, all right then. I'll just wait out here."

"Yes, you will."

By this time, Eric was already being ushered in by the woman who had called out his name. She was short and very thin, and she was dressed in office attire—a pencil skirt and a white shirt. Her hair was tied in a bun at the back of her head, giving her a severe look. Eric threw me a last glance before he disappeared around the corner. I smiled and mouthed, "Good luck."

By the time we left the building, lunchtime had come and gone. We went for coffee down the street instead of our seaside lunch.

"What do you mean she said no?" I asked. We both squinted in the sunshine.

"She needs more information. Except I'm sure I've provided most of it already."

He unfolded the piece of paper with the itemized list she had given him. He looked pale and tired. He threw his hands up and looked away.

"I've provided all of this but now they want more. They even want three months' worth of bank statements."

"What? What for?"

"Something about having enough money for medical emergencies. Or something like that. I don't know, she was hard to understand."

"Did you explain that you have provided all this information already? And that the University of British Columbia is still your employer and is still paying you? And that we have medical coverage?" My frustration increased with each question.

"No, I did not."

"Well, why not?"

"First of all, because I can't speak Portuguese. And second, because she could barely speak English. We could not understand each other."

"Argh, this is so maddening."

I glanced around the coffee shop and noticed that people were looking at us. We weren't arguing, not really, and I thought we had been whispering. But the tension was obvious. We were both sitting upright, backs straight and jaws clenched.

"I'll just gather the information she's asking for—again—and come back in two weeks. That's all. She gave me a letter that grants me interim permission to remain in the country and work until the date of my next appointment. We're fine. Let's not worry. Let's enjoy this coffee. Do you want a pastel?"

"No, I don't feel like having one, but you go ahead," I said. I slouched in the chair.

"I don't feel like it either," he said.

It was still warm in the late afternoon when we got back to Costa so we took Maggie for her walk. Matt and Georgia had been rummaging through the garden shed in the morning and had found two bicycles that they worked on during the day to get them into riding shape. They were now using them to tour around the area, and we weren't sure when they'd be back. We sat on the sand and watched Maggie dig holes. Occasionally we'd throw the ball and watch her run for it, hoping she'd take her time bringing it back. We were too tired to play.

A few surfers remained in the water, but it looked like the tide was going out so they wouldn't be there for much longer. The roar of the sea sounded more distant with each incoming wave. I sat there, knees huddled to chest, arms clasped around, mesmerized by the patterns left on the sand when the water receded. All those frothy bubbles left behind. Eric sat beside me, legs outstretched, arms straight behind him, supporting his weight. Maggie had given up digging and running and was flopped across his legs, breathing hard, sandy tongue hanging out.

"Guess we should think about dinner, huh?" I finally said, breaking a long silence.

We took the long way home through the town centre and stopped at the Churrasqueira Alentejana—a takeout barbecue chicken establishment. We ordered *Menu #4* as we had on several previous occasions—a whole chicken, a vegetable, and a drink—all for under ten euros.

Churrasqueiras are very popular in Portugal. These are delis where you can get ready-made dinners such as arroz de pato (a rice and duck casserole), lasagna, and the signature dish—piri-piri chicken, roasted on coals, Alentejo-style. In some churrasqueiras, you can eat-in but these are primarily takeout establishments. I remember the first time I had come here. The scrumptious aroma had drawn me in from the street. I'd heard the piri-piri chicken was a must-try but I hadn't yet ventured into one of these places. They were usually small, dark, and crowded at dinnertime. I had been too intimidated to go in and order because I didn't know exactly what to do, but on that day, I must have been feeling bold. I walked in and looked at the chalk board and was overwhelmed with all the choices, permutations, and combinations. I had no idea where to start. I watched a few people come in and order, then grab their bag of food, and leave.

During a lull, the man behind the counter looked at me and asked if I was going to order something or not.

"I haven't done this before. How does it work?" I asked.

"You order what you want, I put it together for you, then you pay and leave." He was almost smiling. It must have been unbearably hot behind the counter where he was, so close to the big oven like that.

"Okay, okay. I'll have a chicken please. What's the vegetable?"

"Potatoes," he said. "And you get a drink too—Coke, Pepsi, beer, whatever you like."

"Beer? Okay, beer." I ordered, then paid.

He took a chicken off the rack and wrapped it up, grabbed a large bag of potato chips, put it in a bag, and handed it to me.

"Where's the vegetable?" I asked.

"You've got it there. Potatoes," he said.

"You mean this bag of chips? Chips is the vegetable? Really?"

I found this quite humorous, but he was serious. "Chips are made from potatoes, and a potato is a vegetable."

"Got it. All right then." I was still not fully believing him.

"Grab the beer from the fridge on your way out," he said.

I looked in the glass-fronted fridge, opened the door, and took out a one-litre bottle of Super Bock, the local beer.

I ordered the same thing today, while Eric stayed outside with Maggie. Every time a bus went by, Maggie would jump and bark and bite at the leash. She sounded like a wild dog and people walking by gave her a wide berth. She was most likely just frightened by the noise—it was a busy corner—but people avoided her; I could see that from inside the deli.

I walked out with my bag of chicken and chips in one hand and the large bottle of beer in the other. Eric laughed. "I still can't get over that potato chips count as a vegetable."

"I know!" I said. "Should we stop at the Minipreço to buy some broccoli or something?"

"Nah. Let's just go home. We can have vegetables tomorrow."

"Now that makes me feel like a local." I laughed.

Eric put his arm around me and we walked to the square, then on to a side street to head towards home. Maggie wormed her way between us where she felt safe, protected from all the frightening, loud buses.

. . . .

Spring Market Days

TIME PASSED AS TIME DOES, and as it did, I felt more at home in Costa. By late spring, when the days were bright and the heat was rising from the pavement as if it were already summer, I began to sense that our time in Costa was drawing to a close. My days became tinged with wisps of sadness. I had been thinking that if we were to stay in Portugal long-term, for some reason, I could be quite content.

Since our arrival in January, there had been numerous times when I had wished I could be transported back to the comfort of my Vancouver home, especially when it was cold and wet and our laundry refused to dry—those days when the chill seeped into my bones, and three blankets and a pair of thick wool socks were not enough to warm me up. I had longed for central heating, for warmth, for having friends call or just drop by, but instead had to settle for watching a show on TV, in English. But then the sun came out and we started having our breakfast outside, and lunch too. We watched the surfers walk down our street, barefoot, their tousled hair swinging with each step they took, making their way to the beach from the hostel a few blocks away. There was a liveliness to the town that hadn't been there in the winter. I had survived the cold, and now I was easing into the day-to-day of spring with a sense of comfort, as if I belonged here.

I was glad for the warmth and the sun—and the peace and quiet. For at least six weeks, our house had been a flurry of activity, with friends arriving and departing, with housecleaning and laundry and meal planning and cooking and frequent trips to the market.

For me, the market in Costa was the jewel. I was proud to show it off to our guests. It was one thing I thought they would likely not see if they came to the Lisbon area as regular tourists. But I learned that some of our friends didn't like to be confronted by the reality of dead fish that still have heads, tails, and fins attached. I once caught a friend gesturing to her companion that she was about to throw up. When she realized I had seen her, she said, "How about if I head to the bakery over there and pick up dessert for tonight?" She never mentioned the fish at the market but claimed to have enjoyed the fish dinner I had served.

I loved not only cooking, but also looking at all the fish. I was thrilled with the progress I had made in my cooking lessons too. Now that the season was changing, the daily catch was also changing, and there would be more to learn. The arrival of sardine season was highly anticipated. Everyone talked about it. I could hear conversations in the market, at the beach, and in coffee shops. "It's almost sardine season" was a refrain I heard several times a day.

As if Matt and Georgia sensed our looming departure too, they opted to accompany me on my market shopping trips more frequently. Or maybe it was because there wasn't all that much else for them to do. It didn't matter—I was enjoying having my family all together, even if I sensed that Matt was eager to leave, to discover, to be without his parents. He was busy planning his first solo trip, and I was sensing the loss that comes when your children are ready to leave you for exciting adventures of their own. I was feeling a strange mix of satisfaction and nostalgia, of saudade for my boy, even before he left.

The three of us walked to the market one morning, looking for inspiration for something to make for dinner. We started with coffee (for me), chocolate milk (for Matt and Georgia), and a few tarts (for the three of us) at Nutritiva, the big coffee shop and bakery near the main square. We saw—and heard—a group of four men outside, on the street corner, having an animated discussion. They all looked roughly the same age and sported similar balding patterns. They were short, stocky men, and each one wore a short-sleeved dress shirt and jeans cinched to the waist with a belt. They were gesticulating wildly and pointing emphatically in different directions. One of them hit his forehead with the palm of his hand, then walked away for a few steps, then came back to the group. Their voices rose, then dropped, then rose again, their sentences punctuated with body language and mixed inflections. Around them, life carried on, and no one seemed interested in their conversation. Except us. I wondered if a physical fight would break out. On our way out of the coffee shop, we walked past them, and Georgia asked if I could tell what they were talking about.

"Yes," I said. "They are talking about the location of a particular restaurant. It sounds like they can't agree which street it's on."

Both Matt and Georgia stopped walking.

"You're kidding, right?" Matt said. "They are fighting about that?"

"They are not fighting, they are discussing," I corrected.

It's a mistake I remember my high school friends making when I brought them home after school. Eventually, they would confide in me that it sounded like my family was always fighting. Eric said the same thing after the first time he met my family. I'd invited him for dinner with my parents and my sister Maria. We weren't so many people around the table but at one point, even I noticed that there were several conversations going on at once. A quick glance at Eric who looked overwhelmed, and I knew exactly what he was thinking.

"No, we're not fighting," I assured him. "It just sounds like we are."

The men on the corner were obviously passionate about their opinions.

"Ah," I said to Matt and Georgia. "That little scene makes me feel like I belong here."

"I get that. I really do," Georgia said. "You move your arms exactly like that when you're trying to explain something."

"And you yell like that too," Matt added.

"They are not yelling. They are just raising their voices for emphasis," I said. "It's called inflection. Sheesh."

We walked into the market, and I steered us towards the ice room at the back where about a dozen fishmongers had set up their stands. I was looking for carapauzinhos. In the last few weeks, I had bought these several times and I hoped they were still in season. I remembered eating these fish when I was a child in the Azores, except that we called them chicharros. When I consulted my Portuguese-English fish dictionary, I learned that both are types of stickleback—essentially the same fish.

At first, I had been unsure about buying them because I couldn't remember how to clean them. I needed a refresher. It's a little tricky to remove the guts but keep the tiny fish relatively intact. The first time I bought them, I asked the fishmonger if she could teach me. She said, "Don't worry, we do it for you."

"Yes," I said, "but I'd like to learn how to do it."

"What on earth for? I'll do it for you, and it'll be quick. How many do you want?"

That meal of fried fish had been so simple to cook. When we sat down to eat, I explained to my family how to take the fish apart, which part of the head to eat and which to discard, and how to take the meat off the bone, right to the tail. The most important thing, I remember saying, is to use your hands. No knives and forks allowed.

It had bothered me that I hadn't cleaned the fish myself. It felt like I was cheating. I remember my mother telling me many times that this was a skill I needed to learn. I had watched her do it so often but had never tried it myself. Maybe she believed that she would have a lot of time to teach me, or I thought I'd have forever to learn.

Our move to Canada meant that any fish we bought from back home was frozen and not quite as tasty. Eventually, we started eating less fish and more meat, which is not surprising, given that we were living in beef country—Alberta is famous for top-quality beef.

On this day, I wanted to buy carapauzinhos again, before they went out of season. And I still wanted to learn to clean them myself.

When we walked into the ice room at the market, it was as if we had been transported to a fish lover's heaven. It smelled like the sea—fish and salt intermingled—and all around us, fish. The variety was impressive. The vendors called out to us with their catch of the day, trying to outdo each other with price and freshness. I headed towards the stalls against the back wall, where I'd bought fish before and knew the fishmongers.

I asked for carapauzinhos, enough for three regular appetites and one very hungry young man. The fishmonger looked at Matt, smiled, and started picking fish off the heap of ice on the table and throwing them into a bowl.

"You know, I'm going to be leaving soon," I told her. "I'm kind of running out of time to learn how to clean fish. It's my goal before I leave, remember."

Matt and Georgia stepped back and turned around as if looking at other fish, other stalls. I'd embarrassed them again, brought attention to our being different, and to my ignorance.

"Okay, okay," she said. "How about if I do most of them, you can watch me if you want, and then I'll leave a few for you to do at home. How would that be?"

"Sure, that sounds like a great idea. Leave me a dozen or so?"

I inched up close to the counter and fixed my eyes on her hands while she ripped through the fish so quickly, it was hard to follow.

"You're so fast!" I said. "Can you do a few slowly so I can really absorb it?"

She sighed heavily and turned to her partner, who was also standing there watching her, and said, "See what I have to put up with? I have no idea why she's so adamant about doing this herself." She said all of this as if it were an imposition, but I could tell she was pleased with my request to learn from her. She looked proud of herself.

She took one fish and gave me step-by-step instructions. "You hold the head on both sides, with your thumb and forefinger like this, then take the fish by the neck, like this, watch me, and pull out the guts. If you do it properly it's a quick two-step process."

She wrapped up my fish and weighed the package, then handed me the bill and said, "I gave you a discount since I didn't have to clean them all."

She took my money and gave me a smile and a wink in return.

I met Matt and Georgia in the produce area. They had walked off so as not to witness the special attention I had asked for and received.

We made a stop at my two favourite vegetable vendors near the exit. At the first, I bought some tomatoes and potatoes.

"What are you planning to do with these potatoes?" she asked.

"Fries?" I replied. I wasn't sure; I hadn't thought everything through.

"Then here, take these, they're much better for frying," she said, pointing at the smaller, red skinned potatoes.

My other favourite vendor, a mere two steps away, looked on. I had to buy something from her too, so I picked out two cucumbers, a bag full of cooking onions, and a bunch of radishes.

"You bought some fish today, I see," she said.

"Carapauzinhos," I said to her, and raised my bag to show her how much fish I had bought. "I'll make a salad and maybe some fries," I added.

"Hmm," she said. "With that fish you need to make arroz de tomate, tomato-rice. Otherwise, it's too much fried stuff. You know how to make the rice?"

"Oh, good point. I do know how to make that rice. You've told me before."

"Keep the potatoes for tomorrow," the vendor said with a wink, then handed me a big bunch of parsley. "Herbs are on the house."

We left the market and headed towards the beach. We were taking the long way home. As we passed the outdoor patio of one of the seaside restaurants, we saw the four men who had been arguing earlier, sitting together at a table. There was red wine in their glasses and a bottle in the centre of the table. They were talking and laughing and looking focused on deboning their fish.

"I guess they found their restaurant," I said to Matt and Georgia. "But let's keep going. It sounds like they are talking about soccer, so things could get heated."

Verão
(Summer)

A Dog's Life

MAX WAS A HAPPY DOG. We thought he was a stray because we often saw him wandering by himself all over town—in the central plaza, on the beach, in the residential areas. One day, he was sitting outside the supermarket, as if he were waiting for someone. When we walked past again, about an hour later, he was still there. Matt noticed that he was wearing a collar and approached him to check the tag.

"It says Max," Matt said. "He must have an owner!"

I was quietly relieved that my twenty-year-old son, usually gruff and tough on the outside, had a sensitive side and was showing concern for the well-being of this dog.

Max stood out among the town dogs because he trotted quickly, as if he had somewhere to go or business to attend to. Even that day at the supermarket, he was sitting with purpose and not pestering customers for food. He was alert, as if he were expecting something important to happen. When Max walked, his tail would be up in the air and his mouth would be partly open, as if in a smile. This was in contrast to many of the other dogs we saw on the streets, who would lie around for hours, or root through garbage, or walk as if they couldn't handle their boredom anymore. Other dogs, the guard dogs, seemed imprisoned behind high fences or left to pace back and forth on verandahs. And then there was Max—free to wander but also not abandoned. He belonged to someone.

We had been keeping a close eye on Reybeez, another of the street dogs, because of her tumour, which seemed to be growing. Matt had been startled when he first saw the poor dog looking so lethargic and mangy. When my friend Jennifer came to stay with us, she became openly distressed about the dog's condition. She pondered her options and considered taking her back to Vancouver with her.

"But she could have an owner," I said. "You can't just take her, can you?"

"It bothers me that you've called her Rabies," Jennifer said.

"It's Reybeez," I corrected.

I felt for Georgia. I didn't think she had meant any harm by giving the dog that name, but it clearly troubled Jennifer.

"I think it's different here with dogs," I said. "They may look like strays, but some of them have owners. Look, she has a collar. I'm sure she's someone's dog."

"I find it really upsetting," she said, tears welling up in her eyes.

Our dog, by contrast, was a spoiled pet, a member of our family. By some people's standards, especially here, we pandered to her. We took her for long walks on-leash, for at least an hour, sometimes two; we ensured she had at least one off-leash play session outside every day; we took her to the beach to swim and to play fetch with a ball or a frisbee or a myriad of other toys we'd managed to accumulate; and we brushed her on the deck, in the sun, every couple of days. We clipped her nails, rinsed the salt water off her coat, and dried her off with fluffy towels.

The day that Georgia discovered a tick on Maggie's belly, we all froze. Now what?

At the veterinarian's office, the technician smiled at me when I asked her if she would send the tick away to a lab to test for Lyme disease.

"No, we've never done that," she said. "Would you like me to? I'm not even sure how to go about that."

"Oh no, it's okay. It's just that in our vet's office in Vancouver, there's a sign on the wall with a warning about Lyme disease. And they send ticks for testing, just to be sure. Also, it helps track the disease," I explained.

"Ticks are pretty common here," she said. "And I don't think there's any Lyme disease in this area. I haven't heard of any cases."

"How much for the tick removal?" I asked.

"Don't worry about it," she said. "It was easy."

The third time we took Maggie in to have a tick removed, the technician suggested that we watch her, to see how it's done, so we could do it ourselves next time.

"Eric, can you watch, please? I don't think I can do it," I said, and I walked away.

I used to be against pet ownership. "Too much luxury," I'd tell people if they asked me why. "They're costly, and so many resources go into the whole pet industry that could be better applied to improving people's lives. Also, there's all that poop. It can't be good for the environment." We didn't have dogs in our house when I was growing up, and I remember being frightened of dogs when I was young.

After my sister Maria died, though, I was desperate to add some joy to our lives. It had been a tough four months for all of us. Maria fell ill quickly, and we all scrambled to adapt to the reality that she was very sick. She had complained about being tired and went to the doctor, who sent her for a blood test. That was it. She had cancer, and it had already metastasized, so much so that doctors were not able to figure out the original cancer until an autopsy was done. That was when we found out it had been a rare and deadly form of uterine cancer.

Like me, Maria had not grown up around pets. It surprised me when she became captivated by the therapy dog at the BC Cancer

Agency—a white standard poodle. Maria had frequent appointments at the clinic, and whenever we sat together in the waiting room, the dog would come and lie at her feet. Sometimes, he would sit and put his head on Maria's lap, and we would both pet him.

"I'm becoming very fond of this dog," Maria would say. And for brief moments, she and I would play with the poodle and forget about cancer.

When Maria was hospitalized, my niece would sneak in her chihuahua and put her on the bed next to Maria. Diamond didn't like being petted by too many people, but she would curl up next to Maria and let herself be stroked until Maria fell asleep. Sometimes one or another of the nurses would notice Diamond in bed with Maria, but they wouldn't say anything. They'd smile, then turn and walk away.

When Maria was discharged, I spent a few weeks with her at her apartment. She didn't have much energy so we'd pass the time by looking up pictures of cute puppies on the internet, and of dog breeds that she or I might consider for a pet. I remember we looked up Portuguese water dogs and retrievers and terriers.

"I think if I were to get a dog, I'd get a Portuguese water dog. They're so smart and strong, but affectionate too," I said.

"Not me. I want a smaller dog, one that I can pick up easily and sit it on my lap."

One day, when we were watching TV, we saw a commercial for pet food featuring a West Highland white terrier named Maggie.

"She's adorable!" Maria said. "When I get better, I'm going to retire and get myself a dog. Just like that one. And I'm going to call her Maggie."

After Maria died, each time we saw a white Westie, it made us think of her, and we'd smile. "She's trying to tell us something," I'd say.

Maria was like a second mother to my children. They spent a lot of time together and the kids often went for sleepovers at her house. She took them on special outings and out to dinner, and she'd often pick them up and take them to her place so they could bake or garden together. They would play "store," and Barbies, and dress-up. Maria let them play with her shoes and cassette tapes and books. If ours was the house of rules, Maria's was the freedom palace. She doted on my children, and they adored her.

Maria's death left us all bereft. Four months was not enough time to grasp the idea that we would be living such a large chunk of our lives without her. Hadn't we all thought that we'd have her around forever? I had certainly never contemplated not having her in my life, and I could never have imagined she'd die while still in her fifties. I had lost my parents and that had been difficult enough, but this, the loss of a sibling, was crushing. I suppose on some level we all expect that we will have to deal with the death of a parent at some point, but do we ever think about losing a sister? I never had.

Grief walloped me. It made it hard to breathe. For days it felt as if my chest wouldn't expand enough to take in the air needed to nourish my body. An oppressive darkness enveloped me and moved when I moved. I couldn't shake it. And I didn't just have my grief to deal with, I had my children's. I had to guide them through their feelings and care for their tender hearts even as mine shattered anew every day.

When Maria died, we were living in Quebec City while on another of Eric's sabbatical years from the university. Maria died on the 15th of December and her funeral was the day before Christmas Eve. I don't remember anything about that Christmas in Vancouver. I think our extended family got together for dinner, but did we have turkey? Did someone make dessert? I've tried asking Eric, but he doesn't remember, and neither do Matt or Georgia. It's as if we've all wiped that time from our collective memory. I don't even remember going back to Quebec City, but we must have because that's where we lived for another eight months. I do remember that we all grappled with intense sadness. There were tears and then more tears. We lay around on the couch a lot. Energy was elusive. We were away from the rest of our family, from our close friends, from pretty much our entire support system. We had each other, and that was it.

In many ways, our grief helped us to further bond as a family. As spring drew near and the days grew longer by a minute or two every day, so did our hearts begin to lighten. We made ourselves get off the couch and took ourselves outside. We went skating on lakes and creeks, we went cross-country skiing and marvelled at the beauty of winter, and we appreciated every ray of sunshine. But our experience with grief was not linear. We had good days, but they were followed by hard days. I was easily exhausted, and I cried a lot.

One day, after the kids had gone off to school, I sat and stared out the window at the mounds of snow for what felt like a long time. I decided we needed to do something different, something that would help propel us forward again while also honouring Maria's memory. When Matt and Georgia returned in the afternoon, I laid out a snack and sat with them at the table. I proposed that on the fifteenth of each month, we do something that Maria would have enjoyed. They loved the idea, and we got to planning.

We went to a movie one month, then brunch at the Château Frontenac the next. We enjoyed a horse-drawn carriage ride through the Old City, and took the train to Montreal. We talked more about Maria and remembered humorous events. It felt good to speak her name and not always with sadness.

I also started looking up Portuguese water dogs again on the internet. I learned that they were playful and had a sense of humour. We all agreed that we could use some laughter in our lives, and wouldn't it be fun to have a puppy? Eric was reluctant at first, no doubt thinking about all the care and expense involved in having a dog, but he didn't resist for long. He liked the idea too.

We had to apply to be considered by the breeder. Given that we were new to the dog world, there was an essay to write, forms to fill out, and visits to the breeder's house to meet her dogs once we got back to Vancouver in the fall. She lived about an hour-and-a-half drive from our house, but we made at least three visits so she could see how we interacted with her own dogs, and later, with the litter that included our puppy. When she was satisfied that we would be a good family for this active, demanding breed, she informed us that we would be getting a puppy from the next litter, due in early December.

Historically, Portuguese water dogs worked with fishers on their boats. They dove for broken nets and lost tackle and herded fish into nets. They also carried messages between boats and to shore. They were strong swimmers with stamina for long workdays, and they were highly prized by fishers for being loyal companions. But with improvements in technology, the need for dogs on fishing boats diminished and the breed became nearly extinct. It wasn't until the 1930s that a Portuguese shipping magnate decided to bring it back. By the early 1970s, Portuguese water dogs had been established in the United States, and today they are very popular, perhaps because the Obama family owned two during Barack Obama's presidency.

You'd think with all that history, the water dog would be revered in Portugal, but with the exception of our friend Pedro, who had Beck, few people we met seemed to know about Portuguese water dogs. We made a special trip to the Algarve, in the south of Portugal, to the town of Olhão where Pedro had told us the breed had originated. He said he thought there was an interpretive centre there where you could learn more about the dogs and the efforts to bring back the breed.

The centre was not easy to find and when we eventually got there, the building was boarded up. All that remained was a note on the door with a phone number you could call if you wanted a Portuguese water dog from the next available litter. When we took Maggie for a walk on a nearby beach and saw fishers mending their nets, I wondered if she would instinctively hop into a boat. Would she be drawn to the fishers, or they to her? The answer is no; they ignored each other.

"Bom dia," I said to one man sitting next to his boat mending nets, hoping to elicit some comment about our dog. His reply wasn't audible, though he did look and nod his head in acknowledgement. He must have mumbled something because the cigarette that was dangling from his lips moved, and he took the opportunity to bring his fingers to his mouth and take a long drag. He puffed out smoke and repositioned the cigarette. We carried on.

Back in Costa, on one of Joe John's stops at our house to see how we were doing, he asked, "Have you taken Maggie for a swim in the waves yet?" Only he said her name as "Majee."

I'd tried to correct him several times before, but on that day, I said, "Of course we have! She loves the waves—she's a water dog." And then I added, "And you know her name is Maggie, right? With a hard G?"

"Yes, Majee, she's so cute."

"No, not Majee, Maggie, as in Margarida." Margarida is the Portuguese equivalent of Margaret.

He laughed heartily. "Why haven't you told me that before? I've been calling her Majee all this time! I have a friend named Margarida. Didn't you meet her on the day of the marathon?" I had, in fact.

I had sworn I would never have a pet, and then when I did, I swore I wouldn't give it a person's name. I was good at breaking my own rules. Maggie was born on the first anniversary of Maria's death. How could we have called her anything else?

We had written to the breeder to request a female, but we knew there were no guarantees. Dory, the mother, was due on December 10th but didn't go into labour until a few days later. The breeder kept us up to date with all the developments, and the excitement around our house was palpable. In one of my emails to her, I mentioned that the fifteenth was a special day for us, and wouldn't it be interesting if the puppies were born on that day?

She responded with, "Well, unless you have some pull with Mother Nature, these puppies are ready to be born and they're not going to hold off until the fifteenth."

When we didn't hear anything for several days, I feared that the dam had died during the birth, or perhaps the puppies had all died and we wouldn't be getting a dog after all. My children started walking around with drooped shoulders. They stopped asking if I'd heard from the breeder.

On the morning of the fifteenth, when I had quietly resigned myself to believing there would be no dog, I opened my email and there it was, the announcement that there had been eleven puppies born overnight and all were doing well. Two males had been born before midnight, and nine females after midnight.

When we picked up our new puppy eight weeks later and I held her in my arms, tears filled my eyes. I thought of her as Maria's gift to us—a sign that it was okay to feel joy again, and that indeed, we must.

It turned out that we had been right about the cost of pet ownership. There were vet bills for vaccinations and flea medications, for yearly checkups, for emergency procedures as needed—such as when she ate a box of dark chocolate truffles—and for the odd infection like the one she got when she ran free on the dog beach in Vancouver and feasted on a decaying seal carcass. There was the cost of food, and grooming, and toys—yes, toys—that she destroyed within hours. At least she didn't wreck our furniture.

When I asked Pedro to recommend a groomer in Lisbon, he said he groomed Beck himself, and not all that often. I could see that. Beck's "hairstyle" gave him away as a free spirit. I walked into several grooming salons to ask about Maggie, but they all turned her down, saying that she was too big and that they only groomed small dogs. We decided to forget about grooming for the duration of our stay in Portugal, but we were careful to brush her coat often and untangle the mats, something that became even more important when the weather improved and she started swimming regularly.

I wouldn't say that we pampered Maggie, necessarily, but I sensed that we fussed over her more than is common in Portugal. I got an inkling of that when Joe John pointed to the studio shed in the backyard the day we arrived and said it would be a perfect place for Maggie to sleep.

"Oh, do you mind if she comes in the house?" I remember asking.

"No, no, of course not. But you want her in the house with you, day and night?"

"If you don't mind," I said. "She sleeps in a crate. And she won't damage the furniture, I promise."

We tried to keep track of the strays in our neighbourhood, but there were many. Reybeez troubled us greatly. Neighbours left food out for her, and we often saw her licking cheesy macaroni or leftover sauces on slices of old bread. Dave and Ingrid next door still didn't get walked, and numerous other dogs roamed leash- (and collar-) free.

One evening, as I was walking Maggie down the street to the beach, a big dog came charging towards us. I looked around for an owner, expecting that someone would whistle or call back their dog, but no, it kept running. I had little time to think. The dog lunged and Maggie squealed. And then, just like that, it took off around a corner, and I lost track of it. Maggie whimpered, so I picked her up and carried her home, then discovered blood on her coat.

The vet technician looked at her and assured me she'd be fine.

"It wasn't a deep cut. It barely broke the skin. And she has her shots. Don't worry. Just be sure you keep the area clean." And then she added, "No charge today. I didn't do anything."

Back at home, the look of concern on Matt and Georgia's faces turned to smiles when I said that the damage was minimal. Georgia gave Maggie a treat. Matt sat on the couch, and Maggie jumped up on his lap, happy to curl up and be stroked for a while.

"I followed Max today," Matt said. "And guess what?"

"What," I said, but I wasn't sure I wanted to know.

"He lives in that small apartment down the road! I saw his owner open the door and let him in."

We were all relieved that one of our favourite "strays" had a home after all.

. . . .

Border Services 2

WE WERE BACK IN SETÚBAL at the SEF for the follow-up appointment. This was getting almost ridiculous, but we couldn't see that; we were both frustrated and apprehensive. Even though we were nearing the end of our stay, we were both afraid that Eric would be denied the extension to his work visa, and we'd have to leave the country earlier than we had planned.

Eric had gathered all the documents the last agent had requested, even the ones he'd already provided. He got a new letter from UBC saying that he had a position to return to at the university and that he and his dependants had adequate health insurance. He provided a detailed list of what the health insurance plan covered. He downloaded the last six months of bank statements, and he printed a copy of our savings account balance on that day. All these documents were supposed to reassure the authorities that we would have enough money to cover any medical expenses that might arise during our stay. We had no idea how much was considered adequate, but we hoped that what we had would be enough.

I was still annoyed that the previous appointment had gone so poorly. This time, I was determined to accompany Eric, and I rehearsed what

I would say to the security guard. I would be courteous but persistent. I'd learned over the last few months by watching people at cafés and banks and shops that if you're too polite, you get pushed over, and if you're too assertive, you get dismissed. It's a fine line.

Eric and I drove to Setúbal but neither of us said anything to each other. We did not make plans for lunch, and we gave no thought to spending more time in the area than necessary. We parked the car, then held hands and walked to the SEF building. Just before Eric opened the door, I squeezed his hand.

"We've got this," I said.

We both breathed in deeply and walked through the door.

The same security guard greeted us and asked why we were there. I explained we had an appointment for a work visa for Eric, and I emphasized the "we." He gave me the same spiel as before: that appointments were for individuals only, and translators are not needed because the agents are bilingual. I searched my brain for my well-rehearsed lines.

"Well, you said that last time, but it wasn't the case. My husband and the agent could not communicate and now we've had to come back with more information, so I'll be going in with him today. To avoid any more confusion."

"The appointments are for individuals only," he responded, as if he hadn't heard anything I had said.

We took our seats and waited. I could feel my heart beating faster than usual. Eric kept rubbing his hands on his jeans and looking around. Then he whispered to me, "We really don't want to make things worse. Let's be ultra-careful."

I don't remember exactly how long we waited, but I know we were both feeling sweaty and hot by the time the security guard called out a number, then Eric's name.

We both walked to the front of the room and as I neared the security guard, I said, "I'm going in with him."

He gestured for me to pass, and it was that easy. I was in.

The agent came to greet us and show us the way to her cubicle. She smiled and said hello and made no mention of me going in with Eric. We sat down at her desk, and I explained that I was there to translate because the last time had not worked out so well.

It turned out that this agent spoke English fluently. She apologized about the last time and said it wasn't a big deal to come in with a translator, but as most of their agents speak several languages, it is usually not necessary.

She spent some time reading through the information on her computer screen, then turned to Eric, and said, "It looks like we have all the information we need. Do you have something more for us?"

"Uh, yes, I have a lot of updated information that the last agent requested."

She looked through the bank statements and letters, then closed the file and said, "You have more than enough proof here that you intend to return to your job in Vancouver."

"Yes, of course," Eric said. "In fact, I'm still working, and I continue to be an employee of the university in every official way."

"No problem," she said. "I'm prepared to recommend that your work visa be extended. But I see that you don't have much time left."

"Yes, that's right," Eric said.

"Well, your visa will need to be signed, and unfortunately, there's no one here today who can sign it. You'll have to come back one more time. The next appointment I have available is two weeks from today."

I gasped, and the agent looked at me with concern.

"I'm sorry," I said. "That's one day after we leave for our vacation up north. I can't believe this. We won't have our house anymore, and we'll have to stay at a hotel, and it's not that easy because we have a dog—"

She cut me off with, "Calma, senhora, let's work this out. When will you be back?"

We gave her the date, and then added that we'd have only one more week in Lisbon after that before we headed back home.

"Very well. What is your departure date for Canada? I will book your appointment for the day after you leave."

Eric and I looked at each other, unable to understand what this meant for us.

"I'm sorry, I'm confused," Eric said. "You're making the appointment for the day after we leave?"

"Look, I could give you an appointment for that week that you are in Lisbon, but you won't even be working anymore, you'll be on holidays, correct? And you'll be leaving the country shortly after that?"

"Yes, that's right," Eric said.

"Okay. I will give you interim permission to stay in the country until your next appointment. But by then you'll have left the country already. You understand?"

"Um, not really," I said.

Eric fidgeted beside me, and rubbed his hands on his jeans, as if to wipe the sweat off his palms.

"So you won't have to come back. I'm doing something nice for you, for all the trouble you've been through. It was all unnecessary. A misunderstanding. You can go, you're legal," she said.

She gave Eric a letter to put in his passport just in case we needed to show official documents somewhere, for some reason. She smiled, then said, "Why don't you go for a nice lunch and just relax. Oh, and boa viagem up north. You will love it."

"Muitissimo obrigada," I said. I had to restrain myself because I wanted to throw my arms around her and give her a big hug.

Just before we turned to leave, I double-checked with her that this wouldn't affect Eric negatively the next time he tried to enter the country.

"Because we will want to come back again, for sure," I explained.

"Of course. You will be welcomed back. Always. No more problems, okay?"

The work visa debacle was over. It had been unsettling for Eric and me since that night back in Vancouver when we realized we'd forgotten to even apply for it. Now it was all resolved, and it felt anticlimactic.

"Well, I guess we have to go for lunch," Eric said. "The agent told us to." He smiled and winked.

"Seaside restaurant? Chocos fritos? Let's go."

. . . .

Summer Market Days

ONCE THE MONTH OF JUNE ARRIVED, my trips to the market felt
even more special because I knew that we would be leaving soon.
I was feeling anticipatory saudade. But isn't it strange to experience
nostalgia even before absence, sadness even before loss?

Summer is a busy time in Costa's market. Vendors' stalls are brim-
ming with produce, and fishmongers hawk a new array of fish and
seafood. The market bustles with summertime residents and visitors from Lisbon and nearby towns. The vendors now had less time to
chat, and I faced the realization that our time in Costa was drawing to
a close. I wanted to do so many things for one last time before we left.

I started off my usual Saturday shop with a stop at my two favourite stalls, but with an increased awareness of my appreciation for this
simple routine task. I was surveying the produce and thinking about
dinner when I heard the vendor ask me, "Have you cooked much
seafood yet?"

"Oh hello, bom dia. Come to think of it, no, I haven't. I've been
focusing more on fish, and there's so much to learn," I said.

"Well, you can't go back to Canada without learning to cook seafood our way. Why don't you make carne de porco à Alentejana today," she suggested.

This was a dish I had ordered several times in restaurants and had wanted to try at home but hadn't yet because I thought it was too complicated. It includes cubes of pork loin, fried potatoes, and clams in a traditional sauce and is a specialty from the interior province of Alentejo.

"You'll need some potatoes. Here." She handed me a bag. "And since you love your salads you can buy some lettuce, cucumber, and look at these lovely tomatoes here, and add some sweet onion," the vendor continued.

"Now, there's an idea—pork and clams," I said. "I think I should venture out and try more complicated dishes."

"Nothing complicated about it, amor, it's very easy."

After months of shopping at this market and speaking to the vendors so often, I still didn't know their names and they didn't know mine. I simply called everyone senhor or senhora, and they called me whatever they wanted: amor, querida (love, dear), whatever worked. I chatted with these women (there was one man too), and we talked about politics, the economic crisis, emigration, family living abroad, saudade, how difficult life is, and how much work we homemakers do. We talked about food and cooking and relaxation and travel, but we never crossed the line and exchanged names. Maybe because it didn't matter? I had never felt bold enough to ask their names and they had never asked mine.

"First," she explained, "you go down the aisle here and see my colleague who will sell you some wonderful clams." She fixed her eyes on me with such intensity that I squirmed a bit. She took my arm. She wanted my undivided attention.

"Then you go to the butcher down the street, that way." She pointed, but always with her eyes on me to make sure I was paying attention.

"You'll see my nephew there—he's the only man who is working at this time—and tell him that his aunt sent you and that you're making carne de porco à Alentejana. He will sell you some nice meat. Give you a good price, too. And here..." She reached underneath her counter and put a bunch of cilantro together for me. "Add some of this. Do you have enough garlic? Some good olive oil?"

"Yes, that I do."

"Very well, then, off you go. Come and tell me tomorrow how it worked out. And if your Canadians at home liked it."

I headed down the aisle to the shellfish area and wondered about buying meat at the market. I hadn't done that before. I'd always bought meat at the supermarket where it was sold on foam trays and covered with plastic wrap. What kind of meat would I get here and for what price if I didn't tell the butcher I knew his aunt? I stopped by the seafood stand, and I looked briefly at the clams, and the price—fifteen euros per kilo. I opened my mouth to ask how much I would need for my dish, and the vendor started talking, almost as if she'd heard my previous conversation with the other woman, but I knew she hadn't; she couldn't have. She asked me, "Are you making pork and clams?"

"Uh, yes, that's exactly what I'm thinking," I said.

How did she know that? Surely people eat these clams in other dishes too. I still don't know how she did it, but she seemed to read my mind.

"Muito bem, then take these. A kilo?"

I realized this was not going to be a cheap meal.

"It's so easy to make, you can't go wrong. And it will be so good, you'll want to make a decent amount," she said. "If there's any left over, have it tomorrow. It'll keep for a couple of days."

"Even the clams in the shell?" I asked.

"Yes, yes," she said.

She scooped, drained, and weighed the clams while we chatted. Her life is hard, she told me. She's only here on Saturdays and Sundays now because people are not buying as much as they used to. I told her that I had often thought of buying, that I had wanted to buy, but I'm only here for a few more weeks, and sometimes we've gone away on the weekends so I've often missed her completely, and the opportunity to buy and cook shellfish.

"Where are you from?" she asked.

This is always a complicated question. I explained.

"Ah, Canada is wonderful," she said.

"Yes, it is," I responded.

"Here the government is terrible," she went on. "It cut forty per cent of people's wages overnight, just like that"—she snapped her fingers—"to pay for their blunders."

"It must be very difficult," I said, immediately feeling like a very privileged foreigner. "Canada has its problems too, you know. It's not perfect."

"At least if you work, you get paid, right?" she asked.

I couldn't argue. As if she didn't want to end on an unpleasant note, she said, "Come on a Saturday again next time. My brother goes fishing on Fridays, brings me the best stuff on Saturday morning." She winked and smiled.

"Right," I said. "Now, how about that easy meal? Just how easy is it?"

"Ah, you need instructions. Okay, first, you marinate the pork. Get the butcher to cut it up for you in cubes. Where are you going to buy it?"

"The vendor down there told me to go see her nephew."

"Yes, that's good. He'll give you a nice cut of meat. Chop up lots of garlic, add a little bit of salt, and some paprika, a splash of wine if you wish. Let the pork marinate in that while you fry the potatoes, then set those aside. Then, when you're ready to start cooking the meat, sauté some onion, and add the pork and fry it. Make sure it cooks through. While that is cooking, rinse the clams twice and drain. When the meat is done, throw in the clams, cover and let them steam open.

It only takes a few minutes. Just as they open, throw in chopped-up cilantro. Do you need cilantro?"

"No, thank you. Your friend down the aisle there, at the entrance, gave me a bunch. She's the one who sent me to you."

"Very well. I send people her way too. It's how we work around here. Then you add the fried potatoes, toss, and serve. Oh my, so good. It's what I had for lunch yesterday. You could make it for lunch today. It's so easy."

"Well, I'm going to the beach now. I think I'll make it for supper."

"Right. Good luck. Enjoy. Let me know how it goes." And then, as I walked away, she added, "See you next weekend. You'll have to try some navalhas next time." Razor clams.

Just before I left, I asked, "So I don't have to add wine or water or any liquid when I add the clams?"

"No, nothing. Just the juice of the clams is enough liquid to steam them open. But get some wine, of course, to have with your meal. That goes without saying," she said, and winked at me again.

I went out the back door of the market and headed down the street to the butcher. I walked into the first talho I saw. One man behind the counter. This must be the place, I thought to myself. He had his back to me, and when I said bom dia, he turned around from whatever he was doing, knife still in hand. He was a big guy, clean-shaven except for a bushy moustache that matched his full eyebrows. He had a white cap on to contain his hair. A few curls escaped the edge of the hat and framed the sides of his face. His long, white butcher's apron was stained with brown and red streaks and smears. Blood. Cow, pig, lamb. His forearms were muscular, and dark from the curly hair covering them from elbow to wrist.

Was he the vendor's nephew? He looked about the right age, so it could be him. Should I tell him that his aunt sent me? I felt uncomfortable doing that.

I decided not to say anything—no special favours. I just asked for cubed pork meat for the dish I was making. He didn't chat, didn't give me any cooking tips; he grabbed a hunk of meat from the counter behind him, threw it on the cutting board, and started to cut it up in chunks. I noticed that he hadn't washed his hands. Maybe he had washed them before I arrived, I thought to myself. I stood there, both of us silent, and I watched as he placed a piece of butcher paper on the scale and weighed the meat, added a few more cubes, then wrapped it up. He dabbed his fingers on a towel beside the cutting board, then handed me the package.

He took my money and gave me change, never washing his hands in the process. My Canadian sensitivity for safe food-handling caused a lump to rise from my stomach like a fur ball, and I thought I was going to throw up. I really prefer to buy my meat at the supermarket. I was suddenly glad that I hadn't mentioned his aunt.

I walked out and down the street, grateful for the fresh air. I noticed three other butcher shops, just steps away from this one. I hoped I had picked the wrong shop, hoped that man wasn't the vendor's nephew because in my perfect world, my vendor's nephew would have chatted with me and washed his hands.

I walked home along the beach and stopped at my favourite coffee bar for a cafézinho. I sat at a small table for two on the edge of the patio where I had an unobstructed view of the ocean. It had been my intention to read the newspaper, but I hadn't even brought one to the table. I just sat there with my coffee and stared out to sea.

The staff were getting ready for lunch. They were spreading white tablecloths and setting tables. Dishes and cutlery clanged in the background. A delicious aroma was emanating from the kitchen, and I suddenly felt very hungry. By now, I could even identify the smells— garlic, pepper, seafood. I decided to head home. Maybe I would make my pork and clams dish for lunch after all.

The next-door neighbour was out in the yard, cleaning paving stones. I stopped to talk to her—it had been months since I'd seen her. She seemed eager for a break, so we had a conversation. I told her we'd be leaving in a month or so and I was planning to cook all the seafood dishes I'd been wanting to for so long but only now had the courage to try. I told her we were going to have pork and clams for dinner, maybe lunch. She told me her favourite lunch was ameijoas à Bulhão Pato, the clams in garlic and wine dish named after the ninteenth-century food lover and poet Raimundo António de Bulhão Pato.

"Oh, I really like that too," I told her, and I made a mental note to make that next time. I had enjoyed this dish many times in restaurants and wished I'd tried it at home before now.

The front door of our house must have been open because I could hear Maggie out in our yard. She must have heard my voice or sensed my presence and she was barking as if calling out to me. The aroma of grilled cheese sandwiches wafted out to the street. Eric must be making lunch, I thought.

"You have a dog?" the neighbour asked.

"Yes, we brought her with us from Canada. She's a cão d'água," I said, thinking she'd be impressed that we had a Portuguese water dog. And then I thought, here's my chance to ask about her dogs. I was hesitant because I wasn't sure how much information I wanted. This woman seemed friendly enough, and I liked her, but I couldn't forget that the dogs had been left largely on their own for much of the winter. What was with that?

"And your dogs, what breed are they?" I asked.

"No idea," she replied. "They're mutts, but they're lovely dogs too."

"They are. We've become quite fond of them. But we don't even know their names," I said.

At this point the dogs came to the chain-link fence, almost as if they knew I was talking about them. Then I continued, "My daughter has given them interim names, until we found out their real names, but here we are, in our last few weeks. I'm glad I ran into you today."

"Yes, well, this is pretty much a summer town. Our family is gathering here tonight. The kids are coming from all over the country. Summer is starting just as you're leaving," she said.

"Well, we're not leaving quite yet," I reminded her.

"Dog's names, yes. The dark one is called Sandy, and the other one is Snoopy," she said.

I smiled and thought to myself, so the sandy-coloured one is Snoopy and the dark one is Sandy. Confusing.

"How do they get fed?" I finally asked.

"Oh, we've hired someone who comes to feed them, change their water, and clean up. I don't think he's been here for a day or two—there was a lot of dog mess in the yard."

"Hmm," I said. It was all becoming clear.

And then she added, "We have one more dog. Eli. You may have seen her around. She has a tumour. I'm sure you've seen her."

"We have! And I must admit, we've wondered about her. She did seem to spend a lot of time in your front yard."

"Yes. We don't have to contain her behind the fence because she won't stray too far. She's so lovely and friendly. The neighbours put food out for her. She's been on a waitlist at the vet for surgery, and it's been such a long wait for all the insurance papers. She's going in tomorrow, finally. That's another reason we're all gathering today. And then I'll be staying here while she recovers."

"Oh, so we'll be seeing you more often. That's so great."

Maggie's barking was becoming more insistent. I could barely hear the neighbour now, and I was getting distracted. Eric stepped out onto the verandah and called out, "Is that you, Es? Lunch is ready."

I put away the groceries as Eric set the table out on the patio. I guess it would be pork and clams for dinner after all, and good thing, I was ready to eat now. Eric poured us each a glass of wine and called out for Matt and Georgia to join us. I had a lot to say to bring everyone up to date on the dogs next door.

"So we finally know the dogs' real names now," Georgia said. "I think I'll still use Dave and Ingrid though."

"Sounds like they'll have company all summer long," Eric said. "That's a relief."

"Yeah, and we know that Reybeez is going to be looked after," Matt added. "That makes me feel so much better."

. . . .

An Inheritance of Loss

THE PORK AND CLAMS WERE A SUCCESS. And it had indeed been easy. The hardest part, I found, was that the potatoes had to be fried and then kept warm while I prepared and cooked the rest of the ingredients. But it was quick: sautéing onions—five minutes; searing and cooking the pork—fifteen minutes; and steaming the clams—five minutes. So fast and easy it may well become our new fast-food dish, I thought, as the kitchen filled with a delicious aroma of onions, garlic, cilantro, and seafood. Once assembled, the dish looked as beautiful as it smelled. Eric had sliced some fresh homestyle bread and placed it in a wicker basket beside a bottle of red wine he'd opened earlier and set on the table to breathe.

There were no leftovers. We all had seconds, and Matt had at least three helpings. Even Georgia enjoyed it. I had watched out of the corner of my eye as she took care to dip the bread in the sauce and pick out a few cubes of meat and several potatoes for each clam she tried. I couldn't help but smile. I find it very satisfying to present a meal that is so easy to make and have everyone enjoy it.

Our discussion over dinner turned to Matt's upcoming trip. He had planned a tour of a few countries in Northern Europe—his first trip on his own—and he was ready, but was I? As a mother, I find I am usually playing catch-up, adjusting to my children's new phases of life before I consider myself ready. This little expedition was no exception. He would be gone for only a couple of weeks and, all things considered, he wouldn't be that far away. At least we'd be on the same continent. But the anxiety that arose in me sent me into a whirlwind of reflection and self-analysis as to what it meant to be a mother—a mother following in my own mother's footsteps, a Portuguese mother. I felt that the Canadian part of me wanted to encourage Matt's independence and sense of adventure. The Portuguese part of me wanted to hold on tight. I wondered if my strong sense of attachment to my children was a cultural phenomenon or if it was just related to my family's experience of immigration. Was my need to hang on so tightly a consequence of all the loss I'd experienced? Of all the loss my parents had also experienced?

Poor Matt. He hadn't expected this trip, short as it was going to be, to cause so much angst for his mother. And I knew that my reaction could drive a wedge between us—the exact opposite of what I wanted. I remember being his age and feeling the need to break free from my mother's overprotective grip. "You're smothering me," I remember telling her, more than once. I cringe now as I think about that, and about how I had promised myself that I wouldn't be too protective of my own children. But there I was, trying to micromanage Matt's trip and giving him too many safety tips. It's not that I didn't want him to go; I did. I love to travel, and I was quietly proud that he had been blessed with the desire for adventure, but oh how I worried. And how I needed to be sure that he'd come back to us.

"Of course he'll come back. You're worrying too much about all of this. He'll be fine." This became Eric's mantra, usually when we were away from the kids, mostly when we chatted after we got into bed at night. But my need for constant reassurance was wearing him down and affecting our relationship. It threatened to drive us apart. Our conversations on this topic followed a similar pattern each time.

"You've got to let him go, Es. I want him to be safe too, but I just trust that he will be. You've got to trust him."

To which I'd respond, "I trust him. It's everyone else I don't trust. And bad things can happen, you know." It was a circular conversation, and I knew that I was being unreasonable, but I couldn't help it. Matt was now twenty years old, with his own dreams and plans, but some of them were simply beyond my comfort level.

Matt had planned and paid for the trip himself. He had booked flights with discount airlines, which I knew meant that he'd be arriving in big city airports late at night. He outlined his itinerary at dinner, and it was straightforward. He'd be flying into Amsterdam and meeting up with a friend we didn't know a few days later, then moving on to Oslo on his own, then Stavanger by train to meet another friend, and finally on to Helsinki where he would meet with another friend for part of the time.

"Can I buy you a European SIM card for your phone so you can keep in touch with us?" I asked.

Matt agreed, and I felt relieved. He was well organized, and I knew deep down that he would be fine and the trip would go well. But I was still anxious.

When he arrived at his hostel in Amsterdam and sent me a message on Facebook to inform me that the SIM card didn't work, I panicked. How would we keep in touch?

Eric assured me that our son, now a full-grown adult, had good judgement and would be fine. I realized there was nothing I could do. I stopped hyperventilating and resigned myself to being in touch only sporadically when Matt had access to Wi-Fi.

I wondered how my mother had survived my adventures when I was Matt's age. I had travelled a lot, all over the world, but mostly with my sister Maria. Maybe it was reassuring for my mother that there were two of us. She must have worried too, though I don't remember exactly what that looked like. We did our travelling in the days before cell phones and the internet so we would not have been in constant touch with our mother, nor would she have known exactly where we were on a daily basis. Still, I remember thinking she worried too much.

When I went camping with friends, I'd have to find a pay phone and call my mother to let her know that I'd arrived at my destination safely. When I started outdoor rock climbing, I wasn't exactly straightforward with her. I'd lump that activity under the general description of "camping," and she didn't ask too many questions. I started to feel guilty about that, and one day I decided to show her a few pictures of me on the rock, tied into a harness and hanging from a rope. I was waving at the camera.

My mother was sitting at the dining room table, mending socks. I pulled up a chair beside her and sat down.

"I have some pictures from my last camping trip. Would you like to see them?"

She looked through them, then raised her eyes to mine and said, "You haven't been truthful."

"I didn't lie, Mum, we were also camping," I offered as an explanation and in my defence. She cried. My mother was crying because of me, and I couldn't stand it.

"Rock climbing? How could you do that to me? What if you died?"

It didn't seem like a reasonable fear to me at the time but now, decades later, I understand. I'm afraid of loss too.

My mother's oldest brother, the one she'd been closest to, immigrated to Brazil when my mother was sixteen years old. She never saw him again. They wrote letters and spoke on the phone occasionally, but when he died, my mother hadn't spoken to him in several years.

"Men aren't so great at keeping in touch," she said.

Soon after that, she and my father went to Brazil to visit my mother's sister and all the nieces and nephews. I remember her telling me that she and her sister, my Tia Teresa, had stayed up all night talking, several nights in a row. And then they'd sleep late in the mornings.

"We had so much to say to each other, and we'd start really talking after everyone else had gone to bed. It was so much fun," my mother said.

My maternal grandmother died when my mother was only twenty-four years old, five weeks before my parents were married. My mother didn't talk about it very much, but I can only imagine that it must have been a time of huge turmoil. She'd have been in deep grief over the loss of her mother but also facing immense joy at the start of a new life as a married woman. She sometimes talked about how awful she had felt leaving my grandfather alone with his grief and moving in with her new husband and her in-laws in a different city. She would only be fifteen kilometres away, but in those days a visit would have required hours of travel, making it possible only on weekends, if that. Her father died five years later of complications from diabetes—and a broken heart, my mother said.

My parents' lives were marked by loss, much of it due to emigration. When we moved across the ocean and two-thirds of the way across our new country, my parents believed that their belongings would follow them. They had arranged to ship everything they thought valuable—some furniture, framed photos that had hung on the walls in their house in São Miguel, my mother's paintings, her wedding dress—things that would be of little value to anyone outside our family. But the shipment never arrived. "Lost in transit" was the official reason provided on the form. My parents were devastated. I remember my father saying, "They were just things. At least we are all fine." But even as a seven-year-old, I remember feeling the loss too, and crying because my parents looked so sad.

Five months after we arrived in Edmonton, my father's father died suddenly, in his sleep, back home in São Miguel. We did not have enough money for a plane ticket for my father to go back for the funeral, and my mother resorted to asking a neighbour for a loan. My parents sent a telegram to the priest, asking him to wait a few days before holding the funeral, until my father could get there. By the time my father arrived on the island, it was too late; he had missed the funeral. The priest had not received the telegram in time. My father was shaken by loss yet again when he boarded his return flight to Canada, leaving his newly widowed mother alone.

Our first few months in Edmonton were especially hard. Twelve days after we arrived, there was a family argument and my uncle kicked us out. We were all alone in a new and unfamiliar country, and we were estranged from the only family we had near us. I never knew exactly what had transpired to cause so much insult. There was no yelling or anything—one day my parents just told Maria and me that we would be moving out, and we left hours later. My mother told us that it was a disagreement between the adults, and whenever we saw my uncle and aunt or our cousins, we were to go to them and greet them. But we didn't see them often; they were not active in the Portuguese community. All I know is that my mother and her brother didn't speak for more than fifteen years, not until Teresa died in Brazil and the two siblings decided that whatever had happened all those years ago was not a good enough reason to sever their relationship forever. They made up and got together every weekend over several months so they could chat and catch up on all the time lost.

I understand now that my mother's overprotectiveness with me and my sisters was her way of trying to keep her own family together. After so much loss, how could she fathom losing more? Had my decision to start rock climbing been a selfish one? Should I have thought of the impact it could have on my mother? I don't think I ever considered such things. I didn't think about it then, but I do now.

Several days after Matt left on his trip, Georgia, Eric, and I were relaxing in the living room after dinner, when a message came in from him. It was a warm evening and the French doors to the patio were wide open, allowing the evening breeze to drift inside and fill the room with summer air. We could hear music in the distance, likely from one of the coffee bars on the beach. Eric was sipping wine and reading a book, and Georgia was brushing Maggie. My thoughts were on Matt. I was on the computer when his message arrived.

> *Can you do me a favour plz, i need you to find what baking*
> *soda is called in norwegian, its too hard on this phone*
>
> > *ok. standby. everything ok?*
>
> *Kind of urgent*
>
> > *matt, why??*
> > *natron*
> > *please tell me what's going on.*
> > *you're scaring me.*
> > *where are you?*
> > *MATT! please say something.*
> > *NATRON*
> > *matthew, please tell me what's going on.*

I know it was his use of the words "kind of urgent" that troubled me. My mind wandered, and then it started to spin. I tried to imagine what he could possibly need baking soda for, and all I could come up with was that he had caused a fire in the kitchen of his hostel. I kept waiting for him to tell me what was going on, but he didn't respond for another half hour. I didn't know what to do with myself, it was a very long half hour. Eric tried to reassure me, but I could tell that he was puzzled too. I went for a brisk walk to the beach. Surely by the time I got back, Matt would have responded, and all would be well. But when I got back home and asked if either Eric or Georgia had heard from him and they both said no, I grew more anxious. I went for another walk. It was all I could do to keep from shaking. Eric was a little bewildered, wondering what was happening on Matt's end but also trying to help me settle down. Georgia, on the other hand, was totally relaxed. She continued brushing Maggie, and she rolled her eyes at our concern. Her explanation was that he probably needed the baking soda because his running shoes smelled bad.

It turned out that Georgia was right. Matt was going to spend the next few days with a high school friend and her family in Stavanger and he was worried about how smelly his shoes were.

"How is that an urgent matter?" I asked him in another message when I had finally calmed down.

"That's why I said 'kind of' urgent," he replied, promptly this time.

"Poor choice of words," I said.

It was not the kind of issue we could resolve by exchanging messages, but something happened to me that night. I hit the wall and recognized the futility of my worry. I knew I couldn't stay on high alert for the rest of Matt's trip; I had to let go. I slept very well that night, either because of emotional exhaustion or because I stopped myself from needing to know that he was all right every minute of the day.

Have I inherited the fear of loss from my immigrant parents, or is it just my own losses that have made me who I am? Could it be a combination of both? And how can I manage the unsettled feeling I get when I realize that bad things can happen but likely won't?

I knew that coming back to Portugal might stir up feelings of loss and grief for me. I was still recovering from the "difficult decade." My mother had been diagnosed with Alzheimer's disease on my fortieth birthday. She and my father had moved in with us, into our small bungalow in Vancouver, and for two years, we were a family of six. I became my mother's primary caregiver through her loss of memories, and later, when she was diagnosed with terminal cancer, we provided palliative care for her in our home. It was an intense time for our entire extended family. My sisters, my nieces, even my brother-in-law and Eric, were all involved in looking after my mother and supporting my father. My mother died in our house, on a sunny day in October, after all the family had been keeping vigil for an entire weekend.

The loss of my mother was devastating for all of us, but we leaned on each other for comfort. My father continued to live with us, and I turned my energy to caring for him. We had breakfast together and went for short walks. He suffered from arthritis in his hips and knees so our walks were slow and meandering. I cooked his favourite foods, and he bought Portuguese wine for us to sip while I made dinner. My sisters took turns taking him out for coffee, which was one of his favourite outings. He loved sitting at coffee shops on busy streets, watching the world go by. We watched hockey together, and he and the kids played checkers and cards in the evenings.

Nine months after my mother died, my father fell in our house, hit his head on the floor, and suffered a brain hemorrhage. An accident at home that causes death triggers a coroner's investigation. I was relieved that someone was looking into it. I needed to know whether my father had fallen because he'd had a stroke, or if he'd fallen by accident and his fall had caused the hemorrhage. I really wanted it to be the former.

The report came back as "inconclusive." The coroner called to check on me and to see how I had received the news. She explained that she wasn't going to do a full autopsy because, at my father's age, his veins would have been so fragile that it wouldn't have taken much to cause a bleed. She ended our conversation with, "I'm sorry. You couldn't have prevented this."

I had no room in my heart for more grief. It was as if I were layering on another heavy winter coat while already wearing a cumbersome, fur-lined parka. The movement of my body from day to day was an automatic response to standing still. I felt like a robot. But my children needed their mother, and somehow, I kept going. In time, bits of joy inched their way into the cracks of everyday life. I found myself smiling in the playground one day with my kids as they climbed up the twisty slide, and I noticed that I was on my way back to feeling happy.

Three years later, my sister Maria developed cancer too. She died four short months after her diagnosis. I sank into an emotional void once again. I found it hard to notice when the sun shone or when it rained; I was oblivious to the crocus shoots emerging in the front yard in the spring; and I barely felt Eric's hand as he caressed my cheek or his warmth when he enveloped me in his arms.

Within a few years, I had lost my mother, my father, and my sister. Of the four of us who had immigrated to Canada together, I was the only one left. I am the lone keeper of those early immigration memories, yet I was so young that I can't be sure if I remember everything correctly. My fact checkers are all gone.

I couldn't wait to turn fifty. I wanted to leave my forties behind and start my new decade with a new purpose. I was ready to feel joy away from the shadow of sorrow. So much had changed in me, and I was unsure how I would feel when I returned to Portugal, yet it was something I wanted to do. I wanted to walk the cobblestone streets of Lisbon, the same ones I had walked with my mother and my sister Maria when we would visit Toni during her university days. I knew that the smell of coffee wafting out of the cafés and the sight and taste of pastéis de nata would send me into a whirl of memories and a depth of saudade I would not be able to ignore. But I was ready; I even welcomed the opportunity to feel the enormity of my losses while also knowing that my life was full and happy. I had two great kids, a husband who loved me, and a vibrant and loving extended family. So much to be grateful for, and yet the loss I'd experienced had become an integral part of me. It had changed me.

In many ways, this sabbatical and this return to Portugal signalled for me that I was entering a new phase in my life—one where I was the grown-up without parents to lean on. It was time to revisit the past to make sense of my present and attempt to define my future. Portugal provided me with access to my memories. I listened for the roar of the wild Atlantic and tasted the salt it left swirling in the air. Hearing my first language all around me filled my heart and solidified my identity. I am from this place.

. . . .

Fado Bar

WHEN I HAD IMAGINED LIVING IN COSTA, I saw myself going to fado bars all the time. It hadn't turned out that way, partly because of the difficult logistics.

There are two main areas for fado in Lisbon—Bairro Alto and Alfama. Both neighbourhoods are located across the river from where we lived. It was expensive to drive into Lisbon and park the car so we were limited to using public transportation.

The ferry service ends around one-thirty in the morning, which normally would not be a problem, but fado bars get going late, usually around eleven. If we had to leave by twelve-thirty to make the last ferry, we wouldn't have much time to actually listen to the music. It was doable but it felt complicated. We had to really, really want to go to make it happen and so many times, especially in the winter, it required too much effort.

When spring arrived and we started hosting visitors, I had it in mind that we would be going to listen to fado regularly. I regarded an outing to a fado bar as a social activity, and one that I thought would include more than just Eric and me, so I was looking forward to going with friends when they visited. But most of our guests wanted to start getting ready for bed at ten o'clock, not leave the house for an evening out. With each response of "no, that's too late for me," I became increasingly disappointed. Didn't everyone who came to Lisbon want to hear the fado?

Fado is essential to the Portuguese character and, in many ways, helps to define it. Fado and saudade go hand-in-hand. Portugal is such a small country, both in geographical area and in population, that it is rarely front and centre on the world stage. And perhaps that is just how the Portuguese like it. I know that until recently I'd sometimes have to explain exactly where Portugal was, and I would grumble when people would say, oh yes, it's on the west coast of Spain. Now, Portugal is well known as a funky tourist destination in its own right, one that is still relatively inexpensive, and also as a landing hub and home base for exploring Europe. The Azores remain less well known even now, especially to North Americans, but that too is changing. It seems that the world is coming to know Portugal and discovering its rich literary and musical traditions, including the fado.

At one time Portugal was a prominent nation, famous for the voyages of explorers such as Vasco da Gama, Cabral, and Magellan, and the maritime school founded by Prince Henry the Navigator. But in more modern times, the country became increasingly poor and slid into international obscurity. In the early 1930s, the Estado Novo regime began promoting family values and simple living and discouraged higher education, all of which helped contribute to the survival of the dictatorship, but also to the impoverishment of the nation. The colonial wars in Africa helped drive Portugal into further economic hardship. The military coup in 1974 reflected a change in Portugal's priorities, but four decades later, Portugal is still processing and dealing with its colonial past.

Through all the hardships, there was always fado—the bluesy tunes sung by solo singers accompanied by the Portuguese guitar. The Lisbon style of fado is believed to have started back in the mid-nineteenth century in the taverns of the city and was popularized by the working class as a form of social commentary. While some of the songs were political, others were about love and loss—fate, as it were. Maria Severa, who sang in some of these taverns, is widely accepted as having been Portugal's first fado singer. It is rumoured that she had a love affair with a count, and it was he who then introduced the music to the elite class.

I didn't know much about the origins of fado when I was growing up. I always thought of it as the music of the mainland because there were so many songs about Lisbon. But islanders also listened to it. In my young mind, though, fado was about the other Portugal—the one that lay across the water, the one that I hadn't set foot on until after we had immigrated to Canada and went back for visits.

Like many others, I associated fado with Amália Rodrigues, and I knew that she belonged to all of us. When her voice came over the airwaves on the radio, we stopped to listen. Her words, her anguish, were about heartache. Without effort on my part, I absorbed the ache of saudade for lost loved ones along with my parents and older sisters. We had lost friendships and family to death, yes, but also to emigration. And then we too became part of that cycle, the ones who did the leaving.

Under Salazar's authoritarian leadership, political verses of fado were banned, and only songs about love and melancholy were allowed. Because of this association with the dictatorship, fado fell out of favour with many Portuguese until after the revolution when it was once again reclaimed as the music of the people. I learned about this by accident.

For me, fado had always been about love and loss and saudade. But several years ago, in Vancouver, I watched an episode of Anthony Bourdain's *No Reservations* and listened, fascinated, to a conversation he had with Portuguese writer António Lobo Antunes, who explained this association between fado and the dictatorship as the reason he still cannot bring himself to listen to it. I had no idea. I poked around and did some research, even visited the Fado Museum in Lisbon to learn more, but information on the politics of fado was not well recorded; only now is this history becoming more accessible, decades after the end of the Estado Novo regime.

The portrayal of the Portuguese as a mournful, accepting, non-combative people is a stereotype, of course, but given the decades of oppression under a dictatorship, it is understandable how that depiction of the national temperament developed. With the country's history of losses at sea—of explorers, and later, of whalers and fishers—it is perhaps fitting that our music is more of a lament instead of upbeat and joyful. But it is limiting to think that fado explains the whole story of a whole country.

I admit that fado often makes me cry, although I don't really know why. I'm one of those people who doesn't focus on lyrics, but I am taken with music and melody. There is something so haunting about the sound of the Portuguese guitar and the classical guitar being played together that penetrates my soul. When someone asks me to explain why a particular song is meaningful to me, or what it is about the lyrics that I find so touching or beautiful, I have difficulty answering. Having to translate the sentiment, not just the words, is very hard.

When our neighbours from Vancouver, Douw and Margaret, were in Lisbon for a visit, we decided to get together for dinner and a night of fado. Douw had been teaching a course at the university in Aveiro, a city about two hundred and fifty kilometres north of Lisbon, and Margaret had joined him for a holiday. I knew from our conversations over the fence back home that they loved fado—they are long-time fans of the artist Mariza. They relate to the emotion of fado, but it can't be because of the lyrics since neither speaks Portuguese. Like me, they are probably drawn in by the music and melody. They had told us they wanted a real fado bar experience, not the elaborate shows that are put on primarily for tourists. Indeed, while I enjoy fado concerts and never miss an opportunity to attend one in Vancouver, when I am in Lisbon, it seems more appropriate to sit in a small, intimate bar, sip on red wine, and listen attentively to the fadistas.

On my suggestion, we went to my favourite restaurant and fado bar in Alfama. I was nervous having made the decision because, more than anything, I wanted everyone to enjoy the evening. There is a circuit of fado bars, with singers going from one to another, singing a few songs at each before moving on to the next. The quality of the fado varies depending on who is singing on a particular night. It's the luck of the draw.

My sister Toni was also in Lisbon at the time and was staying with a friend in Lisbon rather than with us in Costa. We had seen each other on a number of occasions but had yet to go for an evening out in the city. When I told her where we were going, she said she'd meet us there later.

I don't remember what we had for dinner—I didn't even write it down in my notebook as I usually do. Even though having dinner and sipping on wine is part of the overall fado experience, it's the music I most enjoy. For our small group, it was what we went for, and it was what we were all looking forward to.

Just past eleven o'clock, a young guitarist walked in, surveyed the room, then looked for a spot near the entrance. He pulled up a stool, sat down, and started tuning his guitar. He was joined by another musician who emerged from the back of the restaurant, Portuguese guitar in one hand, glass of red wine in another. The two of them tuned and plucked strings, while diners finished their meals and spoke in hushed tones. The musicians were so close to our table that they might as well have been sitting right with us. We could see their fingers moving swiftly from one string to another in sequence, producing melodious riffs even though they looked like they were just noodling, and they barely looked at each other. Their faces showed effort, then relief at hitting the difficult notes. Most of the time, their eyes were closed.

At one point, a man walked in, greeted the guitarists, then stood next to them and waited for the room's noise to lessen. He started to sing and the room went quiet. Etiquette dictates that when the fadista is singing, the audience listens attentively. If you are still eating dinner, then it goes cold. It is considered very rude to raise the fork to your mouth, however silently you think you can chew. It would mean that you were not giving the song, and the singer, your full attention, your full heart. You do not chat with your tablemates but rather devote your complete focus to the fado.

The fadista belted out notes, the passion for his song evident to all of us. I was too nervous to allow myself to feel moved. I wanted this evening to be perfect, and I wanted my neighbours to have the best possible experience. I didn't know any of the songs this singer chose, didn't allow any of the words to reach into my soul. I sat back in my chair and closed my eyes and hoped that I would be more taken with the next singer. Once in a while, I'd open one eye and glance over at Eric or our guests, and they looked like they were enjoying the show, but I wasn't feeling it. Partway through the set, a young woman got up and started singing, then the first man sat down. They were sharing a set, which was unusual and something I'd never seen before.

At the break, I explained that the second set is usually when the more well-known fadistas sing so it was going to be even better. The guitarists returned to their spot and the door opened. We expected it to be the next fadista but it was my sister Toni, and her two friends—Barb from Vancouver who was travelling with Toni, and São, a friend from Lisbon with whom they were both staying. I waved and they noticed us right away. Eric got up and found extra chairs so all of us could sit around the same table. They had been doing the rounds of the fado bars, they explained, and had been to two others down the street before they got to this one. I introduced them to our Vancouver neighbours, and they all seemed delighted at this thread of connection. Toni kept saying, "Neighbours from your street? In Vancouver? Really?"

At one point, Barb leaned over to me and half-whispered, "They've taken me all over the place. This is fun but it's way past my bedtime."

I noticed that São had leaned back in her chair and said a few words to the musicians and now she was getting up and straightening her scarf, as if she were getting ready to sing. And then she nodded to them, they started a melody, and she started singing. She belted out the words as well as the performers in the first half, perhaps even better. I didn't recognize the song, but I could see she was emotionally involved. When she opened her eyes, they were teary. She had put in everything she had. The audience burst into applause.

I looked over at Toni as if to ask what on earth was that about. She explained to those of us at the table that fado vadio is fado sung by regular people. Anyone can do it, get up and sing at one of these local bars.

"Fado by the people for the people. It's not all sung by professionals, you know," Toni said, and then, turning to Douw and Margaret, she said one more time, "So cool that you're from Vancouver!" I was impressed by São, not only with her singing ability but her nerve. I could never do that, stand up in a room full of strangers and sing.

We sat back and chatted some more, and then someone else from the audience got up to sing. After that, I looked at my watch; I was getting concerned about making it to the last ferry. Douw and Margaret were ready to go, as well, so we left. I don't know if there was ever an official second set. When I asked Toni the next day, she said, "Oh, I don't know either, we moved on to the next bar up the street right after you left."

. . . .

Sardine Season

THE NEIGHBOURHOOD OF GRAÇA sits atop the highest of Lisbon's seven hills. The houses are crammed onto the hillsides and residents are tightly packed in. There is little privacy—neighbours can hear each other's business without trying too hard. This is the area where Edward and Larissa, our friends from Vancouver, decided to stay when they came to Lisbon for a conference.

The timing was perfect for them to get a good taste of what Lisbon can be like in the summer. The month of June is dedicated to the feast days of the popular saints, three of them—Santo António, São João, and São Pedro—St. Anthony, St. John, and St. Peter. All over the country, there are festivals that focus on food and community with marching bands and parades, but I've often heard that the festivities are most elaborate in Porto and Lisbon.

In June, the sardines are fat and juicy. When Edward called to invite us to dinner, I suggested sardines. It was only early afternoon, but he told me he'd already reached his maximum daily intake. He explained that he had been sitting out on the deck of their suite when a neighbour was grilling sardines. They struck up a conversation and she asked if he'd like to try one, which he did.

"I lost track after the first dozen," he said. I assumed he was exaggerating, but I couldn't be sure.

The four of us went out to dinner, away from the centre of the city, and feasted on salt cod instead of sardines. It was a warm, humid evening and we had the patio to ourselves. As we were having our after-dinner port, the kitchen and wait staff came to chat with us, and we lingered in the summer night for what seemed like another hour or two.

It became obvious when sardine season was in full swing. Restaurants put out signs and sandwich boards announcing the arrival of the celebrated fish. Smoke emanated from barbecues set up in alleyways and on restaurant patios, giving the air a delicious fishy aroma. Whenever we walked around the centre of Costa, especially down the street lined with restaurants, the smell of barbecued sardines flooded over us—it filled our nostrils and stayed there for hours, it set into our hair and lingered, and it permeated our clothes. It was especially noticeable when we re-entered our house. I immediately thought of my mother. What would she think? I know she'd tell me to hang my clothes outside to air them out, so I did that, up on the deck, but after a while I wondered why I bothered; the smell was everywhere.

I wanted to buy sardines and cook them at home, but we had never used the wood oven on the back patio. We considered cleaning it and getting it ready, but it seemed more trouble than it was worth, especially because every restaurant we ventured into had sardines as the daily special. The oily fish was ubiquitous, at least for now.

Walking along the beach near our home became an eventful ritual. Fishing boats would head out regularly and then come in fully loaded. Fishers and their families would sell their catch right on the beach. One afternoon on a dog walk, Eric and I were treated to a complete show.

The sun was out, and it felt like summer. The tide was high, and there weren't many people on the beach, but small groups were scattered here and there, making it hard to pick a spot to play frisbee with Maggie. We kept walking, farther than we normally would on a regular dog walk. Way down the beach, in the distance, we could see two tractors going back and forth from the sand to the edge of the water, as if to flatten or clean the sand. They were so far away that we had to squint to even identify them as tractors. What was going on? There was a big group of people gathering, which piqued our interest.

"Let's go see," Eric said.

As we got closer, we could see one tractor had backed into the water and its winch was turning. It was pulling in a rope under the waves, and if we looked way out, hundreds of metres offshore, we could see a bright orange buoy on the surface, inching towards the shore. The crowd grew. We waited for over half an hour, mesmerized, along with everyone else, watching the slow progress of the buoy. Eventually we could see that the rope was hauling in a massive net full of fish. Near the shore, men in hip waders worked to keep the net closed until it was up on the sand. Others, on shore, spread out giant blue tarpaulins.

I looked around at the crowd. There were families—mothers and fathers and toddlers, mothers holding babies, women and teenagers setting up makeshift tables, several groups of schoolchildren and their teachers, a few tourists. One of the students, a boy of around twelve, looked like he had been assigned to be the class photographer, and he was taking his job very seriously, snapping pictures of every step of the process.

The excitement of the crowd was palpable as we waited to see the size of the catch. For Eric and me, it felt surreal, as if we had walked into an alternate world. We were absorbed into a family of strangers, a community of fishers, but no one seemed to notice we were there, or question whether we belonged. I wanted to capture everything with my camera, but I hadn't brought it with me. We would simply have to be present and watch, and then rely on our memories.

The net was pulled up onto the sand and several men guided it onto the blue tarp. One of the men in hip waders opened it up and the fish spilled out. There were thousands of fish, all flopping and jumping, their skin silver and shimmery in the sun. I could see sardines, fat and shiny, and mackerel with its bluish skin and dark zigzags, but there were so many other kinds of fish too. The schoolchildren asked their teachers to identify them, and I stood nearby, listening in. They called out sea bream, with its stubby body, and gurnard, a red fish with a shark-like spike on its back and spread fins that made it look like it could fly; there were cuttlefish, and more.

There must have been thirty people around the nets with specific jobs to do—three men on either side of the net, still in the water, with their hip waders on; two others sitting at the tractors, working the winches; women gathering buckets and filling them with sea water; toddlers running around; older children keeping track of the toddlers; and a half dozen others on their knees, getting on with their job of sorting the fish. By hand. One by one. Sardines in this bucket, mackerel in that one, sea bream in another. The mackerel were winning, or maybe they were losing because there were many mackerel, Spanish mackerel, almost too beautiful to think of cooking or eating.

There was the odd squid here and there, picked up quickly by a young girl standing guard. She would rinse it in the blue bucket, then place it gingerly in the small red one, which was two-thirds full of sea water. In the excitement, we watched as a fat sardine executed a perfect acrobatic flip and jetted out of the dark mass of fish to land on the sand. It turned over three or four times, showing us how willing it was to fight for its life. A young woman in her twenties, an observer like us, ran over to it, picked it up and ran to the shore and threw it back in the water. A small act of defiance for her, a new lease on life for the sardine.

I watched these fish, at first so full of life but later slowing their fight, their jumps not quite as high, their flops less energetic. Some had given up and lay on the sand, mouths gasping as if for air. Four sardines rested just beyond the blue tarp. The sorters seemed to not see them, or maybe it wasn't worth moving from their positions and their mechanical, precise movements to rescue the fish. Rescue seems an odd term, since they would be rescued only to be sorted and categorized, placed in the bucket, and sold to a customer waiting in line on the beach, or delivered to a restaurant to make their way onto the daily menu. Either way, they would end up on a plate.

I stepped away and noticed a young girl of fourteen or fifteen setting up a table away from the crowd, directly behind six baskets of different colours already spread out in a line. Each basket was full of a different kind of fish. She stood behind the table and sold to a few customers, then the crowd at her table grew. People handed her their bags and asked for fish by the kilo. Another girl next to her did the weighing and another took payment. It was fast and efficient.

I looked at Eric and noticed that his eyes were teary. Like the school photographer, I'd been concerned with mentally documenting the process, determined not to miss any of the steps. Eric had been observing quietly. He was holding on to Maggie's leash and keeping her under control. When I saw the look on his face, I was brought back to the significance of the moment. The whole process unfolding before us was both awesome and disturbing. So much fish, all for food. There was abundance and I hoped there wouldn't be waste.

"I think I'm ready to head back," Eric said. "Are you?"

"I am," I said, and we walked back side by side without saying much to each other, our footprints left behind in the sand.

Eric threw the frisbee and Maggie chased it and brought it back to us. Down the beach, we saw more tractors head out into the waves to meet two more boats. On shore, a different family gathered, a different community, but a similar routine.

This scene played out in my head a number of times, especially when I would sit at a restaurant and order sardines. I didn't do it lightly anymore. Eating fish now, any fish, but especially the sardine, felt like a sacred act.

. . . .

Adeus Costa da Caparica

IN THE LAST TWO WEEKS BEFORE WE LEFT COSTA, my energy
turned to packing, consolidating our belongings, and trying to use up
the food staples we had accumulated. I looked at the pile of things
we'd be giving away or leaving behind at the house—laptop tables for
our computers, hot water bottles, numerous pairs of thermal socks,
heavy sweaters we'd bought at the height of winter—and I felt a pang
of sadness. We had adjusted to life here, I thought to myself, and now
we were packing it up and moving on before any of us really wanted to.

Summer in Costa brought us a heat wave and an introduction to
beach season, the local beaches packed daily with umbrellas and
portable lounge chairs, soccer players, frisbee throwers, and sunbathers.
This meant that Maggie was no longer able to roam the sands as if
they belonged only to her, and she was not keen on sharing. She
chased runners and got her nose into a few too many picnic baskets.
After going in for a swim, she'd pick a nearby stranger and get very
close before giving herself a good shake to dry off her coat. To avoid
awkward moments or worse, we started taking her for her runs and
swims early in the morning or late in the evening.

One night, during a full moon, Eric and I went down to the beach with her at eleven o'clock. It had finally cooled enough for us to feel comfortable outside. There were a few people out but not many. Maggie ran and swam, and we waded in the water up to our knees. One wave caught me by surprise, and I got drenched. It didn't matter much; the air was warm, and I was dry by the time we got home around midnight. That late-night walk and the memory of the light of the moon twinkling on the water remains a highlight for me.

We had planned to leave Costa in the summer and head north where it would be cooler because we all claimed to dislike the heat. Yet now here we were, sorry to be leaving, and admitting that the sun and heat felt wonderful, and we wanted more of it. Couldn't we change our plans and stay longer?

The shift into summer had me reflecting on beach culture in Portugal. I loved the water around Costa because it was cold and clean, and I found it refreshing. There were days when the water was so clear that it felt like I could see right to the bottom of the ocean. I'd heard that the waves get bigger as you head up the coast, and the largest wave ever surfed was recorded near Nazaré a few months before we arrived. I am neither a surfer nor a thrill-seeker and thus found the waves near Costa big enough for me. As of the first of June, lifeguards staffed their observation towers, which added to my comfort level in the water.

The aspect of beach culture that I liked the most was that beach-goers wore whatever they wanted regardless of age, body type, or degree of muscle tone. One afternoon when Georgia and I were lying on the beach reading our books, I noticed that a woman next to us, perhaps in her mid-eighties, was lying topless, enjoying the sun. How great is that, I thought to myself. Farther down the beach, there was a family of five or so, with young children and teens and friends, both adults and kids. Some were topless, others not. Everyone looked relaxed except perhaps for Georgia and me, the two of us trying to fit in with this easygoing crowd but feeling less carefree than we would like.

I thought back to conversations I'd heard at home in Vancouver, also a beach town of sorts, about getting your body "bikini-ready" for the summer, a sentiment also conveyed on billboards and television advertisements. Things appeared to be different here. People seemed to go to the beach to have fun. I noticed that in groups of sunbathers, there were elderly people and forty-somethings and teens and toddlers all sitting together. And yes, I did see groups of just young people too, but I sensed more age diversity than I was accustomed to. Invariably, pick-up games of beach soccer would spring up here and there. I saw nine- and ten-year-olds playing with fifty- and sixty-year-olds and anyone in between.

We ate out more often as our supply of staples at home dwindled, but on our last weekend in Costa, I headed to the market for my last seafood purchase. I bought razor clams and littlenecks to make ameijoas à Bulhão Pato, and I made sure to thank the vendor for all her instructions and tips.

"You keep cooking our foods when you get back to Canada. And come back and visit us again soon," she said.

I bought more than usual, and she threw in extra. Back at home, we had a feast. Eric and I shared a bottle of Muralhas de Monção, a crisp green wine we'd loved since the first time we tried it at Zé's restaurant. The three of us lingered over lunch and relished the familiar and comforting aroma of freshly sautéed garlic emanating from the kitchen. Our conversation turned to what we would miss most about Costa. Our combined list was long: fries and beer at Café do Mar, the coffee, walking two minutes to the beach, walking for hours on golden sand, swimming in the waves, lazy mornings and breakfasts on the porch, the endless blue sky, hanging laundry on the line, my favourite fishmongers, the market women, the fruit stand at the bus stop, the bakery and the yummy bread.

Our list of what we wouldn't miss was shorter and surprisingly dog-centred: dog poop on the street, dogs barking all night long, stray dogs, aggressive dogs. I added sore feet from the long walks on cobblestone streets. And then we talked about the winter storms. The cold and relentless rain of the early days had drained our energy and our spirits, but in retrospect, the winter storms were an exciting part of our adventure, we agreed. It was as if time and sunshine had collaborated to erase those difficult days from our memory banks.

The next day I made my final trip to the market. I bought some fruit but mostly I went to say goodbye. I visited each of my favourite vendors and told them how much I had appreciated their friendly banter and all the cooking instructions and recipes. I told them that they had made my stay in Costa so much more pleasant and meaningful.

"Well, don't forget us," the verduras lady at the entrance said. A few of the women had gathered near that stall. They asked me where we were going on vacation, for how long, when we were going back to Canada, and when we'd come back to Costa. They asked me if I'd go back to serving raw spinach and eating Canadian-style. The woman who used to give me all the herbs waved goodbye and then crossed her arms at her chest before heading back to her stall. The woman beside her blew me a kiss. "Come back and visit," another woman said.

The man from the fruit stall rushed over and said, "Are you really leaving? I never asked my wife where my cousin lives. You can't come back tomorrow?"

"I'm sorry, I am really leaving. Today."

"Ai meu Deus," he said. And then in English, "Too bad."

I wanted to take pictures so I could remember these people's faces, but I was too shy. And somehow, it didn't feel right. Some things you just can't capture with a camera, shouldn't even try. I walked away, and headed towards the beach to take the long way home.

"Adeus," I called out. I looked back before I turned the corner and saw that everyone had gone back to their stalls. Their day would carry on as before.

As I neared our house, I saw that the next-door neighbour was out in her garden, so I stopped and asked how her dog had managed with the operation.

"Oh, Eli, she's recovering. Everything went so well. She's been spending time out in the yard already. Have you seen her? She's sleeping right now though. Such a sweet dog."

I told her that we were leaving in the afternoon, heading north on a vacation, and then going back to Canada from Lisbon.

"So, you won't be back here? That's a shame, and beach season is just starting," she said.

"I know, we all wish we could stay longer," I said.

By the time I opened our gate, I was ready to cry. Eric was stripping the beds in the house, and Georgia was sweeping the living room floor. She had brought out the cleaning bucket and supplies and had put them on the porch. I was about to reach for them and get started with cleaning, too, when I heard a car pull up. Helena and Odete had come to say goodbye.

We greeted each other in the front yard, and Eric and Georgia came out to join us. Eric had an armful of sheets that he was taking to the laundry shed at the back of the house.

"I hope you're not doing any cleaning," Helena said. "I told you that we've hired a cleaner to come in tomorrow, that you didn't have to do anything."

"Oh, I know, but we can't just walk away without tidying up and cleaning a little bit."

"No, no, no," she insisted. "Use your time to pack up your car and then just go. You don't want to be driving into the evening. You're supposed to be on vacation now, relaxing!"

"Okay," Eric said. "I just put this in wash machine." He spoke in broken English as if that would help them understand him better. He also used hand gestures, so they knew exactly what he was saying.

"Yes, yes, that's fine. We'll hang them up first thing tomorrow," they both said, almost in unison.

"Well, I guess we're almost ready to go then," I said. "We just need to finish packing up the car."

"Wait," Georgia said. "I need to say goodbye to Dave and Ingrid."

She went inside to get a bag of dog treats, then stood at the fence and slipped them a few treats through the slats. The dogs barked their excitement.

Helena took a handkerchief from her purse and dabbed her eyes.

"My goodness, I never dreamed that we would become friends like this. That I'd be so sad to see you go," she said.

It doesn't take much to get me to cry, but we were all teary as we hugged goodbye.

"We're going to see you in a month or so, right? For lunch? That'll be our real goodbye," I said.

After they left, we sat on the porch and ate sandwiches and fruit in the sun. A couple of hours later we were packed up and ready to go.

Eric drove the car out of the driveway, and I closed the gate one last time. As I got in the car, Georgia called out from the back seat, "Look! It's Reybeez!"

Little Eli was lying on a paving stone in the yard next door. She had a gauze bandage around her belly and a cone collar around her neck. She was napping in the sun.

. . . .

A Vacation in the North

WHEN WE WENT NORTH on our vacation, we spent much of our time
away from the coast and our food choices reflected the change in
landscape. As expected, we ate less fish. As we toured the mountains
of Peneda-Gerês National Park and Serra da Estrela and made our
way around the terraced vineyards of the Douro region, we feasted on
wild boar, stewed goat, and braised beans, all washed down with the
full-bodied, flavourful red wines of the region.

In Mirandela, a small city in the country's northeast, we stayed
at a bed and breakfast near the outskirts of town. The large heritage
house, owned by two sisters, was situated on a property dotted with
olive and walnut trees. It had two wide porches with comfy uphol-
stered chairs and a hanging hammock, a pool, and a patio with a
barbecue. The pool was especially appealing to me—the water so
clear, it beckoned.

Inside the house, the wood floors gleamed. There were lace
curtains on the windows, decorative washbasins, and dark, antique
furniture throughout. Our beds had embroidered (and ironed!) sheets
and pillowcases. It seemed the perfect place to rest awhile. We'd been
on the road for a couple of weeks already, never staying more than

one or two nights in one place, and we were tired of moving around. We wanted to relax here for a few days, but I wondered about Maggie staying in such an elegant place.

One of the owners assured us that they loved dogs and were happy to welcome ours. In fact, they had two dogs of their own, she said. There were numerous walking trails nearby, and also the river, a perfect spot for Maggie to swim. Indeed, that became our favourite spot. Maggie spent hours swimming and chasing sticks in the current and the three of us took turns on the shore, throwing sticks, while the others sat in the shade and read, napped, or daydreamed.

From what I could tell at the breakfast table, there were two other families staying at the house—one family of four from Porto and a family of three from Lisbon, the children all roughly the same age as Georgia. Eric and I often got into conversations with Graça and Rosário, the owners, and we lingered the longest at breakfast. They practised their English, and when we resorted to speaking in Portuguese, I practised the art of simultaneous translation.

We learned that Graça was a teacher in Mirandela and also ran the bed and breakfast, while Rosário lived full time in Porto but spent the summers here at the house. Their land was vast and lush, with fruit trees, a vineyard, and a magnificent garden. Graça was experimenting with making candied walnuts and had us sample some before she decided whether she would sell them at the market. She also made soap and offered Georgia two lavender-scented, heart-shaped bars. Georgia kept those as souvenirs until the smell grew faint and she decided it was best to use them, but she had trouble letting go of her keepsakes.

Graça also wanted to give us a two-litre jug of their olive oil, but we wouldn't be able to bring that back to Canada on the plane. We were limited to 100-millilitre bottles of liquid in our carry-on baggage, and I wasn't sure I wanted to put a large bottle of oil in my checked luggage. I had visions of an oily mess when I opened my suitcase back in Vancouver.

"I'll wrap it really well," Graça said.

"I think I'd just rather come back sometime and enjoy it here," I said.

"I hope you come back," she said.

It had only been a few days, but I sensed that if I lived here, these women could be my friends. As if reading my mind, Rosário announced that she was putting on a dinner for all the guests that evening. She slammed her hands on the table as she got up and said, "Do you like sardines? I'm going to order some now from Porto. Let's gather by the pool for dinner, shall we?"

"Oh, that sounds so nice. What can we bring?" I asked.

"We have everything we need right here. Except the sardines, and I'm picking those up. Just bring yourselves."

I looked around at their land. There were mature olive trees, as well as fig, walnut, and a variety of other fruit trees. There were grape vines near the pool and off into the distance. Their vegetable garden was lush with lettuce and other greens and teeming with bright red tomatoes. I spotted several lemon trees too, their branches hanging heavy with large fruit ready for picking. I tried to imagine what I could go and buy from the supermarket in Mirandela to add to the feast, but I couldn't think of anything.

When Georgia asked later, "What time is dinner?" I realized I had no idea. Around five or six o'clock, we began keeping watch from the porch to see when the others would gather by the pool area. At dusk, I saw one of the guests head over there with a bucket full of potatoes. Behind her, Eva, another of the guests, brought a folding chair and sat down with the bucket at her feet and started peeling the potatoes— the peels falling to her left, the potatoes into a large pot of water her husband had placed to her right. Graça wheeled out two barrels that looked like homemade barbecues and started laying wood in each one. I realized then that we were still a long way off from dinnertime, but we should make our way down to help with the preparations.

Near the pool, there was a small stone building that I had seen earlier, but assumed it was a storage shed for the pool equipment. I could not have been more wrong. It was a cottage, complete with a beautiful rustic kitchen and pantry. There was a large fireplace and an old farmhouse table with wooden chairs. Pots and pans were stacked on shelves along the walls and bunches of dried herbs and chili peppers hung from the rafters. Strings of lights brightened the counters and wash basin. The doors to the cupboards were open and I could see they were filled with jars and jugs. Olive oil? Jam? I wanted to explore, but this was not the time. Instead, I stood there with my mouth wide open. I was in awe, but I hoped it wasn't noticeable.

Georgia came up to me and whispered, "This is so perfect! I'd love to live in a place like this."

Graça brought in a large bowl full of lettuce from the garden and another with arugula that grew wild on the property. It became my job to turn that into a salad. Georgia was given a cutting board, a knife, and a handful of large cucumbers, Eric another knife and a bag of tomatoes. One of the men told him to slice the tomatoes, just so. Someone was slicing the broa, corn bread, and someone else was cutting up local sausage to have with the bread for an appetizer. Within a few minutes, we were all working, taking breaks to snack on olives, sausage, and bread. The family from Lisbon had brought two bottles of wine from their region, and there was also a large jug of homemade wine. We sipped and chatted.

Rosário arrived, carrying a bucket of red and green peppers in one hand and a Styrofoam cooler in the other, and everyone clapped. She placed the containers on the ground near the barbecue, and we all gathered round to watch her open the cooler. When she removed the top and revealed the sardines layered on beds of coarse salt, there was a chorus of "ooh" and people smacked their lips and rubbed the palms of their hands together. I thought back to the sardines jumping and flopping on the blue tarp on the beach in Costa. The life had long gone out of these fish, yet their skin still glistened as they lay there, motionless. The strong smell of the sea wafted in the air, suspended around the cooler.

One of the guests gathered eucalyptus branches and threw them in the fire. The peppers were placed on the grill first, and once they were done, it was time for the fish. The pot for the potatoes had been placed on an outdoor propane burner and the water was already boiling.

Rosário set the long table under the canopy of grape vines. She laid out an embroidered tablecloth and lit a long row of candles in jars down the centre of the table. Once all the dishes were out and people placed their glasses near their plates, we all stood around the table marvelling at how beautiful it looked. The air was warm and summery but not stifling, and the cicadas and crickets filled the darkness beyond our enclave with the sounds of the night. I hadn't started my dinner yet, but the evening already felt perfect to me.

When all the food was ready, I dished out my plate and thought it looked like a work of art. There were perfectly boiled potatoes topped with a sprig of parsley, a mound of colourful salad, a heap of grilled peppers, both red and green, and a beautiful, plump sardine with charred streaks across its belly. I sat down at the table and took in the salty, fishy aroma, feeling a rush of gratitude. I split my fish open, removed the small sacs of innards and set them aside. Then I used my fork to hold the fish near the head end, and with my knife, I lifted the backbone and ran my knife to the tail, slowly and deliberately lifting it and separating it from the fish. I pushed the discarded bits to one end of my plate and got ready for the first bite. It was a perfect blend of crunchy, salty skin and rich, buttery meat. I closed my eyes, hoping to make that moment last a little longer.

Eric nudged my elbow and said, "I'm making a mess here, how did you do that?" Then Georgia, sitting across from me, followed that with, "Are these hair-like things bones and can I eat them?" I didn't have to answer—others sitting nearby took great pleasure in explaining how to eat the sardine without mangling its flesh and diminishing its flavour. Georgia smiled, proud of her accomplishment, and I was relieved that she seemed to like the fish. I took another sardine from the platter and shared it with Eric. This amused the others and we, the Canadians, were dubbed the light eaters.

For dessert, there were big slabs of smoked cheese and tomato jam. I never would have imagined pairing these two flavours, but the result was delightful. Eric and I turned down the after-dinner cafézinho but filled our cups with chamomile tea that had been made, no doubt, with herbs from the property. I looked at my watch and wondered how anyone could have coffee at this hour. How would they get to sleep?

We'd been together for several hours and dinner wasn't over yet. The port was still to come.

Maggie was sitting up in the room when we got back. She must have heard us coming. Her tail was wagging back and forth, sweeping the floor from side to side. She was ready for a walk. We took her out for a short stroll, but then kept walking. The night was still and warm and we'd been sitting for so long that it felt good to be up and moving. We could hear the soft din of voices still gathered by the pool. We walked much longer than we'd intended, through the town and to the river. By the time we got back, the pool party had wrapped up, and it looked as if most people were asleep. All the lights in the house were off.

Georgia was exhausted, she said, and got into her bed. Eric and I slipped between our embroidered sheets, and we both sighed the relief that comes with finally lying down after a long day. Within seconds I could hear Eric's breathing change into soft, rhythmic snoring. I turned over and listened for the crickets and cicadas, still chatting to each other in the otherwise quiet night.

My reverie ended abruptly the next morning when I woke up feeling a strange need to contact Matt. There was no internet coverage in this area, and it had been a few days since we'd been in touch. We were supposed to be meeting him in Porto the next day, when he would be flying back from Helsinki, marking the end of his solo trip. We were going to spend a few days in Porto together, then head back to Lisbon for our last week in Portugal.

"I feel like something's wrong," I told Eric, "And I really want to try to reach him."

"You often get that sense, Es, and everything turns out fine." Eric was trying to comfort me, but it had the opposite effect. When he added, "Remember the natron?" I got mad.

I grabbed the car keys and said, "I'm going into town to a café. I'll see you later."

Georgia said, "Wait, I want to come with you," and then Eric tried to reason with me.

"Look, we're about to check out, let's pack up and do that and then we can stop in at a café on our way out of town."

It made sense, so I waited until we were ready to leave. It had been an idyllic stay in so many ways, but the last few hours were agonizing for me. I felt unsettled at breakfast and tried to explain to the others, the people we'd had dinner with the night before. They seemed to understand. Rosário said, "It's so hard when they feel the need to go on their own adventures, isn't it?"

When we settled into a café in town and I logged on to my Facebook account, there were at least a half dozen messages from Matt. "Where are you? I'm stuck in Helsinki!"

I tried calling him on Messenger, but the internet connection was terrible. We were still feeling full from breakfast, but we had to keep ordering coffee and pastries from the café. We sat there for at least an hour before I was able to talk to Matt and figure out what was happening. His flight from Helsinki had been cancelled, and the agent had told him that a refund would be issued but not for another ten days. He had been re-booked on a flight to Barcelona (via Riga) that didn't leave until the next morning, and he couldn't find a connecting flight to Porto.

"It's really hard on this old phone of yours. Can you find me a flight? A cheap one!"

I gave Eric one of those knowing looks that says I'm often right when it comes to sensing that something's up with my children. Except for that time with the natron. I felt smug satisfaction on the one hand, but also sheer panic on the other. It is complicated to make travel arrangements for someone else, especially when they're in a different country and communication is difficult.

Eventually, I was able to book Matt on a discount flight out of Barcelona to Porto. We paid for the ticket, and he assured us he'd pay us back. The issue was resolved except that I was concerned that Matt would be hanging around the Helsinki airport for twenty hours, then flying to Barcelona, spending the day there, and then finally flying to Porto. I knew he'd be exhausted, and this would be a disappointing end to his trip. Worse than that, I imagined he'd miss a flight and we'd be going through this frantic scenario again.

Matt said he'd be fine; Eric said Matt would be fine; and Georgia said that Matt would figure out a way to be fine. But I worried. I know what it's like to try to sleep in airport lounges.

We had a quiet drive to Porto, and I was still feeling uneasy. It took a long time to find our rental apartment. It was nestled behind an industrial complex, and we passed it a number of times before we realized it was there. We'd be staying for close to a week, so we found a supermarket and loaded up on groceries. We were all exhausted, more emotionally drained than anything else, and opted for scrambled eggs and a salad for dinner. We watched the World Cup Final on television but much of the game didn't register with us. My mind was on Matt, who was probably pacing back and forth at the Helsinki airport. Or maybe he'd found a television and was also watching the game. Did he have enough money to even eat dinner? I mulled over a few scenarios in my head, and then I knew what I needed to do. At about eleven o'clock, I contacted one of the hotels at the Helsinki airport, explained the situation and paid for a one-night stay for Matt. Then I contacted Matt and let him know what I'd done.

"I'll pay you back for everything," Matt said when we picked him up at the Porto airport the next night.

"The hotel is on us," I told him. "I'm glad we sorted it out and you got some rest."

"I'm glad too. Thanks. And I got to see Barcelona! It was amazing." Then he added, "Too bad you didn't think of the hotel thing a little earlier. I could have used more than five hours of sleep."

. . . .

Goodbye Lisbon

MAGGIE HAD NOT BEEN GROOMED in nearly a year. We'd been careful to clip her nails and brush her coat often but with all the swimming, she was sporting a few tangles and mats. She was starting to look like Beck, our friend Pedro's dog. The two of them played together occasionally, and I credit Beck with teaching Maggie to swim in the ocean even when there were good-sized waves. Although they were the same breed, Maggie was like the tentative, quiet child, and Beck was the wild guy, the daredevil. The first time they got together at the beach near Costa, Maggie seemed hesitant to go in the water, and she watched Beck attentively. Beck jumped into the waves and swam, just as his ancestors were bred to do. By the end of the outing, Maggie was also tackling the waves with abandon.

The coat of a Portuguese water dog is composed of hair, not fur, thus the need to have it cut regularly. When we were weighing the pros and cons of the breed, we noted this as a disadvantage because of the cost of grooming that would be required. But it was also an advantage because it means that they do not shed and are considered hypoallergenic. None of us is allergic to dogs but we were highly attracted to the no-shedding idea.

Pedro made it sound like it was easy to groom a dog yourself, but one look at Beck and it was clear that his "haircuts" were pretty infrequent. After some encouragement from Pedro, I tried to groom Maggie, but she squirmed and wiggled, and I found it stressful, so I gave up. We'd take her to the groomer when we got back to Vancouver, we all agreed. But the summer in Portugal was hot and she panted heavily. I reasoned to myself that the fishers of long ago who worked with Portuguese water dogs on the fishing boats were probably not sending their dogs to the groomer every three months. She would survive.

While we'd been on vacation up north, Maggie had gone for daily swims in rivers or in the ocean. But now that we were back in Lisbon, opportunities for swimming were hard to come by. We'd sold our car back to our landlord's brother, the mechanic, figuring we wouldn't need it while we were staying in Lisbon for that last week or so. We were staying in Joe John's friend's rental apartment, a couple of metro stops away from the city centre, but with dogs not allowed on the metro or on buses, Maggie's walks were limited to the immediate neighbourhood for the rest of our stay.

Eric and I were relishing the city life. Every morning, while Matt and Georgia slept in, we slipped out and went across the street to the café for our usual coffee and pastel de nata combo. It only took a few minutes—we stood at the counter and sipped—but each day we'd have a brief chat with the proprietor, and after a while we knew a lot about each other!

After our coffee it would be time to take Maggie for her morning walk. We'd often lead her to the university grounds nearby, where even in the summer, large groups of students congregated, either sitting on the lawn or leaning against the cement fence bordering the campus. Many of them were smoking. I tried to think back to when I last saw a group of people openly smoking in Vancouver. I couldn't remember.

As our departure date neared, I found myself feeling irritable. Was I stressed about making yet another big move? Perhaps. But if

I allowed myself to think about it for long, I realized that I was not ready to return to Vancouver. I was already looking ahead to the fall and dreading the arrival of the rainy season. I had hoped that after living in Portugal for all this time, and with all the challenges, I would be ready to leave, to return to my normal Canadian life. But I hadn't reached that point. We had survived the challenges and learned to adapt, and I was prepared to settle in for the long haul.

"I feel the same way," Eric said to me during one of our talks over morning coffee. "But it's also good that we're leaving before we're dying to go, isn't it? That way we'll want to come back."

That was one way of looking at it. And there was a part of me that was looking forward to being back in Vancouver. I missed my friends and my extended family—my sister, my nieces, and their families. But I could also easily see myself staying here long-term. I wanted to go, but also, I didn't. The tension made me uneasy.

In our last few days in Lisbon, temperatures neared 40 degrees Celsius. This made me long for the cooler summers of Vancouver and our shady neighbourhood near the woods. Maybe I was looking forward to going home after all.

We talked about buying souvenirs, eating this or that for the last time, packing our bags, weight limits, and carry-on luggage. We would be flying home via Amsterdam, and after a few days of rest there, back to Vancouver. The children and I would fly together via Toronto, and Eric and Maggie would be on a separate, direct flight again.

We grew increasingly concerned about the heat. What if Maggie was left for a long time on a cart on the tarmac as she waited to board? It would not take long for her to get dehydrated. We decided she needed a haircut. As if by sheer serendipity, Eric and I were talking about exactly this on one of our morning walks when we passed a dog grooming salon. I walked in and spoke to the groomer, asked her if she would be willing to take Maggie. She hesitated at first, and gave me the familiar line that Maggie was larger than the dogs she was used to, but sure, she'd give it a try. We made an appointment for the day before our departure.

The next morning, a Sunday, we walked into the centre of town early in the morning to take pictures. We wanted photographs of the streets and plazas before the cafés opened and the patios filled with people. And I wanted one last picture of me sitting next to the bronze statue of Fernando Pessoa. This would complete my photo album of different poses with Fernando and would, for the first time, include Maggie. Matt had stayed in bed, unable to get up before seven, so it was just the three of us and our dog.

The city centre was deserted and Lisbon looked totally different—quiet and almost sombre, as if it too were bidding us goodbye. The cobblestones were glistening from the overnight rain, and the sun was already shining, warming the streets and patios and riverside benches. We walked familiar routes and looked at doorways and verandahs as if for the first time. The city was on display for us, and we were spending time alone together, like lovers getting ready to part.

Given that there was no one around, Georgia also posed for a few photographs, and I was struck by the reality that this was it. Even Georgia was going beyond her comfort zone in order to capture a few moments with a camera. These photos would become our treasured souvenirs. Now when we look at them, we marvel at how Lisbon was all ours that morning. We hadn't planned it that way, but that outing became our personal and private goodbye.

As the day warmed, people emerged from shuttered buildings. Proprietors rolled up the metal screens and opened iron gates, set out tables and chairs on patios, and hosed down the pavement. We could hear clanging dishes in the coffee shops, staff gathering their stash of cups and saucers before the rush began. We peeked inside a café and saw servers cleaning out the coffee machines, one banging the porta-filter on the edge of a container to release the last bit of yesterday's coffee grounds from the basket. Another tested the steamer, then wiped the counter. The smell of coffee wafted out to the street. The day could officially begin now.

Street cleaners were out in force, cleaning up the litter left behind by the Saturday night crowd. Some picked up the larger bits of trash with long tongs, others swept the small bits into long-handled dust pans. Occasionally one would meet our glance and nod in greeting, then follow us with his eyes as if to ask, why are you out here so early? And I would feel like telling them that this was it for us, that we were leaving, going away for a very long time, saying goodbye to this beautiful city, but I said nothing.

Maggie kept her nose close to the ground and delighted in the smells compressed between the cobblestones. We had to tug at her leash to keep her moving.

"Let's climb up to that viewpoint and look at the castle," Eric said.

"I'd like to go down to the river one last time; can we do that?" Georgia said.

We covered a lot of ground.

· · ·

Any nostalgia I was feeling about leaving evaporated the next day when we dropped Maggie off at the groomer.

"I told you I haven't groomed one of these dogs before, right?" the groomer said to me.

"You did. But you know what they're supposed to look like, right? We would just like her coat trimmed so she's not so shaggy. We're mostly concerned about the heat," I said. And then I added, "Are you still willing to do it?"

"Oh yes. Leave her here for a couple of hours. Do you have any special instructions?"

I don't know what made me say it, but I did. I blurted out, "Yes. Please don't hit our dog."

I had seen enough people smack their dogs that I wondered if it was just more acceptable here for some reason, so I decided to say it.

"Well, I will if she bites me."

That was her response. I couldn't believe it. She was not reassuring at all.

"Our dog doesn't bite! Why would you think she would bite you?"

"Then there won't be a problem, will there?"

I hadn't translated any of this for Eric when we were inside the salon, but as soon as we stepped outside, I burst into tears.

"Eric, I can't do it. I can't leave her here."

We tossed around a few options and ended up leaving Maggie there, thinking it important that she get a haircut before the two flights back home.

"Besides, there's no way she'll bite, so we don't have to worry," Eric said.

I was anxious for the entire time she was there. We walked around, went for coffee, browsed in a bookstore, walked some more, and had another coffee. I felt glad that Matt and Georgia were doing their own thing and hadn't witnessed the exchange with the groomer. Eric and I were both filled with dread as we walked back to pick up Maggie at the appointed time. I felt that if anyone were watching us, they'd notice our slumped shoulders.

Maggie was eager to join us and jumped over the counter as soon as we walked in. I let out a loud gasp, then Eric and I both broke into laughter. What had the groomer done?

It was clear to me that she'd been afraid of Maggie because our dog's face looked like it had a halo around it. Her hair was clean and fluffy and framed her face in a near-perfect circle. I don't think the hair on Maggie's head had been cut at all, just washed and blown dry. Her body, on the other hand, had been shaved, as if she were a poodle. Her tail had also been shaved, but there was a tuft on the end. Poor

Maggie. She looked like a rat but with a disproportionately fuzzy head. It was an awful cut.

Back at home, Matt and Georgia could not contain their laughter.

"Oh no," Georgia cried out. "She looks like a flower. And not in a nice way."

"Aw, man," Matt said. "She looks terrible."

Why had we let this happen?

It was important to the young ones that Maggie look good, I think. But even I was now regretting the last-minute grooming. I was comforted only by the fact that we thought we were doing what was best for her.

Maggie survived the ordeal of the flights, the heat, and her coat grew back. Once we all arrived in Vancouver, though, I swore I'd never put her through that kind of stress again. I didn't tell anyone, but I promised myself that we wouldn't be going to live anywhere for an extended period again, not if Maggie had to fly there in the cargo hold of an airplane.

After the grooming, Maggie hunkered down on her dog bed and fell asleep right away. I imagine the stress had been exhausting. We left her in the apartment and headed into the city centre and across the river to Cabrinha for lunch, our last meal there with our now-former landlord and his family. By the time we arrived, Helena, Rita, and Odete were already waiting for us. The restaurant was bustling. Zé was flitting from table to table checking on diners, shaking hands with a few, opening a bottle of wine at one table, collecting a bread-basket from another. He came to greet us at the door and ushered us to the family table. As soon as we sat down, one waiter brought bread, another brought the cheese and olives, and still another delivered a platter of cold cuts, each greeting Helena, showing deference to her as the proprietor's wife. To each one, she explained who we were, and they nodded in greeting. She spoke to one waiter and ordered, I assumed, then asked what kind of wine we would like and what the children would like to drink.

"This is our treat," she said. "If you don't mind, I'd like to do the ordering. If I miss something you really like, you'll let me know, won't you?"

She remembered that the mixed seafood rice was our favourite dish and ordered that, but also a large platter of seafood, almost too beautiful to eat. There were crab legs and lobster tails and massive prawns and squid rings. Our eyes widened at the abundance but also the variety.

Georgia was happy with the rice dish, relieved that there were chunks of fish in there that she liked. As always, her main focus was the bread, which she slathered with butter.

I was enjoying the food, but I had also flexed into simultaneous translation mode again, making sure that Eric and the kids didn't feel left out of the conversation. I made sure I conveyed to our hosts how much we all appreciated this lunch and their generous hospitality throughout our entire stay.

Helena looked at Eric but spoke to me in Portuguese, asking, "What do you think you would like for the meat dish, some lamb?"

I didn't even translate that; I took the liberty of speaking for Eric, for everyone, when I said that we were all full, we couldn't eat anything else. I knew that Matt especially would enjoy the lamb, but we had hardly made a dent in the food that was already on the table.

"Oh my goodness," Helena said. "I forgot how little your family eats. There's so much still here but don't worry, it won't go to waste, I'll take the leftovers home and we'll have them for dinner."

Over coffee, she turned to me and said, "I'd like you to translate this to your family." Then she gave a little speech and told us how much they had enjoyed meeting us and getting to know us, how we'd become friends in such a short period of time. As she spoke, Odete looked down to her lap and folded her napkin over, then again. I bit my lower lip. I tried to translate but I couldn't do it without tears.

Helena wiped tears from her cheek and said, "Anytime you come back, you will always be welcome in our home."

We spent the evening packing. As I rolled up my T-shirts and crammed them in like sardines in a can, I thought back to our lunch earlier in the day, and how hard it had been to say goodbye to our landlord's family. We had made a connection with them that I knew would last for a long time. It had developed slowly but over the course of our stay, they had become like family to us. I knew they had impacted us—the kindness they'd shown helped us to feel settled in a strange, new place. But I'd had no idea that they felt that we were also friends of theirs.

I remembered our first few weeks in Costa and the loneliness in our days. We'd met our landlord by chance. I say by chance because I'd somehow picked their house out of a list of places to live, and we had initiated a business relationship. Slowly though, we developed a friendship, and now I was having a hard time accepting that it was goodbye. I didn't know when we'd be able to come back, and when we did, everything would be different. This experience would never be replicated. This was a definite ending, and as I've learned, I'm not good with endings.

We packed our suitcases. I am a roller, and Eric is a folder. Every single shirt of his was folded neatly and stacked one on top of the other. Georgia relied on a combination of rolling and folding. Matt ruminated on the best approach, tossed around options, and tried different things. I was most concerned that even when I went to bed, his suitcase was still empty, and his belongings lay in heaps. He'd figure it out, I hoped, but it didn't make for a good night's sleep for me. I did not want to be rushing around in the morning, collecting things and stuffing them in different bags. If we did that, we'd inevitably leave something behind.

The next morning, the first thing I did was survey the living room and look for stray clothes, books, and paraphernalia. Everyone's suitcase was closed and standing on end, ready to be rolled out to the elevator.

Joe John drove up to our door and laid on the horn—three beeps, the last one a little longer than the first two. He seemed surprised that we were already in the lobby, waiting for him. He greeted us and grabbed the first of the luggage. He took one look at Maggie and said, "What happened here?" Then, he let out a laugh. "She looks ridiculous."

His grin was wide, and his eyes were smiling along with the rest of him. I remembered that brilliant blue from the first time we met him, all those months ago.

"Yeah, well, it was a bit of a mistake," I said.

"Next time, take her to a proper groomer, will you?"

We sped along the morning streets of Lisbon in his shiny, black suv. I know he was talking but I wasn't paying attention, none of us were. We were all looking out the window, at everything for one last time.

Joe John dropped us off at the entrance to the departure terminal of the Lisbon airport. When our luggage was all together on the sidewalk, it looked like a mountain. Joe John gave us each a big hug, then shook Eric's hand, and mine. He held mine a little longer and looked at me, not smiling for once, and said, "You will come back soon, right?"

After the lineups at the check-in counter, then security and passport control, we were on the other side. For me, it felt like a strange, limbo-like state between Portugal and Canada. I stepped onto the plane, on that first flight from Lisbon to Amsterdam, and it hit me— we were really leaving. I settled into my seat and put my seatbelt on, my mind already whirring with plans and dreams for the next time. I knew I wouldn't be able to stay away for long. Our plane had yet to leave the ground, but I already knew we'd be back.

· · · ·

Back in Vancouver

I STOOD IN MY FRONT GARDEN and looked around. It was one of those glorious late-summer days in Vancouver—sunny, hot but not too hot, with a slight breeze blowing in from the ocean. I was glad we had returned in time to enjoy the last few weeks of the season.

Right now, I was feeling smothered by green; the bushes were overgrown and wild-looking and formed an archway above my head. Those would need a good pruning, even before the fall, I thought to myself. Some of the weeds were knee-high. Oh, there was a lot of work to do. Out on the boulevard the grass was a yellowy-brown. It looked tired and weary, indicating that the last few months had been hot and dry. If it could talk it would be begging me to make it rain.

All the boxes we'd packed and left in our garage were now piled at the front door. Eric and I opened one and put everything away before we opened the next one. I'd forgotten all we had packed even though the labels gave us a few hints: *Dishes, Clothes, Pots and Pans*. We had a lot of stuff, and we had survived nearly a year without it.

Georgia and Matt ran off to their bedrooms, where they stayed for hours, opening their boxes and filing memories and knick-knacks. I unpacked our good china, which I save for special occasions like birthdays and Christmas, and I looked forward to having friends and family over for dinner again. I unwrapped my favourite coffee mugs and ceramic bowls and platters, which I'd put away so I wouldn't come back to find them chipped and cracked. I was most excited to unpack my wok, which I had really missed. Whenever I was at a loss for what to cook in Costa, all I could come up with was vegetable stir-fry, but I had lamented not having a wok. A stir-fry is almost impossible to make in a frying pan. I found that I'd packed two juicers, four cheese graters, and two zesters. I'd left just one of everything for our renters. I made a mental note to devote some time to culling the extras. I was very happy to see my copper cataplana again. Now I could make pork and clams, Alentejo-style, in the proper vessel.

Among the still unopened boxes were three filled with books that I had shipped from Portugal. I opened the first box and felt a twinge of sadness. I was excited to have Portuguese books to read, but I knew that once we settled in our home again, I'd go back to reading mostly in English. It feels easier to read in Portuguese while in Portugal. I thought back to when I had bought and shipped those books. It felt like one way of sending some of my Portuguese life back to Canada. I think it eased the leave-taking.

So much about my life, it seems, has been focused on leaving. As a child immigrant, I absorbed the unspoken refrain of "you leave, you feel sad," which formed the basis of my saudade. I took pride in my nostalgia for my homeland and wore it as if it were a mark of my Portuguese identity. It was the one thing that connected me to the rest of the diaspora—we had all left, and we all longed to return. But now here I was, feeling happy to be back in my home in Canada.

My joy at returning to Vancouver confused me. I did not want to turn my back on Portugal, or to give up my longing to return, but I also wanted to enjoy this moment. I was looking forward to the weeks ahead, to all the gardening and cleaning outside, and the culling and organizing inside. I wanted to put energy into settling into my house again.

Eric went to the kitchen to make lunch, and I sat on the front stoop for a minute before I opened the next box. The remaining boxes were labelled *Clothes*, and I was not looking forward to unpacking winter coats and heavy sweaters. I rested my elbows on my knees and held my head in my hands. I thought back to the memories this house now holds. This has been home for me for my entire married life. What a contrast to the number of times I'd moved before I met Eric. We laughed one day when he said he could count the number of houses he'd lived in on one hand, and I said that would only cover my first year in Canada.

But this house. This was where I'd brought my children home when they were born, where they'd been toddlers and young explorers digging holes in the yard and turning over every rock in the garden. This is where they had their sandbox, and where we set up our tent to listen to the wildlife come alive at night—the owls, the raccoons and coyotes, and the chorus of tree frogs in the spring. This is where, during the day, we listened to the woodpeckers drumming on the metal tops of chimneys and telephone poles in the back lane and watched for bald eagles and great blue herons high above us in the summer sky. In this house, I'd watched my parents shuck corn and top green beans on the deck and sip their coffee and tea in the sun. This was the place of children's birthday parties, large and loud family gatherings, even arguments and the odd shouting match. There was so much history here, I wondered how I could ever think of some-where else as home.

The next morning when I set up my computer in my writing space again, I longed for the French doors of the house in Costa that I could open to the salty air. I missed the roar of the ocean, even the sound of vehicles making their way over the cobblestone street. I logged on to my email to find a message from my cousin Emanuel in São Miguel. I'd met up with him in Lisbon at Easter and we'd reconnected after many years. In his message, he explained that since we'd met, he'd been thinking that we should organize a family reunion. He'd already contacted cousins in Norway and France and Brazil and Canada and the United States and told them he was planning a gathering. "I've set a tentative date for next July," he said. "Will you come?"

I replied right away, before I had time to think about all the implications, and I said, "Of course. We'll be there."

I had just finished unpacking in Vancouver, but I was already making plans to return to Portugal. And that is the essence of my saudade—one of many leavings, but also, always, of returnings.

. . . .

Recipes

FOOD PLAYS A BIG ROLE IN PORTUGUESE CULTURE. We can sit
around a table and eat and tell stories for hours. During our stay in
Costa da Caparica, food—selecting it, cooking it, and eating it—
became a significant part of our days. Cooking helped me, in
particular, feel more connected to my surroundings. I'm grateful to
family and friends who shared meal ideas and recipes with me. I've
included some of my favourites here.

WINTER
Walnut Cake (Bolo de Noz)
From the kitchen of Helena Cabral

Helena's walnut cake is hearty and nutritious and it hit the spot on that
first night in Costa. This is a treasured family recipe that has been
handed down through several generations. I've translated it here, and
as far as I know, this is the first time it has been written down in English!

   150 g white granulated sugar
   150 g margarine (I used butter)

150 g enriched white flour

3 eggs

1 tsp baking powder

125 g walnuts, coarsely chopped

1 shot of port wine (about 90 ml)

Walnut halves and caramel (for toppings)

Cream butter and sugar together until well blended and fluffy. Add eggs one at a time, beating well after each addition. In a separate bowl, mix flour and baking powder, then add to creamed mixture. Add port and chopped walnuts.

Pour mixture in greased cake pan and bake in a medium oven for about 50 minutes.

Remove from oven and let cool. Remove from pan and top with halved walnuts. Drizzle caramel over the top.

Seafood Rice Casserole (Arroz de Marisco)

From my sister Toni's kitchen

Serves 4

There is no doubt that my sister Toni loves to cook. She is a former importer and fishmonger and particularly enjoys cooking Portuguese dishes in which fish and seafood take centre stage. As the matriarch of our extended family, Toni is proud to serve traditional dishes and says that everything tastes better when prepared with love and care. This soupy rice casserole is a family favourite. We had it many times in Portugal. Chefs use whatever seafood is at hand.

500 g Manila clams

1 kg wild shrimp (or prawns)

2 lobster tails, about 100–140 g each (or substitute 500 g of
   monkfish)
6 cloves of garlic (2 whole, and 4 chopped fine)
1/3 cup olive oil
1 onion, chopped fine
3 tbsp tomato paste
300 g short-grain rice
1/3 cup dry white wine
1/4 cup cilantro leaves
1 lemon, wedged, for garnish

Rinse the clams, place in a bowl and cover with cold water and about a tablespoon of salt. Refrigerate for two or three hours. This helps draw out any sand still left inside the clams. When you are ready to start cooking, drain the clams and rinse until water runs clear.

Divide the kilo of raw shrimp into two equal parts. Set one aside and cook the other in plenty of water, approximately 10 cups, with a tablespoon or two of salt and the two whole cloves of garlic. Cook until shrimp float, about five minutes. Drain and reserve about six cups of the cooking liquid. Rinse the cooked shrimp in cold water. Remove the heads and discard, then peel the shrimp and set aside.

Cut lobster tails in half length-wise and remove meat. Cut in small pieces, about 2.5 cm, and set aside.

Wash rice and set aside.

Sauté onion in olive oil until soft and translucent. Add remaining garlic and sauté for one minute. Add tomato paste and stir. Add rice and stir, then add wine. Add enough of the reserved liquid to cover the rice and stir until rice absorbs the liquid. Keep adding more reserved liquid until rice is nearly cooked and you've used the six cups. Add raw lobster pieces, raw shrimp, and the peeled, cooked shrimp. Stir for two to three minutes. Add clams. Stir and cover. Cook for no more than five minutes.

Remove from heat and discard any clams that did not open. Garnish with cilantro and lemon wedges and serve immediately.

Salt Cod with Creamy Eggs (Bacalhau à Brás)

From the kitchen of Odete Roque
Serves 4 (or 1 Matt and 2 Georgias)

Bacalhau à Brás became a favourite of ours during our time in Costa. Odete kindly provided me with a recipe but did not include quantities for any of the ingredients. How much cod? I asked. And how many eggs? How many potatoes? Everything is "a olho," she replied, meaning put in however much you want. I've now tried this dish many times and it is hard to go wrong, but I still like to measure things out. This is Odete's recipe, with amounts of ingredients filled in by me to get you started. Feel free to experiment.

600–700 g salt cod
1 kg potatoes, peeled and thinly julienned*
3 tbsp olive oil (Odete recommends a "healthy" amount of olive oil)
1 onion, diced
1 tsp coarsely ground black pepper
1 bay leaf
3 cloves of garlic, crushed
5 large eggs
1/4 cup chopped parsley
About a dozen black olives (I use Kalamata)

In Portugal, you can buy potatoes already julienned and fried. They look almost like thin potato chips. In Vancouver, I make my own fries, which adds time and complexity, but I've also baked packaged fries and that works too.

Soak the salt cod for at least 24 hours, changing the water once or twice. Drain.

Place cod pieces in a shallow frying pan and cover with cold water. Bring to a boil, then simmer on low until the fish is opaque, about 10 minutes. Drain and let cool. Break up the cod gently, using your fingers, removing the skin and any bones. Set aside.

Fry or bake the julienned potatoes.

In a large pot, sauté the onion, black pepper, and bay leaf in olive oil until onion is soft, about 5 minutes. Add the garlic and sauté another 2 minutes. Add the cod and stir to combine. Then add the potatoes and combine gently.

Whisk the eggs in a bowl and add to the mixture. Stir gently for a few minutes on low heat—you want the eggs to cook but the overall consistency should be creamy. Do not overcook or the eggs will be scrambled, and you don't want that!

Transfer the mixture to a warm platter and garnish with parsley and olives. Serve right away.

Add a salad and fresh Portuguese bread and you should have plenty to feed four at dinner.

Portuguese Kale Soup (Caldo Verde)
This recipe is from my kitchen!
Serves 6, as a soup course

This is a tried-and-true version that I have adapted from my mother's recipe. In Portugal, the "verde" comes from using collard greens. In Vancouver, I started using curly kale and I think I like it better than the original. My mother, of course, would add a cup of mashed white beans for extra oomph and nutrition. I often leave that out because it's a hearty soup anyway.

You can adjust the amount of water or number of potatoes based on how thick you like your soup. Start with the amounts I've used below and go from there.

For a vegetarian version, leave out the chouriço. It won't be quite the same, but it's still tasty.

- 1–2 chouriço sausage (adjust the quantity depending on how much you like meat)
- 3–4 tbsp good quality olive oil
- 1 yellow onion, chopped
- 2 cloves of garlic, minced
- 6 medium russet potatoes (about 3/4 kg), peeled and sliced for quick cooking
- 5–6 cups of water, depending on whether you prefer a thicker soup
- 1/2 tsp salt, plus coarse sea salt to taste
- 1 bunch kale, washed, tough stems removed, and finely shredded

If you're using sausage, pierce with a fork, place in a pot, and cover with cold water. Bring to a boil, then simmer for 20 minutes. Drain and let cool, then slice thinly, cover, and set aside.

In a soup pot, sauté the onion in olive oil until soft but not brown (about 5 minutes). Add the garlic and sauté another few minutes, being careful not to burn the garlic (use low heat). Add the potatoes, water and salt, cover and bring to a boil. Reduce heat and simmer until potatoes are very soft, about 15 minutes. Remove from heat.

Mash the potatoes or purée with a hand mixer or in a food processor. Bring the pot back to the stove and heat through, then add the kale and simmer, uncovered, for 5 minutes. I like the greens to be still crunchy and not limp so I'm careful not to overcook at this stage.

Ladle the soup into bowls and add chouriço if you like. Serve piping hot.

Pork and Clams, Alentejo-Style (Carne de Porco à Alentejana)

My version, based on instructions and tips from market vendors in
Costa da Caparica
Serves 4

3 cloves of garlic chopped, plus 2 more cloves, also chopped
2 tbsp paprika, plus 1 more tbsp set aside
1 bay leaf
Salt to taste
1 cup dry white wine (or beer if you prefer)
1 kg pork tenderloin, cut in cubes
1 kg butter clams or Manila clams
4 tbsp olive oil
1 onion, chopped
2 tbsp chopped parsley
1/4 cup cilantro, plus more for garnish
1 lemon, wedged, for garnish

For potatoes
3/4 kg potatoes, peeled and cut in small cubes
Oil for frying

To make the marinade, combine 3 cloves of chopped garlic, 2 tbsp paprika, bay leaf, a sprinkle of coarse salt, and wine in a non-aluminum bowl. Add pork cubes and turn to coat well. Cover and refrigerate for several hours or overnight.

Rinse the clams, place in a bowl, and cover with cold water. Discard any that are not firmly closed. Add about a tablespoon of salt and let the clams soak in the fridge for 2 or 3 hours. When you're ready to use, drain and rinse clams until water runs clear.

When you're ready to prepare the meal, fry the potatoes first, in batches, in a large skillet or in a deep fryer until golden. Set aside and keep warm.

In a skillet or wok, heat 2 tablespoons of olive oil and brown the pork, in batches, adding more oil if necessary. Turn and brown on all sides, about 4 minutes. Remove from heat and keep warm.

Add remaining oil and sauté the onion and 2 cloves of chopped garlic until onion is soft, about 3 minutes. Make sure garlic does not burn. Add remaining 1 tbsp of paprika and cilantro and stir to combine. Return pork to the wok and stir until cooked through and juices run clear.

Add clams and cover wok, stirring once or twice until clams steam open, about 5 minutes. Add fried potatoes and parsley and stir through. Discard any clams that did not open.

Transfer to a serving dish and garnish with more cilantro and lemon wedges. Serve immediately, with fresh bread to soak up the juices.

Clams in Garlic Sauce (Ameijoas à Bulhão Pato)
From my sister Toni's kitchen
Serves 2 for dinner or 4 as an appetizer

When Toni cooks, she takes care to source the freshest ingredients from specialty stores. No one-stop shopping for her! It's worth it, she says. When I taste-tested the results, I had to agree. For this dish, Toni recommends Manila clams from British Columbia, Russian garlic from Keremeos, BC (very specific!), and wine and olive oil from Portugal. When I have made this dish, I've used half the olive oil and a bit more wine and it still works.

1 kg Manila clams

1/3 cup Portuguese olive oil

6 cloves of Russian garlic, sliced thin

1/3 cup Portuguese white wine

1 cup cilantro leaves

1 lemon

Place clams in a bowl and cover with cold water. Discard any clams that are not tightly closed. Add about a tablespoon of salt and let the clams soak in the fridge for 2 or 3 hours. Then drain and rinse clams until water runs clear.

In a deep skillet or wok, warm the olive oil and cook garlic for a few minutes. Do not let it turn brown. Add cilantro and wine. Cook for 1 minute. Add clams, cover, and increase heat to high until the clams open, about 5 minutes. Stir through and discard any clams that did not open.

Transfer the clams to a warm platter. Bring liquid mixture in the skillet to a boil for a few minutes to reduce slightly, then pour over the clams.

Squeeze half a lemon over the clams, garnish with more cilantro and lemon wedges, and serve immediately alongside fresh Portuguese bread.

. . . .

Further Reading

MUCH OF MY COMMENTARY on Portuguese history and culture comes from my experience of having lived in Portugal at various times and of having grown up in a Portuguese family. In writing this book, however, I did conduct some research to corroborate the stories I had heard for much of my life. I consulted various sources to confirm and expand my knowledge of such topics as Salazar and the Estado Novo regime, the Carnation Revolution, the history and significance of fado, as well as the history of Portuguese water dogs. For those who are interested in reading more about these topics, I include my list here.

ONLINE

American Kennel Club. "Portuguese Water Dog." https://www.akc. org/dog-breeds/portuguese-water-dog/.

Franco, Adriana Gabriela. "Fado, Dictatorship, and Nostalgia: The Centenary of the Life of Amália Rodrigues." *The Catalyst.* January 26, 2021. https://catalystmcgill.com/fado-dictatorship-and-nostalgia-the-centenary-of-the-life-of-amalia-rodrigues/.

Lewis, John. "Tainted Love." *The Guardian.* April 27, 2007. https://www. theguardian.com/music/2007/apr/27/worldmusic.

Sciolino, Elaine. "Fado, the Portuguese Soul Music." *The New York Times*. February 20, 2007. https://www.nytimes.com/2007/02/20/world/europe/20iht-fado.4662292.html.

BOOKS

Gomes, Alfredo e Adelino Cunha. *Os Rapazes dos Tanques*. Lisboa, Portugal: Porto Editora, 2014.

Hatton, Barry. *The Portuguese: A Modern History*. Oxford, UK: Signal Books, 2012.

Page, Martin. *The First Global Village: How Portugal Changed the World*. Cruz Quebrada, Portugal: Casa das Letras, 2002.

FILM AND TELEVISION

Anthony Bourdain: No Reservations, season 8, no. 4, "Lisbon," aired April 30, 2012, on Travel Channel.

April Captains (Capitães de Abril). Director Maria de Medeiros; screenwriter Maria de Medeiros and Ève Deboise. 2000.

. . . .

Acknowledgements

THIS BOOK HAS BEEN A LONG TIME COMING! It took the interest and assistance of so many people to shepherd it through the writing and publishing process. I am thrilled to hold it in my hand, feel the paper, and turn the pages.

I am very grateful that my manuscript caught the eye of the acquisitions editor at University of Alberta Press. Thank you, Michelle Lobkowicz, for believing in my story and championing this project. My thanks also to Alan Brownoff, Duncan Turner, Cathie Crooks, and the rest of the team at the press. I am delighted that my first book is published by my alma mater.

Thank you to my son, Matt Hall, for creating the illustrated map of the Lisbon area, and to Lauren Carter, for the thorough copy edit. The peer reviewers, Scott Edward Anderson and Dr. Manuela Marujo, provided much valuable feedback and supported my work with enthusiasm. Muito obrigada.

An earlier version of the first chapter of this book was published by The Soap Box Press as "A People of Saudade" in the Fall 2021 anthology, *The Hyphenated Generation*. My thanks to Faith Hwang and Tali Voron.

I worked on this manuscript during my MFA program at the University of King's College. Much gratitude to my mentor, Lori A. May, for her constructive critiques as well as her energy and sense of fun. She poked and prodded and challenged me in my writing. I could not have done this without her. David Hayes, enthusiastic foodie and sharp writer that he is, also mentored me at King's and encouraged me greatly, as did the always kind Stephen Kimber. Brenda Copeland may not know this, but in our brief and only conversation several years ago, she came up with the title for my book.

Thank you to Ludger van der Eerden and Carolien van der Laan for accepting me into the OBRAS Arts Residency in Alentejo, Portugal, where I completed my first draft. I benefitted from uninterrupted writing time in a quiet space amid the beauty of the cork oak, and I made lasting friendships. What more could I possibly have wanted?

My thanks to Betsy Warland for her astute comments, which helped to shape the direction of this story. Thank you also to the beta readers of later drafts, Leslie Baxter and Janet Hall, who offered many helpful suggestions.

This book is a family effort. We lived it and breathed it for several years! Eric, Georgia, and Matt provided perspective, feedback, and much-needed encouragement. Georgia, in particular, read these stories So. Many. Times. She is a natural-born editor, and her insights were much appreciated. Thanks, G, for being my biggest fan and cheerleader.

I am so pleased and relieved that both Matt and Georgia agreed to be named in this story. They did not ask to be born to a writer mother, yet they have been unequivocal in their support of me and this book. There would be no story without them.

Costa da Caparica is now a part of our family's history. To the friends from Canada who came to visit us in Costa and to the new friends we made there, thank you for your part in the stories that made it into this book. I am particularly indebted to José João Granjo, and the Cabral (no relation) and Roque families: Helena, Zé, Rita, Odete, and Armando. I treasure our long-lasting friendship.

I would also like to thank the women at the market in Costa who shared stories and dinner suggestions with me. Their smiles and our conversations often made my day.

Helena Cabral, Odete Roque, and my sister António Corby shared their recipes and agreed to have them published here. Thank you.

My writing life predated this book and will go on beyond it, I trust. I am so lucky to be a member of several writing communities that have helped sustain and nurture me as a writer. I am grateful to The Writer's Studio at Simon Fraser University—for all the readings, launches, workshops, and volunteering and work opportunities. Many people I've come to know through TWS continue to inspire me as a writer, and some have become good friends.

The MFA family at the University of King's College holds a special place in my heart. My thanks to the Class of 2019 and the ones who came before and after, for the camaraderie, and the continued connection. King's and Halifax are now woven into the fabric of my writing soul.

I am in regular contact with my virtual Luso-North American writing community, most of whom I got to know through the Disquiet Literary Program and its offshoot initiatives. Special thanks to Diniz Borges who has tirelessly fostered the Azorean diasporic literary community and welcomed me into the fold.

My deepest gratitude goes to Eric. He is always game for the next adventure. We make such a good team when we travel, and even when we don't.

Other Titles from University of Alberta Press

Blue Portugal and Other Essays

THERESA KISHKAN

"Kishkan's lyrical essays glow with the generosity and poetic grace of a richly perceptive mind. *Blue Portugal and Other Essays* explores natural and human histories, the veins and rivers of then and now, with fierce and tender insight."
—Lorri Neilsen Glenn, author of *Following the River*
Wayfarer Series

Tiny Lights for Travellers

NAOMI K. LEWIS

Vulnerable and funny, this award-winning memoir explores Jewish identity, family, the Holocaust, and belonging. Winner of the Wilfrid Eggleston Award for Nonfiction, the Vine Awards for Canadian Jewish Literature, and The Western Canada Jewish Book Awards, Pinsky Givon Family Prize for Non-Fiction. Shortlisted for the Governor General Literary Awards, Non-fiction.
Wayfarer Series

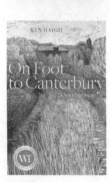

On Foot to Canterbury

A Son's Pilgrimage

KEN HAIGH

Ken Haigh explores the historical and literary landscape of the Pilgrims' Way in southern England. *On Foot to Canterbury* is part travelogue, part memoir, part literary history, and all heart. Shortlisted for the Hilary Weston Writers' Trust Prize for Nonfiction.
Wayfarer Series

More information at uap.ualberta.ca

Printed in the USA
CPSIA information can be obtained
at www.ICGtesting.com
CBHW022123181124
17381CB00003B/5